MINNESOTA'S BEST
BEER GUIDE

A TRAVEL COMPANION

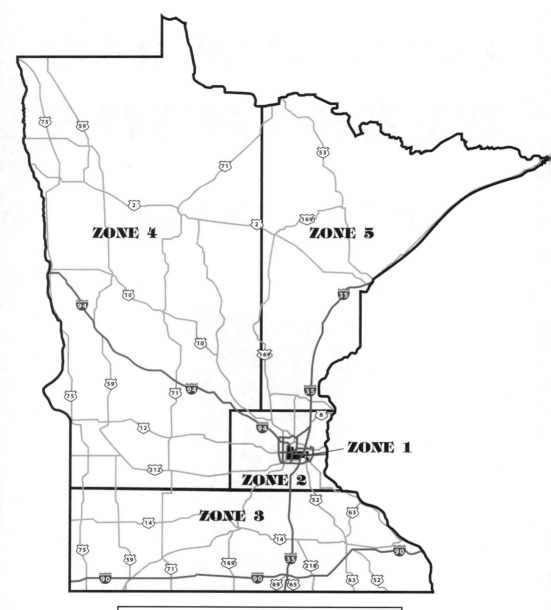

Zone 1: Minneapolis — St. Paul
Zone 2: Twin Cities Greater Metro
Zone 3: Southern Minnesota
Zone 4: Central & Northwest Minnesota
Zone 5: Northeast Minnesota and the North Shore

MINNESOTA'S BEST
BEER GUIDE

A TRAVEL COMPANION

by Kevin Revolinski

Thunder Bay Press

Minnesota's Best Beer Guide
by Kevin Revolinski

Published by
Thunder Bay Press
Holt, Michigan 48842

First Printing, June 2015

19   18   17   16   15   1   2   3   4   5

ISBN: 978-1-933272-53-5
Library of Congress Control Number: 2015941261

Cover Photo: Kevin Revolinski
Except where credited, Interior Photos: Preamtip Satasuk
Book, Map and Cover Design: Julie Taylor

Printed in the United States of America

Acknowledgments

I know full well that my part in this book is just laying down the highway miles, taking notes, and then pulling together all the work of so many others. From the fantastic brewers of Minnesota, the local restaurants and bars, the growers and producers, the tourism boards and visitor bureaus out there touting their communities' brewers, to the locals and fellow travelers—many of whom I didn't even get their names in passing—who gave me the tips to find hotspots and secrets that supplement the breweries here. I say to all of you: Right on, Minnesota! I raise a pint to you all!

Specifically, I have to say thanks to Joe Alton and Brian Kaufenberg of *The Growler* and *Beer Dabbler*; Tim Wilson, Dave Grandmaison and Paul Helstrom of *The Duluth Experience*; Gene Shaw of *Visit Duluth*; Lisa Huber of *Visit Saint Paul*; Mary Gastner of *Visit Rochester*; Kristen Montag of *Meet Minneapolis*; Cindy Wannarka of *Leech Lake Tourism*; Terry Sveine of *New Ulm Chamber of Commerce*; and Amanda Buhman, Lee Jones, and Andrea Foss Manos of *One Simple Plan*. Thanks also to Tod Fyten and Ed Gleeson for the valuable information and fascinating history stories. Finally, Alyssa Ebel of *Explore Minnesota* was nothing short of a rock star in her assistance with this project.

Another huge thanks to my amazing editor Julie Taylor at Thunder Bay Press for eternal patience and speedy quality work that makes me look better than I am, and to the big boss at TBP and Partners Book, Sam Speigel, and his entire staff.

Thanks to Colin Sokolowski, David Higgins, Jon and Kim Hamilton of White Winter Winery, and my brother Bryan Revolinski for some beer drinking help. And finally, thanks to my wife Preamtip Satasuk for playing the challenging role of navigator and taking all the photos for this book while I was free to take notes, sample beers, and talk smack with brewers, bartenders, and anyone who would listen. None of these beer book experiences would be the same without her.

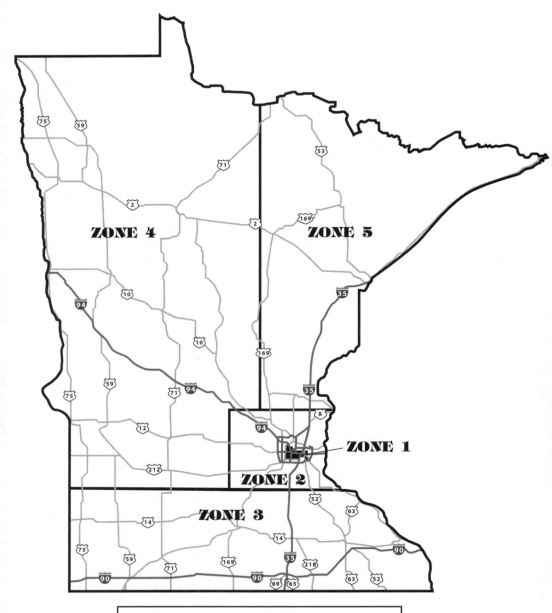

ZONE 4

ZONE 5

ZONE 1

ZONE 2

ZONE 3

Zone 1: Minneapolis — St. Paul
Zone 2: Twin Cities Greater Metro
Zone 3: Southern Minnesota
Zone 4: Central & Northwest Minnesota
Zone 5: Northeast Minnesota and the North Shore

Table of Contents

Table of Contents

The Rules

Every state has its own way of dealing with beer, and Minnesota isn't any different. But rules change all the time, and as Minnesota quickly becomes a giant among craft brewers, outdated laws are going to see some changes.

Breweries

Check the Surly Bill in the index. Up until this bill became law in 2011, breweries (as opposed to brewpubs, which are legally different here) were not allowed to serve pints of their own beer at the brewery. The new law changed that, allowing breweries to have taprooms where they can serve pints of their own beer. They can now also serve food with a properly outfitted kitchen/food preparation area. (Brau Brothers Brewing in Marshall and Surly Brewing in Minneapolis are notably the first of these new taprooms serving food.) Pints can only be sold if the brewery produces *less than 250,000 barrels* of beer each year. They can also only fill growlers and 750ml bottles if they make *less than 25,000 barrels* of beer annually.

Brewpubs

Brewpubs must have a proper full-service kitchen, but they are not allowed to distribute their beer as breweries do—with the exception of serving it at related "sister" establishments. (Minneapolis Town Hall Brewery and Fitger's Brewhouse notably have other restaurants under the same ownership wherein their own beer can be served.) Brewpubs may also run a full bar and serve guest beers. They may be open 7 days a week (ie. serving on Sundays is OK, but read about growlers below), and they are limited to an annual production of 3,500 barrels.

Growler Rules

Growlers, those 64 oz. refillable bottles, are allowed for carryout from both breweries (of under 25,000 barrels) and brewpubs, but you cannot drink them on site and you must have them out the door before the end of growler sales hours (growler sales times align with local liquor store opening times which may be different from the brewery's posted opening hours and vary by community). Minnesota doesn't exactly do half-growlers (32 oz.) but rather 750 ml (25.3605 oz.) vessels and that's defined by law. Many establishments pre-fill growlers, meaning you have to buy the glass with it or exchange an empty growler (presumably that brewer's growler).

However, it is now legal for a brewery to fill another brewery's branded growler as long as it has the required government warnings on it. As of now, most brewers refuse to fill those other branded containers, but a few are noted here in the book who will do it as long as the growler is clean and has the government warning. Law changes also now accommodate non-glass growlers, so the various steel and insulated growlers are OK. Again, be aware that these are off-sale purchases and you must take them to go, not drink them on the property.

As of printing in May 2015, **Sunday growler sales are legal in the state of Minnesota**! Approval of this, however, may still vary among municipalities.

Special Offers

Special offers listed in this guide are NOT guaranteed. The brewer reserves the right to rescind the offer at any time and for any reason. Not all brewers are participating and that will be noted on each brewer's page. Legal drinking age still applies, of course.

Introduction

At one time before the Dark Ages of 1919 to 1933 (Prohibition), many American towns had brewers doing their thing. You couldn't swing a cat without hitting one. When consumption of our veritable holy water became a mortal and legal sin, many were the breweries that went beer belly up. The larger ones survived, a few got by on root beer and soda (Schell's survived with soda and candy), and for this we can lift a pint. Then over the following few decades, many of the mid-sized survivors closed their doors until by the mid-1970s there were fewer breweries in the entire USA than there are today in the State of Minnesota. The few remaining brewers such as Anheuser Busch, Miller, Pabst, Schlitz, G. Heileman, Hamm's, Schmidt, and Stroh's Brewing Co. battled it out, and today all the mass-market beer comes from just a few companies, ultimately owned by foreign entities.

But never mind all that: America is at the cutting edge of the Beer Renaissance. President Carter made homebrewing legal back in 1978. Since the 1980s, we have witnessed a rise in the number of craft breweries. In 1986, Summit Brewing opened in St. Paul and just over a decade later built the first brand-new brewery in Minnesota in 75 years. It is one of the top 50 largest craft brewers by production. A surge and collapse in the 1990s perhaps hinted that opening a microbrewery might be a fad, but such is most definitely not the case. In 2014 the number of breweries in America surpassed the 3,000 mark, and more open every month. Minnesota's breweries have already surpassed 100, and the pace of growth shows no sign of slowing. The big producers—Summit, Surly, Schell's, for example—are still growing by leaps and bounds, and the little guys, like the corner brewpubs or regional production breweries, keep opening—and are staying open. Wineries are adding beer to the production. Small towns we may have doubted could ever support one brewery ten years ago now suddenly have two or three. (Hello, Grand Marais and Waconia!) Minneapolis and St. Paul proper have over 30 breweries (never mind the greater metro area!) and Duluth has become a must-visit beer destination.

Minnesota beer is on the rise. Many Minnesotans are fortunate to have someone looking out for them with a handcrafted lager or ale. Who in this state should not have their own personal hometown beer? (My condolences to those who don't, but don't worry—this book can help you adopt and probably someone already has one planned anyway.) Designate a driver (or pack your sleeping bag in the trunk), turn the page, and set off on a *pils*-grimage to the breweries of Minnesota.

BUT I DON'T LIKE BEER

You'll hear it time and time again when you ask a brewer—pro or homebrewer—why they got into brewing. Many of them will tell you they were dissatisfied with what was on the market back before the advent of the modern craft beer revolution. Maybe they took a trip to Germany. Maybe they were inspired by another homebrewer. But in the end, regardless of that original motivation, it becomes a passion for quality beer. I have to admit, it took me a long time to come to beer. If you had offered me a beer in college, I would likely have gone the choosy beggar path and asked if you had any vodka or rum instead. I really didn't even like beer. I can already hear the collective gasp of horror, but let me explain: beer was social lubricant, something you sipped at with friends at a cookout, bought for the cute woman at the other end of the bar, or beer-bonged on occasion. I didn't like the taste so much and—oh the humanity—often didn't even finish them. I killed many a houseplant at parties and have gotten hordes of bees drunk at picnics with the remains of a bottle of Something-or-Other Light.

It wasn't until craft beer that I became a Born Again Beer Drinker. Beer experts already know and commercial beer drinkers might be leery of the fact that outside of the mass-produced impersonal brews, beers are as different as people. They have tremendous character, and the people who dedicate their lives to brewing are characters as well. Traveling to visit a brewery—what I like to call a *pils*-grimage—is as much about appreciating the subtleties and variations of beer as it is about taking a peek into local communities and beer's place in them. Part of what makes Minnesota great, and what makes brewing great, is that even the little guy can get in on the action. All respects to the giants of the mass-market beer industry, but how cool is it to walk into a local place and see the brewmaster standing at the bar sharing suds with the guy next door?

This book is a compilation of all the places that brew their own beer in Minnesota from the big boys Summit, August Schell, and Cold Springs all the way down to the most modest of producers such as Borealis Fermentery. The list continues to grow, and even at the moment I closed the book on this first edition of my Minnesota brewery roadtrip guide, at least a dozen more were likely planned to open by the end of the year. That's the nature of the beast.

Using the very latest cutting-edge state-of-the-art rocket-science-level technology, I established the locations of all of the breweries in the state. OK, actually it was a Sharpie and a **free Minnesota highway map** from *Explore Minnesota* (exploreminnesota.com, 888-868-7476). You can also contact them for loads of free paper or downloadable brochures and guides, including the annual Minnesota Travel Guide. They even offer personal assistance from Travel Counselors at explore@state.mn.us or 1-888-VISITMN (1-888-847-4866). I sat down with the list and divided the state into five zones. Each of those zones is listed in the Where's the Beer At? section and shows the brewtowns alphabetically. If you already know the name of the brewery you are seeking, look for it in the cross-referenced lists at the beginning of Where's the Beer At? Make sense? Worked for me!

WHAT IS BEER?

Beer is produced by fermenting some sort of starch product. In many cases this is barley, wheat, oats, or rye, but even corn, rice, potatoes, and certain starchy roots in Africa have been used. In parts of Latin America, corn is chewed, spit out, and left to ferment becoming a sort of corn beer called *chicha*. I've tried it... *before* my traveling companion told me about the chewing process. We are no longer on speaking terms. Don't expect MillerCoors or Anheuser Busch to be rolling it out in mass quantities very soon. And since you don't hear anyone advertising "brewed from the finest Senegalese cassava roots" you can guess barley is still the primary grain of choice. (Burning Brothers Brewing has got your back if you have gluten issues.) There's no distilling for beer—that would make it some kind of liquor, and it's not strictly sugars or fruit juices—which is where your wine comes from.

The History of Beer

MANNA FROM HEAVEN

Yes, your craft beer is pure brewed right here in the State of Minnesota, but it wasn't always so. Egyptians loved it long before, Sumerians wrote down recipes for it on stone tablets, and you can imagine the drunken bar brawls over at the Viking lodge. Beer dates way back beyond 5000 BC, which is even before *writing*. (I think Ernest Hemingway, F. Scott Fitzgerald—Minnesota native—and many other writers have also put the one before the other.)

The word itself comes to us by way of Middle English *ber*, from Old English *bEor* which goes to show you just how difficult life must have been without spellchecker. The English version surely comes from *bior* which was Old High German which became Old Low German by the end of a serious night of drinking.

BEER IN MINNESOTA

In 1998, I traveled to Czech Republic to see a bit of the land my forefathers left behind for the sake of the American Midwest. I landed in Frankfurt, Germany (cheaper flight!), and with a rental car drove to Prague. In fact, as I bundled up in a jacket and faced an unseasonably cold June in Plzen, this is pretty much what struck me: My great-grandparents had packed up all they had into small trunks or had a big barn sale perhaps, left behind everyone they knew on this earth—friends, family, perhaps a few creditors—spent much of their remaining money on ocean-liner tickets, braved the long and sometimes dangerous Atlantic crossing, had their names misspelled at Ellis Island, and went overland halfway across a continent to settle in the same damn place they left behind. Seriously. Change the highway signs to English and set up some road construction detours, and I may as well have been driving down MN-95 outside of St. Cloud. But these immigrants' absurd notions of improving their lots worked to our benefit: conditions were perfect here for making the same great beers of Northern Europe—and so they did.

BEER TERRITORY

How serious were the European settlers about beer? Consider this: Minnesota became a state in 1858. Bavarian immigrant Anthony Yoerg opened the first brewery in 1849 in St. Paul. Another German, John Orth opened one a year later. Many early brews were ales, but political turmoil pushed a wave of Germans immigrants to the US in the 1840s, and this also brought more beer and brewers and the German love of lagers. By 1858, there were over thirty breweries; a decade later, over fifty. Some of the beers of the late nineteenth century brewers would go on to be nationally famous: Hamm's, Grain Belt, and Schmidt's. (A couple old school breweries even survive today: August Schell Brewing, 1860, and Cold Spring Brewing, 1874!) Orth's brewery joined four others to become part of Minneapolis Brewing Co. (original makers of Grain Belt Beer) in 1890, and together with Gluek and Hennepin Brewing Co. made Northeast Minneapolis ("Nordeast") a center of brewing. (Today, approaching a dozen craft breweries, the Northeast Minneapolis "neighbrewhood" is still a hotspot for beer.)

The first brewery in Duluth was opened in 1857 by Sydney Luce and would eventually pass into the hands of a German brewmaster August Fitger. The Fitger's brewery buildings are still there, reclaimed as a hotel and commercial property. A few contract brews exist under the name, and the unrelated Fitger's Brewhouse is rocking it as an exceptional brewpub within the complex.

Minnesota's massive grain production industry played no small part in fueling the brewing. Go see the Mill City Museum in Minneapolis. In fact, Rahr Malting, founded in Manitowoc, Wisconsin, in 1847, opened a facility in Shakopee in 1937 that remains the largest single malting site in the world (380,000 metric tons per year).

PROHIBITION

The Prohibitionists had already been on the boil since the middle of the nineteenth century for religious and social motivations. But while beer-haven Wisconsin bordered on one side, Iowa went through dry periods, and North Dakota was dry at statehood. In the late 1800s, temperance was gaining traction and turning some Minnesota counties dry. Some towns revoked saloon licenses or stopped issuing them. In 1890, Northern Minnesota's 5th district sent Kittel Halvorson, the first Prohibition Party member to congress. On January 16, 1919, the 18th Amendment to the U.S. Constitution received enough votes to be ratified for the entire nation. (Minnesota's ratification came the next day, actually.) The amendment banned the production, sale, and transportation of intoxicating liquors but did not define them. For this purpose the National Prohibition Act was enacted. Though written up by lobbyists of the Anti-Saloon League, it is better known as the Volstead Act, named for Congressman Andrew Volstead of Minnesota's 7th district who introduced it to Congress on June 27, 1919. And if you were looking for loopholes, the Volstead Act defined alcoholic beverages as containing over one-half percent of alcohol. So do the math here. At best, you'd need about NINE BEERS to drink the equivalent amount of alcohol as a normal picnic beer! Even the most ambitious drinkers weren't going to be getting a buzz. Both legislative branches passed it, and though President Wilson vetoed it, the veto was quickly overridden. On midnight January 17, 1920, Prohibition went into effect. The first offenders were busted in Chicago less than an hour later.

Brewing was a productive industry in Minnesota, and it had just been banned. Minneapolis Brewing Co. started making near beer and soft drinks as the Golden Grain Juice Co. Some made dairy products. (Ironic, as in recent decades much dairy equipment has been converted to make beer.) The best way to make something attractive? Prohibit it. This also goes a long way to making it profitable on the black market. Stories of Al Capone and bootleggers and the mob in Chicago are widely known. Something as crazy as outlawing beer was doomed to fail, and when Prohibition was repealed by the Twenty-first Amendment in 1933, there was much celebration.

THE FALL OF THE MIGHTY, THE RISE OF THE CRAFT

Only 25 Minnesota breweries survived Prohibition; by the end of World War II there were 18. Slowly, those last remaining breweries competed in what primarily became a marketing war. Many went beer belly up. The struggling Remmler Brewing in Red Wing was bought in 1948 by Goodhue Brewing and failed three years later. Hauenstein Brewing in New Ulm gave up the ghost in 1969. Duluth's Fitger's Brewing made it to 1972. By 1983, only four brewers remained: Schell's and Cold Spring (still alive today!) and the ill-fated Hamm's (by then owned by Stroh's) and Schmidt. The Schmidt Brewery was taken over by Wisconsin-based G. Heileman Brewing Co. (which brewed Grain Belt and Schmidt together there until 1989) but is now reclaimed as artist lofts. The Hamm's brewery is now home to Saint Paul's Flat Earth Brewing. Grain Belt Beer is still brewed by August Schell Brewing. The Minneapolis Brewing Co.

building—now artist studios—is on the National Historic Register and you can still see the magnificent structure when you visit the Northeast Minneapolis neighbrewhood. You can also still see the big Grain Belt sign out on Nicollet Island when you cross the Hennepin Avenue Bridge.

The arrival of craft beer took things the other direction. In 1986, Mark Stutrud pioneered the first craft brewery in Minnesota. You may have heard of Summit Brewing? In 2014 Stutrud's creation was #28 on the Brewers Association list of top producing craft breweries by beer sales volume in the country (one spot behind the second oldest continuously family-owned brewery in the nation, August Schell Brewing, which, though founded in 1860, has kept pace with the craft beer trend).

James Page Brewing opened the same year Summit did (notably in the beer-centric Northeast Minneapolis neighborhood very near where Indeed Brewing is today) and made it to 2002 as a physical brewery. (Stevens Point Brewery in Wisconsin has the label and still produces a version of the beer.)

The state's first brewpub, Taps Waterfront Brewery and Comedy Club, opened in Minneapolis in 1989 but only made it a couple years. Others followed, notably Bill Burdick's Sherlock's Home in Minnetonka, which poured real ales until 2002. Great Waters Brewing set up in the historic Hamm Building in 1997; Town Hall Brewery opened several months later. Lake Superior Brewing brought beer back to Duluth in 1994, and Fitger's Brewhouse soon followed and made its mark as a highly regarded brewpub.

The history of Minnesota brewing continues as we speak, with new breweries opening every month, and while there may be the occasional unfortunates falling by the wayside, the trend shows no sign of slowing. You can play your part in making history: support your local brewers!

INGREDIENTS

Hops
Malt
Water
Yeast
Other

THE "SURLY BILL" AND POWER OF THE PINT

There was a time when craft breweries in Minnesota couldn't serve pints of their own beer at the brewery. Crazy, right? Like the Jack Daniels distillery being in a dry county where it can't sell its own bourbon. Surly Brewing owner Omar Ansari had expansion plans, and this outdated law, which clearly defined the three-tier system of manufacturers, distributors, and retailers, was holding them back.

Like Mr. Smith going to Washington, Omar went to St. Paul. Senator Linda Scheid and Representative Jenifer Loon wrote much of what would officially be known as bill SF 416.

The Minnesota Licensed Beverage Association didn't much like the idea, worrying it might cut into the business of the other two tiers. Surly hired lobbyists, and the Surly Nation—a grass-roots army of craft beer—also went to the capital to call for a change. In May 2011, Governor Mark Dayton signed the bill into law. Lift a pint to that!

Municipalities can now grant breweries a special license to sell their own beer at their brewery. (Brewpubs, obviously, already had that permission but have their own unique restrictions.) This law only applies to pouring draft beer. Bottles and can sales are not allowed, and neither are growler fills at the moment. In fact, the law still prohibits serving pints at a brewery if that brewery makes more than 250,000 barrels.

THE DIVINE PROCESS

The first step in brewing beer is *MASHING*, and for this you need a malted grain, such as barley, and it needs to be coarsely ground. The brewer will add hot water to the malt to get the natural enzymes in the grain to start converting the starches into the sugars necessary for fermentation. Think of your bowl of sugared breakfast cereal growing soggy and then making the milk sweet. It's kind of like that, only totally different.

The next step is *SPARGING* when water is flushed through the mash to get a sweet liquid we call *WORT*. The wort is sent to the brew kettle and filtered to remove the barley husks and spent grain. Wort then needs to be boiled to kill off any unwanted microcritters and to get rid of some of the excess water. This generally goes on for about an hour and a half. It is at this stage that any other flavoring ingredients are generally added, including hops.

Once this is all done, the fermentation is ready to begin. A brewer once told me, "People don't make beer, yeast does." Yes, yeast is the magical little element that monks referred to as "God is Good" when they were making their liquid bread in the monasteries. If you wanted to grab a brewsky in the Middle Ages (and believe me you didn't want to drink the water), the best place to stop was the local monastery. The monks made beer, the travelers spent money, the church got along. Everyone happy. How the Church ended up with Bingo instead of beer we may never know. Bummer!

Yeast eats sugars like the little fat boy eats candy in *Willie Wonka and the Chocolate Factory,* and as we all know from a long afternoon of drinking and stuffing our faces, what goes in must come out. As Kurt Vonnegut once put it, and as unpleasant as it may seem, beer is yeast excrement: alcohol and a little bit of gas. Reminds me of a night of Keystone Light, actually.

ALES vs. LAGERS

There are two basic kinds of beer: ales and lagers. It's all about yeast's preferences. Some yeasts like it on top; some prefer to be on bottom. Up until now, yeasts have not been more creative in their brewing positions, but we can always fantasize.

Ale yeasts like it on top and will ferment at higher temperatures (60–70 °F) and so are quicker finishers than lagers (1–3 weeks). Usually ales are sweeter and have a fuller body, which really starts to take this allusion to extremes.

Lagers, on the other hand, use yeasts that settle in at the bottom to do their work and prefer cooler temps (40–55 °F). They take 1–3 months to ferment. Lagers tend to be lighter and drier than ales and are the most common beers, often easier to get along with for the average drinker and they don't mind if you leave the seat up. (In fact, you may as well, you'll be coming back a few times before the night is done.) For lager we can thank the Bavarians who—when they found that cold temperatures could control runaway wild yeasts in the warm summer ale batches—moved them to the Alps. The name lager comes from the German "to store."

Ale is the first real beer that was made, and it was sort of a mutation of another alcoholic drink called mead. This was made with fermented honey. Remember the mead halls when you read *Beowulf* in high school? OK, I didn't read it either, but the Cliffs Notes mentioned it some. This is the sweet and potent concoction that put the happy in the Vikings as they ran wild, pillaging and plundering. Someone added a bit of hops, and later some malt, and the hybrid *brackett* evolved.

THESE ARE NOT YOUR MALTED MILKBALLS

Malting is a process of taking a grain, such as barley or wheat, getting it to start germinating, and then drying it quickly to cut off that process. I like to call this *germinus interruptus,* but then I like to make a lot of words up, so take that with a grain of barley.

So the malting process is 1: get grain (seeds) wet; 2: let germination get started; 3: roast in a kiln until dried. And here's where the specialty malts come in. You can roast the malted grains to different shades, a bit like coffee beans, and you can even *smoke* the stuff for a real twist on flavor (check out Rauchbier). I mean like you smoke bacon, not like you smoke tobacco—don't get any ideas.

Why is barley the most common grain? It has a high amount of those enzymes for beer. So although corn, wheat, rye, even rice can be used, you'll see that barley is the king of the malts. If you have trouble with gluten, this is bad news because barley has it, but fear not! Burning Brothers Brewing in St. Paul does nothing but gluten-free brews.

I know you're wondering, because I was too: What about the malt in malted milk balls? There *is* a connection, in fact. William Horlick of Racine, Wisconsin, sought to create a food for infants that was both nutritious and easy to digest. He mixed wheat extract and malted barley with powdered milk to form malted milk. Walgreen's Drugstores almost immediately started selling malted milkshakes.

WHAT'S HOPPENIN', HOP STUFF?

So why the hops? It's a plant for cryin' out loud; do you really want *salad* in your beer?? Actually, without refrigeration beer didn't keep all too well. The medieval monks discovered that hops had preservative properties. The sun never set on the British Empire which meant it never set on the beer either. So the Brits hopped the ale hard to get it all the way to India. Thus India Pale Ale was born. (No, the color is not really pale, but compare it to a porter or a stout and the name makes sense.)

The point in the process when you put the hops in makes all the difference, and generally it goes in the boil. Boil it an hour and it's bitter; half an hour and it's less bitter with a touch of the flavor and aroma; toward the end of the boil and you lose the bitter and end up with just the aroma and flavor, making it highly "drinkable." (You will hear people describing beer as very "drinkable," and it would seem to me that this was a given. Apparently not.) There is another way to get the hoppiness you want. Dry hopping—which sounds a lot like what some of yous kids was doin' in the backseat of the car—is actually adding the hops after the wort has cooled, say, in the fermenter, or more commonly in the keg.

But let me tell you this, when I first sipped a beer back in the day, I only stared blankly at brewers when they asked me, "Now, do ya taste the hops in this one?" How was I to know? I mean, if someone from Papua New Guinea says, "Do you get that little hint of grub worm in that beer?" I really have nothing to go on. Before touring or on your brew tour, if you aren't already hops-wise, ask someone if you can have a whiff of some. I did, and suddenly the heavens parted and Divine Knowledge was to me thus imparted. I could then identify that aroma and flavor more accurately, and I have to confess I'm still not sure I taste it in those mass market beers.

WHAT ARE IBUs?

Compounds in hops are what bring bitterness to your beer. IBU stands for International Bittering Units and gives beer drinkers something else to say about how bitter a beer is besides "really really" or "very very very" or "just a bit." Brewers use a spectrophotometer which measures how light passes through or reflects off a solution and thus determine the chemistry of their beer. This system offers an objective scientific accounting of a beer's bitterness, which, of course, is harder to otherwise pin down with our subjective tongues. The higher the number, the greater the actual (not *perceived* necessarily) bitterness. However, this number may not always predict your own experience of the beer. A beer with a lot of malt and a higher IBU of 60, for example, might not taste as bitter as a pint of bitters made with less malt and rated at 30 IBU. There is a limit to how much of the bittering compounds are actually soluble, so one cannot simply add hops infinitely and go screaming toward 100s of IBUs. (Heaven knows, because someone would have done it by now!) Plus, there's a limit to how much your tongue can even perceive. Debate goes on about what those limits are, but pretty much after about 110 IBUs you are likely near the limit.

REINHEITSGEBOT!

Gezundtheit! Actually, it's not a Bavarian sneezing, it's the German Purity Law. Want to know how serious the Germans were about beer? By *law* dating back to 1516, beer had to be made using only these three ingredients: barley, hops, and water. (The law later added yeast to the ingredient list once Louis Pasteur explained to the world the role of the little sugar-eating microorganisms in the process.) But this meant you wheat, rye, or oat lovers were out of luck. Barbarians! Bootleggers! Outcasts! Why so harsh on the alternative grains? Because these grains were necessary for breads, and these were times of famines and the like. Fortunately, times got better and we have the wide variety of ales and lagers that we see today. In the end, the law was used more to control competitors and corner a market— so much for its pure intentions. But there's more to beer quality than a list of ingredients anyway; it's the *purity* of those ingredients that makes all the difference. It's also the time, patience, and care of the brewer that lifts the brew to a higher level. Am I talking about craft brewing here? I most certainly am!

THERE'S SOMETHING FUNNY IN MY BEER

So you know about the German Purity Law and the limits on what goes into a beer, but obviously there is a whole range of stuff out there that thumbs its nose at boundaries. Some of this is a good thing, some of it not so much. These beyond-the-basics ingredients are called *adjuncts*.

Let's talk about the type of adjunct that ought to make you suspicious and will elicit a curse or look of horror from a beer snob. In this sense an adjunct is a source of starch used to beef up the sugars available for fermentation. It is an ingredient, commonly rice or corn, used to cut costs by being a substitute for the more expensive barley. Pale lagers on the mass market production line commonly do this. It doesn't affect the flavor and often cuts back on the body and mouthfeel of the brew, which is why if you drink a mass market beer and then compare it to the same style (but *without* adjuncts) from a craft brewer you will taste a significant difference.

You may hear beer snobs use the word adjunct when ripping on the mass produced non-handcrafted brews, but there are other ingredients which are also adjuncts that we can't knock so much. Wheat, rye, corn, wild rice, oats, sorghum, honey—many are the options that don't just serve to save a buck or two on the batch ingredients but rather bring something to the beer. Maybe a longer lasting head, a silkier mouthfeel, or a sweeter taste. And in the case of a wheat beer, can one really call wheat an adjunct? Most would say no. Word dicers will say yes. Whatever.

Fruits and spices are also friendly adjuncts. Think of cherry, orange, or pumpkin flavors in certain brews, or spices such as coriander in Belgian wit beers, ginger, nutmeg, or even cayenne pepper. Brewers can add chocolate, milk sugar, or even coffee as in the case of a good coffee stout. By German Purity Law, of course, this is a big no-no, but there's nothing wrong with pushing the envelope a bit for some new tastes. It's not cutting corners, but rather creating new avenues.

BARRELS OF FUN

It's a trend that's gone so widespread that even many of the smallest breweries do at least a little bit of barrel aging. This can be done with a fresh oak or other wood barrel (or by throwing oak chips or oak spirals into a beer as it ages) or by using a previously owned/used barrel. Bourbon barrels are the most common, but chardonnay, brandy, rye and other barrels can be used as well. The wood and the bourbon, for example, impart an amazing flavor to the beer the longer you leave it sit there.

How long does a beer have to wait? Some brewers suggest one month of aging per alcohol percentage point. So seven months for a 7% alcohol beer. The beer takes on some of the bourbon flavors but also develops a relationship with the charred wood. Just like wine, beer can mellow and age, and some beers might be best drunk fresh, while others just keep getting better over time.

SOUR ALES

Throw out what you think you know about keeping your brewing equipment all squeaky clean so as not to spoil a brew. Yes, that is extremely important for brewing typical beers, but it's a rule that gets a little bending when making a sour ale. This is not a beer gone wrong but an actual style of beer that is gaining in popularity in the US and so is worth noting here.

Most commonly associated with Belgium (lambics or Flanders red ales), sour ales are intentionally allowed to go "bad." And by bad, we mean good. Wild yeasts and/or bacteria are purposely introduced to the beer to give it a sour or tart acidity.

Fruit can be added for a secondary fermentation, but many sours use bacteria such as Lactobacillus or Pediococcus, or a special yeast, such as "Brett" (Brettanomyces), which occurs in nature on fruit skins. Brewing such a beer can be challenging in that by introducing these wilder elements into the brewhouse, a brewer increases the risk of infecting other beers that aren't intended to be soured. But when done well, this is a unique beer experience, another alternative for those who claim they don't like any kind of beer, and maybe a crossover for those wine drinkers.

TASTING YOUR BEER

Back in the days of youth, I suppose savoring the taste of your beer meant you belched after pouring it down your throat. Since you have evolved to drinking craft beers, you may take a bit more time to savor it. Beer geeks will talk about the odor, taste, mouthfeel, warming, and after flavor.

Here are a few pointers for savoring the stuff:

Sniff it for aromas. Remember your nose works with your tongue to make you taste things. Kids plug their noses to eat liver for a reason! Get a bit of that beer in your sniffer before you sip by swirling it around in your glass to raise that aroma like you would with wine.

OK, now sip it. Swirl it a bit around on your tongue. Gargling is generally frowned upon, however. Is it watery or does it have a bit of body to it? Squish it against the roof of your mouth with your tongue to appreciate the "mouthfeel." Some beers have more body than others and are thicker, heavier, or smoother.

Swallow! Wine tasters can spit it out during a tasting, but beer has a finish that you can only get at the back of the tongue where the taste receptors for bitterness are. The most graceful option is to swallow. (Remember what I said about gargling!)

Everyone's tastes are different, of course, and some may prefer a bitter IPA to a sweet Belgian tripel, but the test of a good beer is that bittersweet balance. Now if you want to be good at this tasting business, you need to practice. I know, I know—oh, the humanity of it all! But you can suffer all this drinking if it really matters to you. Repeat the process with various craft brews and really appreciate how different all the beers are. Is this one too bitter? Too malty? Is the hops aroma strong, fair to middlin', barely noticeable? Hints of chocolate? Coffee? Caramel? Is it citrusy? Creamy? Crisp? Even smoky? (See "rauch beer" in the glossary.)

Is that *butterscotch* I'm tasting?!?

Shouldn't be! Beware of diacetyl! This natural byproduct of yeast is actually used in artificial butter flavoring. At low levels diacetyl gives a slippery mouthfeel to the brew. A bit more and the butterscotch flavor starts to appear. Brewers need to leave the yeast a couple days or so after the end of fermentation and it will reabsorb the flavor-spoiling agent. The warmer temp of ale brewing makes this happen faster.

Here's something that will sound crazy: a good beer will even taste good when it has gone warm in your glass. (Some will even taste better!) Now try *that* with your crappy picnic beer!

SOME FOOD WITH YOUR BEER

PAIRING AND PALATES with Lucy Saunders

Think about your taste buds, and what you savor: the five elements of taste—salty, sweet, bitter, sour and savory umami—are foremost. Pour a glass of beer and ponder its possible pairings.

But start with sniff, not a sip. In tasting beer, often aromatics can suggest herbs, spices or other ingredients that might make a bridge for a potential food pairing.

Hops can be piney and resinous—which suggests rosemary or juniper berries. Citrusy hops meld well with tropical flavors such as mango or lemons and limes.

Witbiers brewed with coriander and orange zest bring out the best in seafood and many salads. Malty, bready notes suggest caramelized flavors and meld well with rind-washed cheeses. Peppery, high ABV brews will extend the heat of chiles and spicy foods. Yeasty dark ales balance the acidity in dark chocolate.

Since everyone's palate and threshold of sensitivity differs, know how to approach a pairing.

I interviewed Chef Jonathan Zearfoss, a professor at the Culinary Institute of America, about pairing tips. "The standard approach to flavors is to complement, contrast, or create a third new flavor through the synergy of flavor," he says.

For example, Zearfoss read a menu description of a rauchbier that suggested pairing it with smoked foods. "I had the rauchbier with a lentil salad made with smoked bacon and a vinaigrette. On my palate, the acidity of the vinegar cut through the smoke. But my friend, who was eating a pasta with cream sauce, found that the smoky taste coated her palate and became cloying."

"The taste memory is composed of the synergy between the drink and the food," says Zearfoss, "and that's especially true with beer since it has a definite aftertaste." Texture elements in beer—carbonation, residual yeast—also contribute to flavor.

When tasting a beer that's new to you, try sampling both bottled and draft versions of the same beer. Fresh beer tastes best, and be sure you know what the brewer wanted the beer to taste like.

There's a delightful weaving of the experience of drinking beer: your sensations, your palate and overall enjoyment. With literally hundreds of beer styles from which to choose, allow experimentation and sampling beyond your usual preferences. It's an adventure you can enjoy in Minnesota. Cheers!

© 2012, 2015 Lucy Saunders

Lucy Saunders is the author of five cookbooks and has written about craft beer and food for more than 20 years. One of my favorites of her books is Grilling With Beer *and her most recent is* Dinner In the Beer Garden. *For more tips on beer and food pairing, plus free recipes, follow her @lucybeercook*

BEER ENGINES AND NITRO

On your exploration of the brewpubs, you may find a beer engine. No, I'm not talking about an alternative motor for your car that runs on brewsky. The beer engine looks suspiciously like a tap handle, but not exactly. Normally, beer is under pressure from carbon dioxide—or air you pumped into the keg at a party—which pushes your pint out at the tap. Now this can affect your beer, of course. Air will eventually skunkify it (which is why pubs aren't using it; at a party you will probably finish the keg in one go, so it doesn't matter anyway) and too much CO_2 increases the carbonation of the brew, sometimes beyond what is desirable. There are a couple of tricks that can avoid all this.

The beer engine is one. It is a piston-operated pump that literally pulls the beer up from the barrel or holding tanks. This is what you can expect for many cask ales. So when it looks like the barkeep is out at the water pump in an old western, he or she is actually using a beer engine. When you use this, the beer gets a cascading foam going in the glass (very cool and hypnotic, really) and a meringue-like head. Look for the tap with the long curved swan-neck spout that delivers the beer right against the bottom of the glass to make that special effect.

In Ireland, the Guinness people came up with an alternative to the barkeep arm-wrestling the pump handle. They put the beer "under nitro." This was not some sort of IRA terrorist plan (talk about hitting the Irish where it hurts!), it means nitrogen. Unlike CO_2, nitrogen does not affect the natural carbonation of the beer and yet it still provides the pressure to get the brew up the lines and into your glass. You'll mostly see stouts coming out this way, though a few great exceptions are out there.

PRESERVING YOUR BEER

You probably know enough to cool your beer before you drink it, but remember that many craft brews are not pasteurized. Yes, hops are a natural preservative, but let's face it, we are not sailing round the Cape of Good Hope to India eating hardtack and hoping for the best for the ale. This is fine beer, like fine wine, and deserves some tender loving care.

If during your brewery travels you pick up a growler, put that thing on ice! If you don't refrigerate unpasteurized beer, you are getting it at less than its best and perhaps eventually at its worst. Basically, anything above 75 degrees may begin to produce some off flavors. Excepting bottle-conditioned live yeast beers, beers degrade over time; they get old. The higher the temperature, the faster that process goes. (A beer in a hot room for a week will taste perhaps twice as old as one kept at normal room temperature.) If you are picking up brew on a longer road trip, take a cooler along or bring it inside to your hotel room. The longer you leave good beer exposed to light and heat, the more likely the taste will deteriorate until you have the infamous beer of Pepé Le Pew.

That said, beer is not milk, so don't freak out if the temperature is a little high for a short while or if it is being re-cooled a few times. The hot trunk coming back from the liquor store? Not a big deal. A week in the trunk on vacation in July? Don't do it.

BREW YOUR OWN

OK, I know what you're thinking: if so many of these brewmasters started in their basements, why can't I? Well, truth is, you can!

Homebrewing supply stores are many nowadays. A basic single-stage brew kit includes a 6.5 gallon plastic bucket with a lid and fermentation lock, a siphoning tube, bottle brush, handheld bottle capper and caps,

CANS VS. BOTTLES

Because you couldn't spend your entire life at the saloon—though many have tried—we developed methods of taking some brew home with us. Growlers and the like worked fine but didn't last long. Bottling was the best method back in the late nineteenth century. But canning beer was in the  works, at least in research, even before Prohibition, but that dark space between the 18th and 21st Amendments put cans on hold. Beer reacts with steel, so to prevent that American Can Co. developed a can liner. G. Krueger Brewing of New Jersey became the first to use the "Keglined" cans in 1935, and from that point forward, cans grew to take over the market. Continental Can Co. gave us the "cone top," a can with a tapered top capped like a bottle. Minnesota brewers Gluek and Fitger's were early adopters of the cone tops.

Most cans were flat-topped cylinders. Initially, one needed a pointed can opener (a "church key") to puncture the top to get at the beer. Then the pull tab arrived, invented by Ermal Fraze in 1959, and this was big news. You can still find old Pabst steel cans touting "No opener needed!" A prized can for collectors. After a couple decades of cutting our feet on those tabs at the beach, the Sta-Tab came into favor—the little lever we still use today that stays with the can—unless you are collecting them for the Ronald McDonald House.

As the craft brewing age came upon us, bottles became the favored packaging. Beer tastes better from glass, we said. The bottles are sexier, we believed. In a bar brawl one couldn't break a can and cut someone.

Pragmatism, however, is bringing back the cans—both in 12 and 16 oz sizes. And it all makes good sense. No returns or deposits, easier to recycle. Easier to stack, and thus easier to ship and store. Lighter, quick to cool, and not so fragile like glass. Plus, it keeps the beer-damaging light out completely. We still think it tastes different, but that's why you should always pour your beer into the proper glassware anyway, even the bottled variety.

and hopefully, instructions. You then need a recipe pack and about 50 returnable-style bottles (not twist-offs). (Grolsch bottles with the ceramic stopper also work great; you only need to buy new rubber rings for the seal.) The kit starts around $50. A two-stage kit throws in a hydrometer, thermometer, and a 5-gallon glass "carboy" where the brew from the bucket goes to complete fermentation. Now you can watch it like an aquarium. Don't put any fish in it though.

Ingredient kits have all you need for a certain recipe. Simple light ales might start around $25 while an IPA with oak chips can get up around $50. Each makes about 50 bottles of beer. In many cases you are using malt extracts thus skipping the grinding of grain in the wort-making process. As you go deeper into the art you will likely want to do this yourself as well.

If your future brewpub patrons are really slow drinkers or Mormons, this basic kit will do you fine. That said, the pros are by no means always using the state-of-the-art equipment either. Remember Egyptians and Sumerians were already making beer over 5,000 years ago, and they didn't even have toilet paper yet. Um… my point is big brewers might have the funds to get the fancy copper brew kettles made in Bavaria and a micro-biology lab, while others at least got their start with used equipment that had other original purposes. Old dairy tanks are popular.

Or if you want to try it before you buy it, go use someone else's equipment. Vine Park Brewing in St. Paul offers brew-on-premise, which means you rent the time on their equipment and brew a batch, leave it to ferment, then come back and take it home.

Before you get all excited about naming your beers and what the sign on the brewpub is going to look like, there is much more to consider. When I wrote my first beer guide back in 2006 (*The Wisconsin Beer Guide: A Travel Companion*), I had the pleasure of meeting Tom Porter of Lake Louie Brewing Co. in Arena, Wisconsin, who had a thing or two to say about the challenges of starting a brewery. I got such a kick out of it that now I include it in all my brewery guidebooks.

ON STARTING A BREWERY: TOM PORTER

If you want to start a brewery, use somebody else's money. Because you can go big to start, big enough to make it a profitable minimum, and then if it goes belly up you just tell them, "Sorry, guys, I did the best I could!"

I'm on the hook for it, win or lose. It *does* give you tremendous impetus to not fail. There's no doubt about it. "Hey, you gotta make good beer." That's a given. There's nobody out there making really crummy beer anymore, they all went belly up and we all bought their used equipment. It's a given that the beer is pretty darn good. Yeah, there are different interpretations of style, but it's really all about costs.

I could be in the muffler business, or I could be in the hub cap business; I could be making paper clips for chrissakes, as long as the paper clip quality is as good as everybody else's, it doesn't matter. The reality is you better be darn good on cost control and you better know business, and I didn't. I was an engineer. Engineers sit way in back of a great big company. Someone else goes and sells it, someone else decides if there is profit in it. By the time the paper ever gets to your desk, it's a done deal. I went from the engineering business to having to *do* the business, the books, the capital decisions, the sales... *inventory* control. All those things: debt amortization, accounting... ggarrggh, accounting? Man! I never went to accounting classes. I got out of those thinking they were like the plague to me. "A credit is a debit until it's paid?!?" *What?!?*

My accounting system that started out when I started this brewery is I had a bucket of money. And every time I get some more I put it in the bucket. And when I need it, I take it out of the bucket. When the bucket's empty I got to stop taking money out until I get some more to put in. Well, that system still works here, but there's a WHOLE—SERIES—OF BUCKETS now! There's literally *dozens* of buckets. It gets hard to remember which one do I put it into and which one do I take it out of. And sometimes you don't notice one's empty. So business and accounting—that's really been my learning curve. I went from going "What's a balance sheet?" to a profit and loss statement, and now I work off cash flow statements and sometimes I split them up. I want to know where the push and pull is of my cash flow, because that's really what makes a good businessman. And I'm learning this because I HAVE to. And it has had NOTHING to do with making good beer. The good beer part is a given. You've gotta have it. If you don't have it, don't even think about it. But having that is not enough. I have a lot of people here coming through the door on tours and such saying, "I'm thinking of starting a brewpub. Gees, I make really good homebrew." And I say, "That's a really good first step." But the second through fortieth steps are... how are your plumbing skills? How're your carpentry skills? Can you pour concrete? Can you weld? And then can you balance a balance sheet every thirty days?

BARLEY'S ANGELS

Few things are more irritating than the notion that women somehow don't like beer. Testament to the nonsense of that idea is an organization called Barley's Angels (barleysangels.org). An international network of local chapters—100 chapters in 7 countries—Barley's Angels unites women around the world who appreciate good beer. They host events, both for fun and education, such as beer and food/chocolate pairings or cooking with beer discussions, and they organize beer outings. Bringing women together over beers is their mission as is helping breweries, beer bars, and restaurants grow their beer-wise female client base. Join a chapter or start one if there's not one near you. Follow them on Twitter @barleysangelsor and Facebook.com/barleysangels.org. There are five chapters currently in Minnesota:

Duluth
Barley's Angels – Duluth
Contact: Elissa Hansen | BarleysAngelsDS@gmail.com
www.BarleysAngelsDS.com
Twitter @BarleysAngelsDS
Facebook.com/BarleysAngelsDuluthSuperior
Meets every other month at changing location

Mankato

Barley's Angels of Southern Minnesota
Contacts: Angi Drynock-Proehl & Jennifer Johnson
barleysangelssomn@gmail.com
Meets monthly at changing location

Minneapolis – St. Paul

Barley's Angels – MN Twin Cities
Contact: Megan Parker | barleysangelsmn@gmail.com
Facebook.com/barleysangelsmn
Meets last Thursday of each month at changing location

Saint Cloud

Barley's Angels – MN Saint Cloud
Contact: Christy Zietlow | Christyzietlow@hotmail.com
Meets monthly at changing location

Willmar

Barley's Angels Willmar, MN
Contact: Elise Winter | ejw@usfamily.net
Meets monthly at The Oaks at Eagle Creek, 1100 26th Ave NE, Willmar

BIKING FOR BEER

It ought to be an Olympic event. Nothing like pedal power to get you out enjoying fresh Minnesota air… and on to the next fresh Minnesota beer. The state has a growing network of great bike paths. Whether you're pedaling the **Gitchi-Gami State Trail** from Two Harbors to Grand Marais along the North Shore of Lake Superior, or following the Mississippi River on the **West River Parkway** path, you are not far from a craft brewery. Within the brewery listings in this book, in the Directions, nearby or connecting bike trails are listed. In some cases, you can go from brewer to brewer almost without ever leaving the multiuse path for a city street. **Bike Walk Twin Cities** (BWTC), a program of Transit for Livable Communities, is a great resource and offers some maps. (bikewalktwincities.org) If you plan to carry a growler home, you might consider **Frost River's** (frostriver.com) cool growler packs made up in Duluth. Let me just remind you: wear a helmet and don't start pedaling if you've had too much. But if you are looking for pedal tour to some brews, here are a few suggestions:

MINNEAPOLIS:

Dinkytown Greenway (dinkytowngreenway.org) and **University of Minnesota Transitway** (a path but also a full sized road open only to bus, bicycle, and emergency vehicles) connects *Surly Brewing, Bang Brewing,* and *Urban Growler,* and connects across the river on a trail bridge to put you close to *Town Hall Brewery* and *Day Block Brewery.*

North Cedar Lake Trail connects the city of Hopkins (*LTD Brewing*) into Minneapolis, passing close to *Steel Toe Brewing.* The trail branches due east onto **Midtown Greenway** (midtowngreenway.org) which can get you to *The Herkimer* and *LynLake Brewery.* Or stay toward downtown and you'll pass within striking distance of *Sisyphus Brewing* (also near **Bassett's Creek Trail** intersection with **Cedar Lake Trail**) and *Fulton Brewing* and *The Freehouse* after passing Target Field. The Cedar Lake Trail can connect you to the **West River Parkway** path as well.

Hiawatha LRT Trail brings you close to *Northbound Smokehouse & Brewpub*

OTHER MINNESOTA BEER BIKING:

Duluth Lakewalk is a multi-use asphalt path that follows the Lake Superior shoreline for 3 miles and connects *Fitger's Brewhouse* to *Canal Park Brewery.*

Cannon Valley Trail (cannonvalleytrail.com) is a nice ride near *Red Wing Brewing* in Red Wing, naturally.

Gitchi-Gami State Trail (ggta.org) connects *Castle Danger Brewery* in Two Harbors to *Gun Flint Tavern & Brewpub* and *Voyageur Brewing* in Grand Marais.

Lake Minnetonka LRT Regional Trail spans the distance between *Excelsior Brewing* in Excelsior and *ENKI Brewing* in Victoria.

Minnesota River Bluffs LRT Regional Trail (connects to North Cedar Lake Trail) brings you between *Lucid Brewing* and *LTD Brewing.*

Where's The Beer At?

(INTRO TO THE LISTINGS)

The listings for all the commercial brewers in Minnesota are divided here into five zones: 1—Minneapolis and St. Paul, 2—Greater Twin Cities Area, 3—Southern Minnesota, 4—Central and Northwest Minnesota, and 5—Northeast Minnesota (including the North Shore). Each section has a map of that portion of the state with the brewtowns marked. (Minneapolis-St. Paul includes a separate map for the Northeast Minneapolis neighbrewhood.) Within each zone the communities are listed in alphabetical order by city with the brewpubs and breweries below the city/town heading. Watch for textboxes that contain a few extra non-brewing but brew-related attractions and other interesting bits you can read during your journey.

HOW TO USE THE LISTINGS

OK, this isn't rocket science, but let's go over a brief summary of the finer points of the listings.

Brewmaster or Head Brewer: So you know who to ask brewing questions.

Number of Beers: This may indicate the number of different brews in a year and/or the number of beers on tap.

Staple Beers: Always on tap.

Rotating Beers: Like roulette only with beer, the beers that may come and go, often seasonal brews, series beers, or in some cases one-offs that are listed here only to show the breadth of their brewing styles. Mention of casks, barrel-aging, or other specialties might be here as well.

Best Time to Go: Be aware that opening hours, happy hours, or trivia nights, etc. listed here may change, especially seasonally. Best to call or check websites to be sure.

Samples and **Tours**: Prices (and tour times) may change from what you see here.

Got food? A recent law change does allow **brewery** taprooms to get approval to serve food, though most probably still don't. In that case, most are likely "food friendly," meaning you can order delivery or bring your own grub into the taproom. **Brewpubs** by legal definition serve food and may offer a full bar and other breweries' beers.

Directions: For those without a GPS, these written directions should indicate the nearest major highway and specific driving directions and distances. Sometimes bus and metro lines/stops are also shown in italics, as are nearby trails and paths for cyclists.

Special Offer: This is NOT a guarantee. The brewer reserves the right to rescind this offer at any time and for any reason. This is something the management of the place you're visiting suggested they'd give to a patron who comes in and gets this book signed on the signature line of that particular brewer in the back of the book. This is a one-time bonus and the signature cancels it out. You must have a complete book, and photocopies or print-outs don't count. I didn't charge them and they didn't charge me; it's out of the goodness of their hearts, so take it as such and don't get all goofy on them if the keychain turns out to be a bumper sticker or supplies have run out or the bartender that night didn't get the memo about how the offer works. And if they are offering a discount on a beer, it is assumed that it is the brewer's own beer, not Bud Light or some such stuff or that fancy import you've been wishing would go on special. Legal drinking age still applies, of course. Not all brewers are participating and that will be noted on each brewer's page.

Stumbling Distance: Two or three cool things near the brewery that are very local, very beery, very Minnesotan, or just plain cool. Some may be more of a short car ride away. If you really are stumbling, get a designated driver for those.

And that's about it, the rest should be self-explanatory. Enjoy the ride! Last one all the way through the breweries is a rotten egg. Or a skunk beer.

LISTINGS BY BREWERY

56 Brewing . . . . Zone 1 — Minneapolis
612Brew . . . . Zone 1 — Minneapolis
Able Seedhouse & Brewery. . . . . Zone 1 — Minneapolis
Angry Inch Brewing . . . . .Zone 2 — Lakeville
August Schell Brewing Co.. Zone 3 — New Ulm
Bad Weather Brewing Co.. .Zone 1 — St. Paul
Badger Hill Brewing Co.. . . . . Zone 2 — Shakopee
Bang Brewing . . . . .Zone 1 — St. Paul
Bank Brewing Co.. . . . . .Zone 3 — Hendricks
Barley John's Brew Pub . . . . .Zone 2 — New Brighton
Bauhaus Brew Labs . . . . Zone 1 — Minneapolis
Beaver Island Brewing. . . . . Zone 4 — St. Cloud
Bemidji Brewing Co. . . . . .Zone 4 — Bemidji
Bent Brewstillery. . . . . .Zone 2 — Roseville
Bent Paddle Brewing Co. . . . . Zone 5 — Duluth
Big Wood Brewery . . . . Zone 2 — White Bear Lake
Blacklist Brewing. . . . . Zone 5 — Duluth
Boathouse Brew Pub. . . . . Zone 5 — Ely
Boom Island Brewing Co. . . . . Zone 1 — Minneapolis
Borealis Fermentery. . . . . Zone 5 Knife River
Brau Brothers Brewing Co . . . . Zone 3 — Marshall
Bryn Mawr Brewing . . . . Zone 1 — Minneapolis
Burning Brothers Brewing . . . . Zone 1 — St. Paul
Canal Park Brewing Co. . . . . Zone 5 — Duluth
Carmody Irish Pub & Brewing . . . . Zone 5 — Duluth
Castle Danger Brewery . . . . Zone 5 — Two Harbors
Dangerous Man Brewing Co. . . . . Zone 1 — Minneapolis
Day Block Brewery . . . . Zone 1 — Minneapolis
Eastlake Brewery & Tavern. . . . . Zone 1 — Minneapolis
ENKI Brewing . . . . .Zone 2 — Victoria
Excelsior Brewing Co.. . . . . .Zone 2 — Excelsior
Fair State Brewing Cooperative . . . . Zone 1 — Minneapolis
Fitger's Brewhouse . . . . Zone 5 — Duluth
Foxhole Brewhouse . . . . Zone 4 — Willmar
The Freehouse . . . . Zone 1 — Minneapolis
F-Town Brewing Co.. . . . . .Zone 3 — Faribault
Fulton Brewing Co. . . . . Zone 1 — Minneapolis
Goat Ridge Brewing Co.. . . . . Zone 4 — New London
Granite City Food and Brewery . . . . .Zone 2 — Eagan
Granite City Food and Brewery . . . . Zone 2 — Maple Grove
Granite City Food and Brewery . . . . .Zone 2 — Roseville

LISTINGS BY BREWTOWN

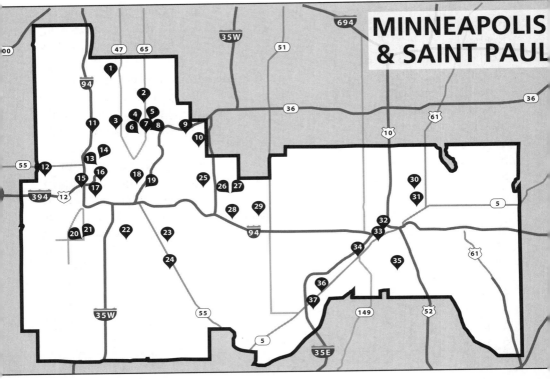

MINNEAPOLIS & SAINT PAUL

1: 56 Brewing
2: Fair State Brewing Cooperative
3: Dangerous Man Brewing Co.
4: Indeed Brewing Co. & Taproom
5: Sociable Cider Werks
6: Able Seedhouse & Brewery
7: 612Brew
8: Bauhaus Brew Labs
9: NorthGate Brewing
10: Insight Brewing
11: Boom Island Brewing Co.
12: Bryn Mawr Brewing
13: Fulton Brewery
14: The Freehouse
15: Sisyphus Brewing
16: Rock Bottom Restaurant & Brewery
17: Lakes & Legends Brewing
18: Day Block Brewing
19: Minneapolis Town Hall Brewery

20: LynLake Brewery
21: The Herkimer Pub and Brewery
22: Eastlake Brewery & Tavern
23: Harriet Brewing Co
24: Northbound Smokehouse & Brewpub
25: Surly Brewing Co.
26: Urban Growler™
27: Bang Brewing Company
28: Lake Monster Brewing
29: Burning Brothers Brewing
30: Sidhe Brewing Co.
31: Saint Paul's Flat Earth Brewing
32: Tin Whiskers Brewing Company
33: Great Waters Brewing Company
34: Bad Weather Brewing
35: Wabasha Brewing Co.
36: Vine Park Brewing Co.
37: Summit Brewing Co.

ZONE 1
Minneapolis – Saint Paul

56 Brewing . . . . .Minneapolis
612Brew . . . . .Minneapolis
Able Seedhouse & Brewery. . . . . .Minneapolis
Bauhaus Brew Labs. . . . . .Minneapolis
Boom Island Brewing Co. . . . . .Minneapolis
Bryn Mawr Brewing . . . . .Minneapolis
Dangerous Man Brewing Co. . . . . .Minneapolis
Day Block Brewery . . . . .Minneapolis
Eastlake Brewery & Tavern. . . . . .Minneapolis
Fair State Brewing Cooperative . . . . .Minneapolis
The Freehouse . . . . .Minneapolis
Fulton Brewing Co. . . . . .Minneapolis
Harriet Brewing Co. . . . . .Minneapolis
The Herkimer . . . . .Minneapolis
Indeed Brewing Co.. . . . . .Minneapolis
Insight Brewing. . . . . .Minneapolis
Lakes & Legends Brewing . . . . .Minneapolis
LynLake Brewery . . . . .Minneapolis
Minneapolis Town Hall Brewery . . . . .Minneapolis
Northbound Smokehouse & Brewpub . . . . .Minneapolis
NorthGate Brewing . . . . .Minneapolis
Rock Bottom Restaurant & Brewery . . . . .Minneapolis
Sisyphus Brewing Co. . . . . .Minneapolis
Sociable Cider Werks . . . . .Minneapolis
Surly Brewing Co. . . . . .Minneapolis
Bad Weather Brewing Co.. . . . . .St. Paul
Bang Brewing . . . . .St. Paul
Burning Brothers Brewing . . . . .St. Paul
Great Waters Brewing Co. . . . . .St. Paul
Lake Monster Brewing . . . . .St. Paul
Saint Paul's Flat Earth Brewing Co. . . . . .St. Paul
Sídhe Brewing Co.. . . . . .St. Paul
Summit Brewing Co.. . . . . .St. Paul
Tin Whiskers Brewing Co.. . . . . .St. Paul
Urban Growler ™ Brewing Co.. . . . . .St. Paul
Vine Park Brewing . . . . .St. Paul
Wabasha Brewing Co.. . . . . .St. Paul

NORTHEAST MINNEAPOLIS OR "NORDEAST"

This northeast corner of the city north of Hennepin Avenue and tucked up against the east bank of the Mississippi River has long been the place to find beer. Back in the late 19th century, John Orth built his brewery here. Just down the street from his was Gluek Brewing (now just a park called Gluek). In 1890, four breweries merged to make Minneapolis Brewing & Malting Co. and operated out of John Orth's brewery before making a new brewery on that site. Notably four different architectural styles were used. The flagship beer was none other than Golden Grain Belt and it would go on to be a household name as Grain Belt. In 1967, the brewery changed its name to Grain Belt Brewery and brewed its namesake here until 1976 when Heileman Brewing took it over and closed it, moving the beer to the old Schmidt Brewery.

THE OLD GRAIN BELT BREWERY AT 1220 MARSHALL STREET NE, MINNEAPOLIS

But this lovely building with its cream colored brick remains standing thanks to being listed on the National Register of Historic Places. It is now home to RSP Architects, which led its restoration and redevelopment.

If you are in the Northeast Minneapolis neighbrewhood, give it a drive by and take a photo of history. This is four blocks west of *Dangerous Man Brewing* along 13th Ave.

If you are entering this part of town from Hennepin Avenue in the southwest corner of the 'hood, you can see the 1940's Grain Belt sign as you cross the Hennepin Avenue Bridge going east. The sign, which used to light up at night, stands high above Nicollet Island in the Mississippi River. Until 2014 it was actually the property of a family trust; the Eastman family once owned the island and the old sign upon it. But that year August Schell Brewing, which had purchased the beer brand in 2002 (and still brews it), sought to acquire the sign, and with cooperation from the Preservation Alliance of Minnesota, they'd restore the sign. The façade is porcelain and depicts a giant Grain Belt bottle cap. Plans are to turn the lights back on as well after an update to modern bulbs.

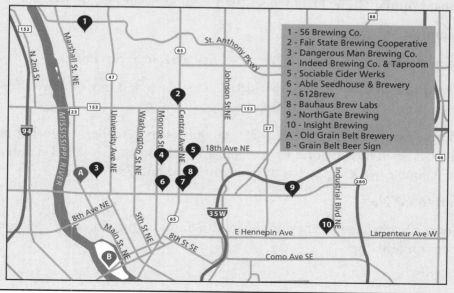

1 - 56 Brewing Co.
2 - Fair State Brewing Cooperative
3 - Dangerous Man Brewing Co.
4 - Indeed Brewing Co. & Taproom
5 - Sociable Cider Werks
6 - Able Seedhouse & Brewery
7 - 612Brew
8 - Bauhaus Brew Labs
9 - NorthGate Brewing
10 - Insight Brewing
A - Old Grain Belt Brewery
B - Grain Belt Beer Sign

56 BREWING

Opened: 2015
Head Brewers: Nick Chute and Kale Johnson
Address: 3134 California Street NE • Minneapolis, MN 55418
Phone: 612-404-0056
Web Site: www.56brewing.com
Annual Production: up to 450 barrels
Number of Beers: 4 core beers, various seasonal and limited releases

Staple Beers:
» AMERICAN PALE ALE
» DARK CHOCOLATE COCONUT STOUT
» HONEY KÖLSCH
» RYE LAGER

Rotating Beers:
» KELLERBIER
» MAPLE SYRUP PORTER
» OKTOBERFEST
» PILSNERS and lighter beers in summer
» THE PRESIDENTIAL STREET SERIES (special brews named for the first 17 presidents streets in NE Minneapolis)
» … plus some barrel aging.

Most Popular Brew: Dark Chocolate Coconut Stout (also in barrels)

Samples: Yes, free sips.

Brewmaster's Fave: Kale: APA | Nick: Maple Syrup Porter

Best Time to Go: Open on Saturday 11AM–6PM and most Friday afternoons until 6PM. Check the website.

Where can you buy it? Here in 750 ml bottles and growlers to go, but no pints. Also in liquor stores in kegs and 750 ml bottles. Glass and stainless steel double-walled growlers available in 64 oz and 750 ml sizes.

Got food? No.

Tours? Yes, whenever they are open. Sip and ask questions. By appointment on other days.

Special Offer: A highly prized piece of swag during your signature visit.

Directions: There are many ways to get here, but here's a general method. University Ave runs north/south through the city, crossing Hennepin Ave near downtown and Broadway in the Northeast Minneapolis neighborhood. From Broadway go 1.3 miles more north on University and then turn left on 27th Ave. Two long blocks later turn right (north) on California St. Go 0.3 mile and it's on your left.

Cyclists: *The brewery is a block south of the 55-mile bike loop of the Grand Rounds National Scenic Byway which passes along St. Anthony Parkway. The best map may be online at Peddle Minnesota (pedalmn.com) but the municipal park system also has one.*

The Beer Buzz: You know those CSAs, the Community Supported Agriculture groups that you join or subscribe to and they send you a box of fresh veggies every week in summer? Well, this is a CSB—Community Supported Brewery—and Minnesota's first. Members pay a fee to receive a certain number of growlers throughout the year, the frequency depending on which of the three membership plans they choose. Members get a discount on the typical non-member growler price, plus free swag and first dibs on beer releases. Sure beats a weekly box full of eggplant, beets, and zucchini.

Co-founder and brewer Kale is schooled in engineering and science but has long had a passion for homebrewing. His wife Kerry told him, "You've got to live your dream," and they started making a plan. Brewer Nick was a tenant of Kale's, and one day when they started chatting, Kale saw his homebrew kit and they became friends. Things were falling into place. Kale and Kerry turned their house into an office full of paperwork to get the approvals for the brewery. Brewer Nick joined them as a partner, along with Kristin Noraker as chief financial officer, Joe Wirth as chief technology officer, and Micah Godfrey as facilities director.

Brewer Nick has a philosophy degree, in case you were wondering what one could do with that major. He also has a food background and really gets into the technical side of brewing. He likes to use local ingredients as much as possible. Maple syrup used in some of the brews comes from Nick's family's farm, for example. As part of 56 Brewing's "Garden to Growler" mission, the brewery keeps a nice little garden outside with hop vines and some varieties of kale and rhubarb, spices, and herbs. Much of this will end up in small batches of beer. And then the spent grain finds a local home as well: *Mississippi Mushrooms* (mississippimushrooms.com) uses it to grow their 'shrooms.

The brewery occupies a 710 square foot space in an old warehouse and manufacturing area, but they weren't the first brewer to operate here. NorthGate Brewing started in this very same space before growth compelled them to move to their current location (still in Northeast Minneapolis). The timing was perfect: NorthGate was looking to sell the 10-barrel system on site right around the same time 56 Brewing was moving forward with their plans in late 2014. Kale chatted with NorthGate in August and by the end of October took over the equipment. By March 2015, they were brewing and organizing a Kickstarter program to get a canning line going.

For now, Kale is keeping his full-time engineering job. There is no tap-room here—just bottles, growlers and kegs, all of which, when purchased, need to be consumed somewhere else according to state law. They are also contemplating a limited delivery service by bike. And speaking of bicycles, *PedalPub* (952-703-9000, twincities.pedalpub.com) begins its Nord'East Minneapolis tour right across the street, and pedaling clients stop in for samples before a pedal tour. Be aware the PedalPub does not allow glass on the tour.

Facebook/56brewing and Twitter @56brewing

Stumbling Distance: *Riffs Smokehouse* (3134 California Street NE, Suite 106-B, 612-208-1623, facebook.com/riffssmokehouse), in the same complex, sells smoked meats and pulled pork and offers samples. *Stanley's Northeast Bar Room* (2500 University Ave NE, 612-788-2529, stanleysbarroom.com) has good bar food, 32 taps, and happy hours every day. *Jax Café* (1928 University Ave NE, 612-789-7297, jaxcafe.com), a family-owned steakhouse since 1933, has become an institution. Have an old German experience at *Gasthof Zur Gemutlichkeit* (2300 University Ave NE, 612-781-3860, gasthofzg.com) complete with accordion music, boots of German beer, and sauerbraten.

612BREW

Founded: 13 February 2013
Brewmaster: Robert Kasak
Address: 945 Broadway St. NE • Minneapolis, MN 55413
Phone: 612-217-0437
Web Site: www.612brew.com
Annual Production: 3,400 barrels
Number of Beers: up to 8 on tap, plus a firkin

Staple Beers:
- » GATEWAY PARK PRE-PROHIBITION LAGER
- » SIX AMERICAN PALE ALE
- » UNRATED RYE IPA

Rotating Beers:
- » MARY ANN GINGER LAGER (summer)
- » PAYBACK OATMEAL PORTER (winter)
- » ZERO HOUR BLACK ALE (summer)
- » Various seasonals, always at least one dark brew on tap. Weekly firkins.

Most Popular Brew: Unrated Rye IPA

Samples: Yes, four 7-oz. pours for $11

Brewmaster's Fave: SIX American Pale Ale

Best Time to Go: Open Wed–Thu 4–10PM, Fri 2:30PM–12AM, Sat 12PM–12AM, Sun 11:30AM–9PM. Live music on the patio in summer. Friday firkins. Art-A-Whirl® in May when they host 20+ bands for the Art District weekend (see text box).

Where can you buy it? Draft accounts and in cans in the Twin Cities area. Growlers on site and will refill other brewers' growlers.

Got food? No, but food friendly and a food cart is typically outside.

Tours? Free with a canned food donation. Typically on a weekend and frequently led by the brewer himself. Check the calendar on the website.

Special Offer: Buy one beer, get one free with your book signature.

Directions: From I-94 take Exit 229 and turn east on Broadway Ave (from the south at Exit 229 you need to take Washington north to

Broadway first) and after 1.9 miles, turn left (north) on Tyler St. The parking lot is behind the first building on your left. (From the east side, I-35W Exit 21A will get you onto County Road 88/New Brighton Blvd. Go south and turn right (west) on Broadway and it's 0.6 mile to the brewpub. Turn right on Tyler St and the lot is on the left.)

The Beer Buzz: Stop in for some Six One Two brew (the number is the area code, in case you weren't paying attention). Brewer Robert started homebrewing in the mid-2000s, and by 2009 he was working on a business plan and looking for a site. For years he was a "corporate desk jockey" putting in time at Best Buy, Target, Lifetime Fitness—negotiations and business experience that would help him when he went out on his own. He found three other partners, Ryan Libby, Jamey Rossbach, and Adit Kalra, and they financed the effort themselves and did much of the work.

Where Hennepin Avenue crossed the bridge into downtown Minneapolis, the Gateway District, there once was a fountain. Nearby stood the famous Metropolitan building, which was razed in 1961. The fountain was a gathering place; the building an historical landmark. The flagship lager takes its name from that park. Stones from the ruins have been worked into 612Brew's own gathering place around a fountain and tiny amphitheater outside.

Back in 1924, this building, The Broadway, was a mattress factory—you can still see Land of Nod on the side. It's been reclaimed as retail and office space and stands as a sort of gateway to Northeast Minneapolis, popularly known as an arts district, but now also a notable brewery district. Inside the brewery a colorful mural faces the door. The space shows high ceilings with exposed brick walls, a concrete floor, and large wood beams and columns. At center is an L-shaped bar counter around a central space full of tables, plus a proper bar with a reclaimed bowling lane for the bar top. Above the bar are two TVs plus an LED menu of the beers. Tanks gleam in the back of the taproom beyond a rope. A glass garage door opens to the patio outside (dog friendly) in pleasant weather and here's where you find the amphitheater and fountain as well as live music performances. A food truck is parked here every night. Also, there are board games (kids are welcome and there are Pepsi products) at the bar and a private event space.

There's a parking lot for The Broadway plus a lot of bike racks for pedaling pint seekers. From the parking lot, walk to the far end of the lot from the street and go left behind the building to get to the brewery entrance.

ATM on site. WiFi. Facebook.com/612BREW and Twitter @612Brew

Stumbling Distance: *Spyhouse Coffee* (612-345-4348, spyhousecoffee. com) roasts its own in the same building, selling baked goods. *Uncle Franky's* (728 Broadway St NE, 612-455-2181, unclefrankys.com) is a simple place for burgers, Chicago dogs, and malts.

Bauhaus Brew Labs is just down the street from here and *Indeed Brewing* and *Sociable Cider Werks* are each about a 10-minute walk.

ART DISTRICT MEETS BEER DISTRICT

Brewing's an art, right? So it's only fitting that so many brewers make their home in Northeast Minneapolis, the city's Art District. You can find abundant galleries throughout this part of town, and artist studios even inside the former Grain Belt Bottling House and Warehouse (now Grain Belt Studios at 77 & 79 13th Ave NE).

Watch for Art-A-Whirl® the third weekend in May. This free event organized by the Northeast Minneapolis Arts Association (NEMAA) sees over 60 artist studios, galleries, and other art sales and displays open for tours and artist meet-and-greets, the largest event of its kind in North America. More than 500 artists are represented. The breweries get involved as well, hosting live music events, displaying local artists, and, of course, satisfying everyone's thirst. Pick up a guide and map at the event or download both beforehand. If you miss this—and you shouldn't—check the NEMAA website for other art events throughout the year.

www.nemaa.org/art-a-whirl

@NemaaMN on Twitter! Use #ArtAWhirl

ABLE SEEDHOUSE & BREWERY

Planned opening: End of 2015
Brewmaster: Bobby Blasey
Address: 1121 Quincy Street NE • Minneapolis, MN 55413
Phone: TBD
Web Site: www.ablebeer.com
Annual Production: 2,000 barrels
Number of Beers: up to 8 on tap

Staple Beers:
» IPA
» Pale wheat pub table ale
» Red or an amber
» Sessionable Stout

Rotating Beers:
» Various seasonals

Samples: Yes, sample flights available.

Best Time to Go: *Tentative hours* (call or check website to confirm): Open Wed–Thu 3–11PM, Fri–Sat noon–close, possibly Sunday.

Where can you buy it? On tap here and to go in growlers, plus on tap in local bars and restaurants.

Got food? No, but food friendly, and food trucks are likely.

Tours? Yes. Check website for schedule.

Special Offer: A free sticker with your book signature.

Directions: From I-94 take Exit 229 and turn east on Broadway Ave (from the south at Exit 229 you need to take Washington north to Broadway first) and after 1.6 miles, turn left (north) on Quincy St, and the brewery is on your right. From the east side, I-35W Exit 21A will get you onto County Road 88/New Brighton Blvd. Go south and turn right (west) on Broadway and it's 0.8 mile to Quincy, turn right, and the brewery is on the right.

The Beer Buzz: Co-founder Casey Holley used to live in Lodi in Northern California. The sense of community and their agro-economic focus inspired him to want to create something similar. What better place than the Northeast Minneapolis community? Here's something you aren't going

PHOTO BY BRANDON WERTH

to read often in this book. Casey did *not* start out as a homebrewer. While everyone around him had homebrews going, Casey was doing home *malting*. So any brewery plan he was going to make started with the malt production. This is a rare opportunity for beer fans: an in-house malting facility. It's such an important part of the brewing process but few get to see the process up close. The grain is all regional with farmers producing rye and barley in northern Minnesota, wheat in western Minnesota, and barley and oats in nearby western Wisconsin.

The brewing stage is handled by Bobby Blasey who initially got into craft beer as a restaurant manager overseeing the beers. He graduated from the American Brewers Guild program and spent some time brewing at Mankato Brewery. Oh, and he plays the bagpipes. Casey initially approached Bobby asking him if he knew anyone interested in his malthouse/brewery idea. That turned out to be Bobby, who has a similar food philosophy. The two hit it off and Bobby spent the next 6-8 months developing recipes.

Able is located in the Highland Center at Quincy and Broadway, a 10,000 sq ft brick building from 1915 that used to be a light bulb factory for GE. In recent years it had served as a maintenance facility for City vehicles, especially buses. Now it's malting grains and serving beer in a 2,000 sq ft taproom. Outside is another 1,200 sq ft of patio space. The parking lot is huge and right across the street.

WiFi. Facebook.com and Twitter @AbleBeer
Instagram @ablebrewery

Stumbling Distance: *Brasa* (600 E Hennepin Ave, 612-379-3030, brasa.us) is a Creole-style rotisserie restaurant you shouldn't miss. *Red Stag Supperclub* (509 1st Ave NE, 612-767-7766, redstagsupperclub.com) ain't your typical supper club. Local, organic, great beer and cocktail list and Friday fish fry.

Indeed Brewing is two blocks from here up Quincy street. (The former James Page Brewing once occupied a building halfway between the two breweries.) *612Brew* is 3 blocks east.

Bauhaus Brew Labs

Founded: July 2014
Brewmaster: Matt Schwandt
Address: 1315 Tyler Street NE • Minneapolis, MN 55413
Phone: 612-276-6911
Web Site: www.bauhausbrewlabs.com
Annual Production: 5,000 barrels the first year, but expanding fast
Number of Beers: 5 on tap plus a cask on a beer engine

Staple Beers:
- » Sky-Five! (Midwest Cöast IPA)
- » Stargrazer (German-style Schwarzbier)
- » Wagon Party (West Cöast-style lager)
- » Wonderstuff (Neü Bohemian Pilsner)

Rotating Beers:
- » Copperpop Red Lager (spring)
- » Jingle Fever Baltic Porter (winter)
- » Schwandtoberfest Bavarian-Style Festbier
- » Über Düber Hoppy Bock (winter)

Most Popular Brew: Sky-Five! in distribution, Wonderstuff in the taproom.

Samples: Yes, four 5-oz. pours for about $7.

Best Time to Go: Open Wed–Thu 4–11PM, Fri 3–11PM, Sat 12–11PM.

Where can you buy it? Here on tap and in growlers to go (will fill other's 750 ml and 64 oz. growlers if clean and showing the required government warning). Distributed in cans, some 22-oz. bombers, and draft accounts throughout the greater Twin Cites Metro area and growing. See the brew map on their website for the liquor store, bar, or restaurant nearest you.

Got food? No, but food friendly, and a food truck is typically on site.

Tours? Yes, a one-hour tour for $5 on the first Saturday of the month at 11AM. Book a spot and pay on their website.

Special Offer: "A free high-five and a flight of our tastiest brews" with your book signature.

Directions: From I-94 take Exit 229 and turn east on Broadway Ave (from the south at Exit 229 you need to take Washington north to Broadway first) and after 1.9 miles, turn left (north) on Tyler St and continue 0.2 mile. The parking lot is beyond a passage through the buildings on your right. (From the east side, I-35W Exit 21A will get you onto County Road 88/New Brighton Blvd. Go south and turn right (west) on Broadway and it's 0.6 mile to the brewpub. Turn right on Tyler St, go 0.2 mile, and find the brewery beyond the brick buildings on your right.)

The Beer Buzz: The name Bauhaus (not brauhaus!) actually comes from an art school in Germany that existed from just after World War I until 1933. Its concept was to bring all the arts together in a building sense, from the craftwork of furniture and pottery to the design of architecture. Bauhaus Brew Labs brings that spirit of creativity to their beer. This family-run 30-barrel production brewery occupies the former Crown Iron Works building set back from Tyler Road—go between buildings like a short tunnel to a factory-looking structure across the parking lot beyond.

Three months after opening to the public they were ordering additional 60-barrel fermenters, and another three months after that they were hiring an assistant brewer for Matt.

Inside is a wide open industrial brewing space with cans stacked to the ceiling, and a 2,000-square foot taproom with a nice view of the large-scale brewing just beyond. Communal tables fill the space before the bar built of reclaimed wood, and a stage is in the corner for live music. Two industrial-sized garage doors at the taproom end of the building open to a patio area and typically a food truck. Some brewery graffiti adorns the bricks outside and the patio is sheltered from part of the former iron works high above. The taproom and patio are dog friendly and there are board games to entertain.

The brewery's logo, painted high up on the bricks in the taproom, is the silhouette of a human head with the combined icons of the flagship beers—a red asterisk for Wonderstuff, a blue crescent moon and stars for Stargrazer, a green sun for Sky-Five!, and a pink pinwheel for Wagon Party—plus the yellow light bulb of inspiration, all inside a white circle. Each beer has this head and its respective icon on its label.

WiFi. Facebook.com/bauhausBrewLabs and Twitter @BauhausBrewLabs

Stumbling Distance: You can walk to *612Brew* from here or even *Sociable Cider Werks* and *Indeed Brewing*.

Boom Island Brewing Co.

Founded: February 2014
Brewmaster: Kevin Welch
Address: 2014 Washington Avenue N • Minneapolis, MN 55411
Phone: 612-227-9635
Web Site: www.boomislandbrewing.com
Annual Production: 1,500 barrels
Number of Beers: 8–10 on tap

Beers:
- » Brimstone Tripel
- » Hoodoo Dubbel
- » LoMoMo Palooza
- » Silvius Belgian Pale Ale
- » Thoprock IPA
- » Witness
- » Yule Ale (holiday ale with different spices each year)

Most Popular Brew: All sell very similarly.

Samples: Yes, flights of 4, 6, or all.

Best Time to Go: Open Wed–Fri 4–9PM, Sat 1–9PM, Sun 1–6PM. Happy hour is 4–6PM Wed–Thu. Watch for Boom Days in July, with live music, food, and special beers. Belgian National Day is the second weekend of July.

Where can you buy it? Here on tap and in growlers to go, and in 750ml bottles throughout MN.

Got food? No, but food friendly, and food trucks visit throughout summer.

Tours? Yes, every other Saturday for $5 with a flight of 4 tasters.

Special Offer: $1 off your first pint when you get your book signed.

Directions: From the north heading south on I-94 take Exit 229 and turn east on Broadway Ave. After 0.1 mile, turn left (north) on Washington Ave. (Or from the south, take Exit 229 and turn left (north) on Washington Ave and go 0.3 mile.) The brewery is on the right, but entrance is in back.

Cyclists: *The West River Parkway trail is just two blocks east, along the Mississippi and connects south to downtown Minneapolis.*

The Beer Buzz: Welcome to the Boom Room. Kevin and Qiuxia Welch, the two owners, are classically trained professional French horn players, and they met at a French horn convention in China. How is that relevant to the brewery? Well, they've been known to break out the horns for fanfare purposes during beer releases. They continue to play professionally in the area. Kevin took homebrewing to professional levels after years of pleasing his friends with free beer. When he was playing in the orchestra, he'd bring his brews to dress rehearsals. Silvius, his Belgian Pale Ale, won a homebrew contest, and he ended up winning two more medals at the Upper Mississippi Mash-Out before making the decision to open a brewery. He became certified in tungsten inert gas (TIG) welding for stainless steel, so he could create his own brewing equipment.

In pursuit of deeper knowledge of his favored Beglian brews, he set off for Belgium on lengthy *pils-grimages* over two summers, visiting 13 breweries there, meeting brewers and sitting down to drink and talk shop with them. And when he returned home, he brought nine yeast strains with him. The couple chose to open their brewery in this neighborhood, a sort of rough part of town at the time, which is already changing for the better. Their first location was a couple blocks from here.

Boom Island brews creative bottle-conditioned Belgian-style beers, corked and caged, right here in Minneapolis. Some of the beers are exclusive to the taproom. Horns and flags hang across the ceiling. In the corner is a short L-shaped stainless steel bar. You can play Sjoelbak (Dutch/Belgian shuffleboard). There is a small fenced-in parking lot around back where the entrance also is. Boom Island was an actual island above the dam in the Mississippi where there's now a park with a great skyline view of Minneapolis.

WiFi. Facebook.com/boomislandbeer and Twitter @BoomIslandBeer

Stumbling Distance: *Merwin Liquors* (700 W Broadway Ave, 612-529-9639, shopmerwins.com) has quite a nice craft beer selection and delivers free in the local metro area. *Element Pizza* (96 Broadway St. NE, 612-379-3028, elementpizza.com) is a family joint offering some of the Cities' best wood-fired pizza. Though closer to *Target Field* and *Fulton Brewing*, *Eli's Bar & Grill* (elisfoodandcocktails.com) is popular for good eats and serves Boom Island's beer. The breweries of Northeast Minneapolis lie across the Mississippi River from here if you follow Broadway east.

Bryn Mawr Brewing Co.

Planned to Open: Late 2015
Brewmaster: "Ewald"
Address: 225 Thomas Avenue North • Minneapolis, MN 55405
Phone: TBD
Web Site: www.brynmawrbrewing.com

Directions: Take Hwy 55 west of I-94 for about 1 mile, turn left on Penn Ave, right on Glenwood, and left again on Thomas. The brewery is on the right, across the tracks.

Cyclists: *Part of Bassett's Creek Trail, which connects to Cedar Lake Trail, is right out front.*

The Beer Buzz: Go big or go home. That's what brewery president (and former co-owner of Vine Park Brewing) Dan Justesen says. Located on the banks of Bassett Creek, this will be a nice addition to the redeveloped former Glenwood Inglewood bottling facility. Their 50-barrel brewhouse was custom built in Bavaria, and they are bringing in some very cool new brewing technology that lowers pressure to achieve a boil at a lower temperature. Be sure to watch for a tour schedule once they are open. A taproom for 200 people and a huge beer garden are planned.

Facebook/Bryn.Mawr.Brewing and Twitter @brynmawrbrewing

Stumbling Distance: *Milda's Café* (1720 Glenwood Ave, 612-377-9460) open until 3PM, does great breakfast, rolls, and pasties. *Sisyphus Brewing* is a 5 minute drive from here.

Dangerous Man Brewing Co.

Founded: 2013
Brewmaster: Rob Miller (Owner), Keigan Knee
Address: 1300 2nd Street NE • Minneapolis, MN 55413
Phone: 612-236-4087
Web Site: www.dangerousmanbrewing.com
Annual Production: 1,000 barrels
Number of Beers: up to 12 on tap, with rotating casks/firkins

Staple Beers:
- » Chocolate Milk Stout
- » "a dark one, a light one, a hoppy one and a strong one"

Rotating Beers: (constantly changing and exploring)
- » Belgian Golden Strong
- » Cream Ale
- » Imperial Golden Rose Ale (with steeped rose petals)
- » Belgians (dubbel, tripel, table, etc.)
- » Porters (with coffee, hazelnut, or peanut butter, etc.)
- » Single Hop Series IPAs

Most Popular Brew: Chocolate Milk Stout

Samples: No flights.

Brewmaster's Fave: Chocolate Milk Stout

Best Time to Go: Open Tue–Thu 4–10pm, Fri 3pm–12am, Sat 12pm–12am. Busy like crazy on weekends.

Where can you buy it? Only here on tap in imperial pints (20 oz.) and half pints. Growlers and growlettes (half-growlers 750ml) to go are pre-filled and limited so as to keep beer on tap.

Got food? No food, but food friendly and food trucks come out on Saturdays. Also, there is house soda, kombucha, and cold-press coffee on a nitro tap. (Matchbox Coffee next door provides the coffee beans.)

Tours? Yes, based on a posted schedule on the website where you should sign up. Cost is nonperishable food items.

Special Offer: Your first pint is free when you get your book signed.

Directions: From I-94 take Exit 229 and turn east on Broadway Ave (from the south at Exit 229 you need to take Washington north to Broadway first) and after 0.9 miles, turn left (north) on 2nd St NE. (Or from the east side, I-35W Exit 21A will get you onto County Road 88/New Brighton Blvd. Go south and turn right (west) on Broadway and it's 1.5 mile to 2nd St NE.) Turn north on 2nd St NE, and go 0.2 mile and the brewery is on the corner on your left across 13th Ave.

The Beer Buzz: Local and intimate, this family friendly brewery occupies an old brick bank building on a corner in a residential area. You can still see the bank manager's office. This is the epitome of a neighborhood taproom, with almost a coffee shop feel to it. Coincidentally, they have cold-press coffee on a nitro tap. You can add a shot of it to that Chocolate Stout. The Growler magazine once named this flagship stout the Best Stout in Minnesota. That may be the only recurring beer you can count on as the brewer loves to play and explore. Red Ale with Rooibos Tea and Vanilla? That happened. Expect creative twists on other beers, such as the Cream Ale with papaya, for example. Many brews end up on nitro taps as well.

Brewer/owner Rob Miller, a Minnesota native, had been homebrewing for over a decade but had moved away from his home state, when the Surly Bill became law, allowing breweries to operate taprooms. He came back to Minnesota to take advantage of that and this is the result.

Tall tables stand along the windows and longer communal tables line up in the middle of the room in front of the bar. A company called Rogue Arc built the cool back bar with reclaimed wood, and the bar top goes around a couple of the high-ceilinged room's octagonal columns. Local art adorns the walls, and there are plenty of board games for groups or families.

The staff is a tight-knit group like a family; most of the staff members have been there since the brewery opened. The brewery also has a lot of community involvement, especially with East Side Neighborhood Services (esns.org), and "Dangerous Volunteers" do a lot of volunteer work.

The brewery name comes from an experience Rob had years ago. He attended a wedding in Austin, Texas, and after the reception crashed on a friends' couch. His crazy beard and long hair made quite an impression on the little girl of the house who discovered him in the living room the next morning. She reported back to her parents: "There's a dangerous man in the house!" Rob has turned that to a badge of honor and a quote by T. E. Lawrence is lying around the taproom: "All men dream, but not equally. Those who dream by night in the dusty recesses of their minds, wake in the day to find that it was vanity: but the dreamers of the day are *dangerous men*, for they may act on their dreams with open eyes, to make them possible."

Parking is on the street or their small lot is west of the building.

WiFi. Facebook.com/Dangerous-Man-Brewing-Co
Twitter @DangerousMan7

Stumbling Distance: *Anchor Fish & Chips* (302 13th Ave NE, 612-676-1300, theanchorfishandchips.com) offers its namesake, plus other Irish pub fare and beers. *Element Pizza* (96 Broadway St. NE, 612-379-3028, elementpizza.com) is a family joint offering some of the Cities' best wood-fired pizza. *331 Club* (331 13th Ave NE, 612-331-1746, 331club.com) offers a ton of free live music. Thai food rocks at *Sen Yai Sen Lek* (2422 Central Avenue NE, 612-781-3046, senyai-senlek.com) and you can bring takeout to the taproom. *Boom Island Brewing* lies just west of here across the Broadway Ave bridge over the Mississippi River, and while not strictly counted in the "Nortdeast" neighborhood, the brewery is close and shouldn't be missed.

MIDWEEK BEER GEEK

Nothing to do on a Wednesday night? Get your beer geek on and join Nomad World Pub and Minnesota Beer Activists (mnbeeractivists.com), for a social gathering to partake in some special or even rare beers. The event typically starts at 6PM and you get a chance to meet the people behind the beer. Plus there's trivia, prizes, and did I mention beer?

Nomad World Pub
501 Cedar Ave, Minneapolis | 612-338-6424
nomadpub.com

Minnesota Beer Activists
Facebook.com/MNBeerActivists
Twitter @MNBeerActivists

Day Block Brewing Co.

Opened: January 27, 2014
Brewmaster: Paul Johnston
Address: 1105 Washington Avenue S • Minneapolis, MN 55415
Phone: 612-617-7793
Web Site: www.dayblockbrewing.com
Annual Production: 800 barrels
Number of Beers: 12 on tap

Staple Beers:
  » Batch 035 IPA/Leonard Day IPA
  » Frank's Red
  » … plus a porter and a wit

Rotating Beers: (many come and go)
  » Belgian Blonde Abbey Ale
  » Belgian Triple IPA
  » Berliner Weisse
  » Extraordinary Bitter
  » Molé Porter
  » Oatmeal Stout (nitro)
  » Smoked Roggen
  » Russian Imperial Stout
  » Rye Mild
  » Steam Beer
  » Witte Noire

Most Popular Brew: IPAs

Samples: Yes, flights of four/six 4-oz. pours for about $8/$12.

Brewmaster's Fave: Porter

Best Time to Go: Mon–Wed 11AM–11PM, Thu–Sat 11AM–1AM, Sun 10AM–11PM. Live music Thursday, Friday and Saturday as well as Sunday Brunch.

Where can you buy it? Here on tap or to go in growlers and limited bottles.

Got food? Yes, including pizzas and bacon flights.

Tours? Yes, by appointment.

Special Offer: $2 off your first pint during your signature visit.

Directions: From I-35W take Exit 17C for Washington Ave. Turn northwest on Washington and go 0.3 mile (two blocks) and the brewery is on the corner of Washington and 11th Ave on the left. (Washington Ave spans downtown area and connects to Hennepin Ave to the northwest.)

Cyclists: *About 1.5 blocks northeast of the Hiawatha Trail and not far from the Bluff Street Bikeway to the east and 2 blocks south of the West River Parkway path.*

The Beer Buzz: In 1883, Leonard Day built this building with intentions of developing the entire block. Thus the name of the building, and thus the name of the brewery within. Back during the height of the mill days, this was a bit of a seedy area, even a red light district. You can still visit the mill, now a museum set in ruins, a short walk away. Before the brewery moved in, the building housed a plumbing supply shop as well as a casket maker. I'll just have beer, thanks.

Jeff Hahn bought the Day Block building in 2005 for his web development company Internet Exposure which occupies the third floor. He and his brother Chris, along with some friends, homebrewed in here, sharing the goodies on Beer Fridays. The brewpub, you could say, is Beer Friday times 12 gone daily. When it was decided to open a brewpub, Jeff and Chris hired Brewer Paul Johnston who has a Master Brewer certificate from Siebel and has worked at *Harriet Brewing* and *Lucid Brewing*. For the brews here, Paul uses locally sourced ingredients as much as possible.

There are two bars and bar areas: one on the kitchen side to the right and the other on the left where the brewhouse can be seen in the back behind glass. This bar on the left has a cool pressed tin back bar with perforations in it backlit with colored light. The whole place has high ceilings of pressed tin, exposed brick, and hardwood floors. *Minneapolis Star Tribune* rated it Best New Brewpub in 2014. The food is as notable as the beer. The pizzas are creative—a Bahn Mi pizza?—and who can argue with bacon flights? Pair bacon samples with beer tasters.

WiFi. Facebook.com/DayBlockBrewing and Twitter @DayBlockBrewing Instagram @dayblockbrewing

Stumbling Distance: Next door is *Grumpy's Bar & Grill* (1111 S Washington Ave, 612-340-9738, grumpys-bar.com) which has a full menu, craft beers, and specials such as Firkin Fridays. The venerable *Guthrie Theater* (818 S 2nd St, 612-377-2224, guthrietheater.org) with its three stages is a short walk. *Mill City Museum* (704 S 2nd St, 612-341-7555, millcitymuseum.org), built inside the ruins of what was the largest mill in the world, is impressive as is their rooftop observation deck overlooking the Mississippi River. *Izzy's Ice Cream* (1100 S 2nd St, 612-206-3356, izzysicecream.com) just makes amazing stuff. *Minneapolis Town Hall Brewery* is a 6 minute walk south down Washington Ave.

RAILS TO ALES: THE TWIN CITIES METRO

Minneapolis and St. Paul have a very nice metro system connecting you to a lot of places. With the opening of the Green Line in 2014, craft beer drinkers can easily get to 18 craft breweries divided between St. Paul and Minneapolis. Walks from metro stations to the breweries are typically less than a mile and often just a few blocks. Directions on most brewers' pages mention the closest station.

The Green Line   *in order from west to east*
The Freehouse
Fulton Brewing
Rock Bottom Restaurant & Brewery
Sisyphus Brewing (1.2 miles)
Lakes & Legends Brewery
Day Block Brewing
Minneapolis Town Hall Brewery
Surly Brewing
Urban Growler
Bang Brewing
Lake Monster Brewing
Burning Brothers
Tin Whiskers Brewing
Great Waters Brewing
Bad Weather Brewing (1 mile)

The Blue Line   *in order from north to south*
EastLake Brewing (1.1 miles)
Harriet Brewing
Northbound Smokehouse & Brewpub

Eastlake Brewery & Tavern

Founded: 11 December 2014
Brewmaster: Ryan Pitman
Address: 920 East Lake Street #123 • Minneapolis, MN 55407
Phone: 612-217-4668
Web Site: www.eastlakemgm.com
Annual Production: 600–800 barrels
Number of Beers: up to 12 on tap, at least one malty, one light, and one hoppy beer

Staple Beers:
> » Blue Liner Pale Ale
> » Increasingly Lost Saison (Belgian IPA)
> » Nicollet Mauler Black IPA
> » Slop City (American Rye Stout)

Rotating Beers: (a variety of seasonals and one-offs)
> » Almond Milk Stout
> » Devil's Kettle (Belgian IPA)
> » El Aramtoste Spiced Brown Ale (with coffee, anise, cinnamon, piloncillo)
> » Eye of the Tiger (Vietnamese/Belgian Strong Ale)
> » Good Ol' Gnarly Brown
> » Gustav Mauler's Fifth (Double IPA)
> » One Two Punch (Radler made with kombucha)

Samples: No.

Brewmaster's Fave: Nicollet Mauler Black IPA

Best Time to Go: Open daily: Sun 11AM–6PM, Mon–Wed 11AM–8PM, Thu–Sat 11AM–11PM. When local sports teams are leading in a game, there may be a discount on the saison. Watch Facebook for events partnering with one of the local restaurants.

Where can you buy it? On tap here and to go in growlers (will fill other's) and pre-filled 750 ml bottles.

Got food? Other than possibly pork rinds or bison jerky, no. But food friendly and surrounded by food vendors inside *Midtown Global Market* (open until 8PM). The taproom also serves Deane's Kombucha (deanes-kombucha.com), plus local root beer and ginger ale.

Tours? Not really, but you can watch brewing through the window during lunch.

Special Offer: A free beer with your book signature.

Directions: From I-35W you can take Exit 14 and go east on 36th St 0.5 mile, turn left on Park Ave and go north 0.7 mile to East Lake St. Turn right and the brewery is 0.2 mile on the left. Alternatively, 8th St out of downtown onto the MN 55 ramp and follow Hiawatha Ave just over 1 mile to East Lake St. Turn right (west) and the brewery is 1.1 miles west on the right side of the street.

1.1 mile walking west on Lake Street from the Lake Street Midtown Station on the Blue Line.

Cyclists: *One block south of the Midtown Greenway at 10th Ave.*

The Beer Buzz: The historic Sears Roebuck building has been brought back to life as a fantastic international market, and now that market has beer. Brewer Ryan homebrewed for six years before making the jump to opening his own brewery. He likes the multiple challenges of brewing or what he calls the "mechanical, creativity, and science trifecta." In a previous job he was a bus driver. His route took him past this building and he always thought it would make a good location for a brewery; with all that food in there, it was the one missing piece. So he cashed in his pension and became that piece.

One could almost call this a Craigslist brewery. The bear and the elk on the wall were found there. So was the reclaimed gym floor from Eau Claire (you can still see the blue and gold lines), which became the bar top and the tall communal-style tables. The cedar tongue-and-groove planks had "too many knots" and so a lumberyard gave that up. Ryan took a blowtorch to it in his backyard to give it that scorched look. A friend painted the mural by the door based on an old photo of someone working on a Duquesne Pilsener sign in Pittsburgh.

Ryan's sister works at Mercury Mosaics and did the tiled brewery name below the taps. You can park at the Midtown Exchange parking ramp across 10th Ave for up to 1.5 hours with validation from any vendor in the market. There is also metered parking in a lot a block to the west (Elliot Ave).

Find them on Facebook.com/EastlakeMGM and Twitter @EastlakeMGM

Stumbling Distance: The brewery's home here in *Midtown Global Market* (612-872-4041, midtownglobalmarket.org) has a wide variety of vendors, but you can actually place your orders for *Manny's Tortas, El Burrito Mercado,* and *Hot Indian Foods* right at the bar and your food will be delivered. Across the street and west is *Chicago Lake Liquors* (825 E Lake St, 612-825-4401, chicagolakeliquors.com) with good prices and a decent selection of local craft beer.

FAIR STATE BREWING COOPERATIVE

Founded: January 2013
Brewmaster: Niko Tonks
Address: 2506A Central Ave NE • Minneapolis, MN 55418
Phone: 612-444-3574 (Taproom), 612-444-3209 (Main line)
Web Site: www.fairstate.coop
Annual Production: 1,000 barrels
Number of Beers: 6–10 on tap; 30 beers/year

Staple Beers:

> » Expect at least 1 lager, 1 lactose sour beer, and 2 hoppy brews

Rotating Beers: (many and varied)

> » HEFEWEIZEN (summer)
> » OKTOBERFEST
> » RAUCHBOCK
> » STOUT or SCHWARZBIER (all winter)

Most Popular Brew: IPA

Samples: Yes.

Brewmaster's Fave: Pilsner

Best Time to Go: Open Mon 4–11PM, Wed–Thu 4–11PM, Fri 4PM–12AM, Sat 12PM–12AM, Sun 12–9PM.

Where can you buy it? Here on tap in pints and half-pints, and growlers and 750ml half-growlers to go. Limited 750 ml bottle runs. Will fill outside growlers with Surgeon General's legal warning on them.

Got food? No, but food friendly. Kombucha is served here too.

Tours? Yes, 1PM on Saturdays and Sundays or randomly when slow.

Special Offer: $1 off your first beer during your signature visit.

Directions: From I-94 take Exit 229 and turn east on Broadway Ave (from the south at Exit 229 you need to take Washington north to Broadway first) and after 1.8 miles, turn left (north) on Central Ave. (From the east side, I-35W Exit 21A will get you onto County Road 88/New Brighton Blvd. Go south and turn right (west) on Broadway and its 0.6 mile to Central Ave, turn north/right.) Take Central Ave 1 mile north and the brewery is on the left.

The Beer Buzz: Minnesota may be the land of co-ops. There are many, but this was the first brewery cooperative in the state. Up the street is a food co-op, and even the landlord of this building is a sort of co-op.

Brewer Niko went to graduate school for Humanities in Texas but brewmanities got the best of him. While living in Austin, he started cold calling brewers, offering to work for free. He found an internship, turned it into a job, and then another job, and another. For a while he was commuting to Houston (3 hours) and learned he loved it. One evening Niko, Evan Sallee, and Matt Hauck were hanging at the The Draught House Pub & Brewery in Austin getting smarter over beers. Austin's Black Star Co-op had become the first cooperative brewpub ever in 2010, and they all agreed this was something that would work in Minneapolis. In 2012, they started planning. Fundraising started in March 2013 and they acquired more than 250 members. On September 6, 2014, they opened their doors.

The taproom is an inviting space with exposed light brick, pale hardwood floors, and bright track lighting. At the big windows of the storefront are chairs and a bar to sip brews and people watch. Pass a long fixed communal table and then come to the long bar and some tables. The back wall shows the coop's logo painted on the bricks and 3 LED screens with beer information. The wall opposite the bar is covered with little clipboards holding photos of all the coop members.

Minnesota residents can actually pay and become a member of the cooperative. Membership comes with voting rights, a share of the brewery, and a whole slew of beer-related benefits.

Parking is on the street, and there are bike racks out front as well.

Facebook.com/FairStateBrewing and Twitter @FairStateCoop

Stumbling Distance: *Aki's Bread Haus* (akisbreadhaus.com) has some great pretzels to go with your beer, and a door connects directly from the taproom to the bakery. *El Taco Riendo* (2412 Central Ave, 612-781-3000, eltaco-riendo.com) is cheap and delicious. *Holy Land Deli* (2513 Central Ave NE, 612-781-2627, holylandbrand.com) is the neighborhood pick for hummus, falafel, etc.

THE FREEHOUSE

Opened: December 2013
Brewmaster: Tim "Pio" Piotrowski
Address: 701 North Washington Avenue • Minneapolis, MN 55401
Phone: 612-339-7011
Web Site: www.freehousempls.com
Annual Production: 1,750 barrels
Number of Beers: 20 on tap (including guest taps) plus casks; 23+ beers per year

Staple Beers:
- » No. 1 KÖLSCH
- » No. 2 INDIA PALE ALE
- » No. 3 ENGLISH-STYLE BROWN ALE
- » No. 4 IRISH-STYLE DRY STOUT

Rotating Beers:
- » No. 9 GERMAN-STYLE BOCK (spring)
- » No. 11 BELGIAN-STYLE WITBIER (summer)
- » No. 15 OKTOBERFEST (fall)
- » No. 20 BARLEYWINE
- » No. 21 DOUBLE IPA
- » No. 22 HONEY RED ALE
- » BOURBON BARREL-AGED IMPERIAL STOUT (winter/anniversary ale)
- » …plus a special Minnesota State Fair beer only

Most Popular Brew: No. 1 Kölsch

Samples: Yes, free sips for decision making or 4-oz. "pony" servings for about $2 each.

Brewmaster's Faves: Belgian Witbiers, IPAs, Porters

Best Time to Go: Open daily 6:30AM–2AM. Happy hour is 4–6PM and latenight as well.

Where can you buy it? On tap here in pony (4-oz.), middy (10 oz.), and pints, and to go in growlers and howlers/squealers.

Got food? Yes, a full menu and bar. Food includes fresh oysters, unusual "Beer Bites" (wings and curds but also bone marrow and bulgogi), "Jars" (from Cheez-Its to trout dip), salads, burgers and sandwiches, entrees (Thai pork, Steak 'n' Pierogies, shrimp tacos, beer-battered fish), and breakfast and kids menus.

Tours? Yes, by request or watch for a schedule on the website.

Special Offer: Buy one pint of Freehouse beer and get one free, during your signature visit.

Directions: From I-394, take Exit 9C for Washington Ave. Keep left at the fork for 3rd Ave, then turn left on Washington and continue 0.3 mile. The brewery is on the left with a parking lot. (Take Washington Ave south from Broadway if you are coming from the "Nordeast" Minneapolis neighborhood.) From the south on I-94, Exit 229 brings you to Washington Ave; turn right. From the north on I-94, Exit 229 takes you to Broadway. Go left and take the first right on Washington Ave.

The Target Field Station on the Green Line is about a 10-minute walk from here.

Cyclists: *About 3 blocks north/northwest off the Cedar Lake Trail, which connects a few blocks east to the West River Parkway Trail.*

The Beer Buzz: Stephanie Shimp and David Burley used to work together at The Nicolett Island Inn back in the 1990s. Over drinks after work, they laid plans to go it alone and start a restaurant. They opened Highland Grill in 1993, and as Blue Plate Restaurant Co. followed with a series of great eateries, not the least of which was this huge brewpub which serves everything "From Breakfast to Beer." In 2012 at Minnesota Public Radio and Walker Art Center's annual summer festival Rock the Garden, the two were chatting over drinks again—this time, appropriately, beer—and decided a brewpub would be the next great project.

The Freehouse is located on the ground floor of the Loose-Wiles Building, an early 20th century brick building listed on the National Register of Historic Places, where Sunshine Biscuits used to make Animal Crackers and Cheez-Its. A free house is a the opposite of a "tied house," which is a pub that only serves beers from a single company. A free house is free to serve whatever it wants. While The Freehouse does make its own beer, the brewpub designation in Minnesota allows it to offer a full bar and offer guest taps as well.

Entry is from the parking lot on the side of the building. Inside, the sections of the restaurant rise like terraces from the door. The first is the bar area, then a dining area and the kitchen beyond, and finally, a back room: the Volstead Lounge where you can see a portrait of Andrew Volstead, the Minnesota legislator who sponsored the National Prohibition Act (the Volstead Act), made out of bottle caps by Jason Hammond of Bolster Creative. The ceiling there is keg tops, including the light fixtures. The bar is a long rectangular island with a stainless steel counter and racks of growlers hanging down from above. Diners sit at tables and booths, and the brewhouse is visible through glass at the back of the room. The kitchen is open and the flames of a rotisserie are visible from across the room. Outside is a patio for seating in nicer seasons and a grain tower.

Brewer Pio, a Wisconsin native, homebrewed through college and studied in the American Brewers Guild diploma program doing his apprentice work at Oskar Blues Brewery in Colorado. He also worked as an assistant brewer in three Rock Bottom brewpubs out there which led to the head brewer position back in their Minneapolis location. Blue Plate Restaurant Company picked him up from there for this big brewery project. The production grew quickly—there are three brewers on staff now—and with eight restaurants in the company, they are allowed to serve Freehouse beer in all locations according to current state law. Additionally, they keep The Blue Barn, their outlet at the Minnesota State Fair. They make a special brew that can only be found there.

The beers aim to stay true to style with the thought of food pairings in mind, and none of the brews wants to bowl you over with a hop bomb or anything too aggressive. The menu also features several beer cocktails, such as The Brewer Press made with No. 3 Brown, cold pressed coffee, simple syrup, and heavy cream. The food menu incorporates spent grain into pancakes and English muffins. The place is lively with a 21–35 crowd during happy hour, and for dinner it can get quite busy so you might want to call ahead to get on that wait list.

WiFi. Facebook/FreehouseMPLS and Twitter @FreehouseMPLS

Stumbling Distance: This is a short walk from *Fulton Brewery* and *Target Field*, where the Minnesota Twins play. *Boom Island Brewing* is 1 mile north on Washington Ave.

FREEHOUSE BEER AROUND TOWN

Check out the other *Blue Plate Restaurant Co.* offerings, including *The Blue Barn* at the Minnesota State Fair (mnstatefair.org) the 12 days leading up to Labor Day. The company even has its own free app—"BluePlate"—for Apple and Android. The other restaurants include:

Longfellow Grill (2990 West River Parkway, Minneapolis, 612-721-2711, longfellowgrill.com)

Scusi (1806 St Clair, St Paul, 651-789-7007, scusistpaul.com)

Edina Grill (5028 France Ave S, Edina, 952-927-7933, edinagrill.com)

Groveland Tap (1834, St Clair Ave, St Paul, 651-699-5058, grovelandtap.com)

The Lowry Café (2207 Lowry Ave N, Minneapolis, 612-677-2233)

Highland Grill (771 Cleveland Ave S, St Paul, 651-690-1173, highlandgrill.com)

3 Squares (12690 Arbor Lakes Pkwy N, Maple Grove, 763-425-3330, 3squaresrestaurant.com)

Fulton Brewing Co.

Founded: June 2009
Brewmaster: Pete Grande **Head Brewer**: Mike Salo
Address: 414 6th Avenue N • Minneapolis, MN 55401
Phone: 612-333-3208
Web Site: www.fultonbeer.com
Annual Production: 25,000 barrels
Number of Beers: 6–8 on tap; 20+ per year

Staple Beers:
  » The Lonely Blonde
  » The Ringer APA
  » Sweet Child of Vine IPA

Rotating Beers:
  » The Expat (spring)
  » The Libertine Imperial Red (fall)
  » Patience Barleywine
  » The Randonneur (summer)
  » Ursa Black IPA
  » Worthy Adversary Russian Imperial Stout (winter)

Limited Series Beers:
  » Brewer's Series
  » Garage Series:
  » Batch 300
  » Insurrection
  » Maitrise
  » MPLS Mild
  » Rye Whiskey Barrel-Aged Libertine
  » War and Peace
  » … includes barrel-aged brews, cask and infused versions of their beers

Most Popular Brew: Sweet Child of Vine

Samples: Yes, sips for decision making.

Best Time to Go: Open Wed–Thu 3–10pm, Fri 3–11pm, Sat 12–11pm, Sun 12–6pm. Also open one hour before any Twins home game, even on Mon–Tue. Live music periodically.

Where can you buy it? On draft in the taproom (no growlers per current law for brewers brewing over 20,000 bbls). Staples and seasonals are distributed throughout MN in 6-pack bottles, some others in 750 ml bottles and 22-oz. bombers.

Got food? No, but food friendly, and food trucks park outside.

Tours? Yes, Saturdays at 1, 2, 3, and 4PM. First come, first served.

Special Offer: Buy one regularly priced beer, get one free during your signature visit.

Directions: From the north on I-94, Exit 230 takes you 0.9 mile to 7th St. Turn left, go 0.4 mile, and go left onto 6th Ave. The brewery is 0.3 mile more on the left. From the south on I-94, Exit 230 brings you 0.5 mile to Olson Memorial Highway. Turn right, go 0.4 mile as it continues onto 6th Ave, and the brewery is on the left.

A short walk from the metro at Target Field Station on the Green Line.

Cyclists: *Near Target Field about 2 blocks north off the Cedar Lake Trail which connects east to the West River Parkway Trail.*

The Beer Buzz: Never mind garage bands, how about garage brewers? Fulton Brewing's humble beginnings were in co-founder Pete Grande's two-car garage in the Fulton neighborhood in southwest Minneapolis. They sold their first beer at The Happy Gnome. As they got bigger and bigger they contract-brewed at Sand Creek and Stevens Point Brewery in Wisconsin to meet demand until they could build a new 51,000 square-foot production brewery off site. That is where the bulk of their beer is

produced, but they still brew at this location as well, and many brews throughout the year may only be available in the taproom. The Garage Series, small batches of limited releases, pays homage to their roots. The Brewer's Series gives individual brewers or other employees a chance to brew a small batch for the taproom. A few of these may end up going into bigger production based on their reception.

The taproom has a concrete floor and high industrial ceiling, and there are picnic tables and a few tall tables about plus a few perches at the bar. The bar top is polished concrete and the wall behind it shows a large "Hop Star," part of the brewery's logo, as well as the beer menu. To the left of the bar you can see into the brewhouse through glass. Music is playing and there are board games, one large TV, and cribbage. In nicer weather, the loading dock door is rolled up and there's an outdoor patio and a dog-friendly beer garden in the parking lot. Parking is on the street and it's metered.

ATM on site. WiFi. Facebook.com/FultonBeer, Twitter @fultonbeer and Instagram fultonbeer

Stumbling Distance: This is the place to start your beer drinking before hitting *Target Field* (353 N 5th St) for a Twins game. Craft beers are typically sold inside the stadium, particularly in sections 126 and 320. A new "destination bar" may also serve the good stuff. *Corner Coffee* (514 N 3rd St #102, 612-338-2002, yourcornercoffee.com) showcases art and live music with soups, salads, sandwiches, and breakfast. Burgers, bacon-wrapped hot dogs, and beers (an extensive list of craft and the other kind) await at *The Depot Tavern* (17 N 7th St, 612-338-1828, thedepottavern.com).

BASEBALL AND A BEER HERE!

Peanuts and Crack Jacks are all well and fine, but what's baseball without beer? And wouldn't you rather it be a craft beer? With all the amazing craft brewing going on in the Twin Cities, it'd be a crime not to offer it at the ballpark.

Minnesota Twins
1 Twins Way, Minneapolis
866-800-1275
minnesota.twins.mlb.com

Target Field, home of the Minnesota Twins, has some craft beer stations inside the stadium. Look for Minnesota brews and more at Minnesota Brews Portables in Sections 126 and 320, as well as in Section 140 and at Twins Pub in Section 141. The stadium also offers public tours on game days and non-game days. Fulton Brewing is always open on game days even outside of normal hours and it is a short walk for a pre- or post-game craft brew.

St. Paul Saints
360 Broadway St, St. Paul
651-644-6659
saintsbaseball.com

CHS Field has a Craft Beer Corner near left field with a great selection including many Minnesota brews. Right next to it is a picnic area known as the Craft Beer Bullpen which is reservable for a fee for groups of 50–75 and serves those same beers.

HARRIET BREWING CO.

Opened: January 29, 2011
Brewmaster: John Prusilla
Address: 3036 Minnehaha Avenue • Minneapolis, MN 55406
Phone: 612-315-4633
Web Site: www.harrietbrewing.com
Annual Production: 1,400 barrels
Number of Beers: 6–8 on tap, 14 per year

Staple Beers:
- » DARK ABBEY Belgian-style Dubbel
- » DIVINE OCULUST Belgian-style Golden Strong
- » WEST SIDE Belgian-style IPA

Rotating Beers:
- » ELEVATOR (doppelbock released on their anniversary)
- » HARRIET'S GRANDE ZOMBI Belgian-style Stout
- » HARRIET'S PILS
- » JUHLA BRÜ Finnish-style Sahti (with red cedar twigs and juniper)
- » LUV JUS Belgian-style Wit
- » MÄRZEN/OKTOBERFEST
- » RAUCHFEST (late September)
- » SOONER OR LATER Belgian-style Blonde
- » SOUR DIVINE OCULUST
- » WACHEN BOCK
- » WODAN WEIZEN
- » WOLUPTUWEISS DUNKELWEIZEN
- » …also various barrel-aged sours

Most Popular Brew: West Side Belgian-style IPA

Samples: Yes, flights available.

Brewmaster's Mother's Fave: Divine Oculust

Best Time to Go: Open Wed 4–10PM, Thu 4–11PM, Fri 4PM–12AM, Sat 1PM–12AM. Happy hour Wed–Fri from 4–6PM. Watch for their anniversary party every January.

Where can you buy it? On tap here plus in growlers to go (even your own growler if clean). Draft accounts and kegs at select liquor stores in the greater Twin Cities area.

Got food? No, but food friendly and food trucks park outside most nights. Joia sodas (joialife.com), a Minnesota brand, are served here.

Tours? Free tour (30 minutes): Wed 6PM, Sat 1PM; Full Brewery tour (1 hour): $5 Thu 6PM, Fri 5:45PM, Sat 3:45PM. Book at least a week in advance on the website.

Special Offer: Not participating at this time.

Directions: Heading east on I-94 just east of its juncture with I-35W, take Exit 235A toward 9th St. Turn right on 26th Ave and go 1.3 miles (it becomes Minnehaha after 1.1 miles) and the brewery is on the right. Heading west on I-94, take Exit 235A for Riverside and turn left on 25th Ave, which becomes 26th Ave. Go 1.3 miles (it becomes Minnehaha after 1.1 miles) and the brewery is on the right.

Walking distance from the Lake Street Midtown Station on the Blue Line.

Cyclists: *About 0.3 mile from the Midtown Greenway/Hiawatha LRT Trail*

The Beer Buzz: If you love live music, this is arguably the Live Music Brewery. This building was once a repair shop for municipal vehicles and in the 90s it became an underground grunge venue. Founder Jason Sowards was a chemical engineer who got laid off and took up homebrewing as a sort of stress relief. The Wachmann Brautechnik brewhouse you see here is previously owned and came from Germany by way of Japan. The brewery opened shortly before the Surly Bill became law making taprooms legal, and suddenly they were scrambling to create a taproom.

Brewer John had homebrewed for a few years and worked in bars and restaurants. He knew one of the staff who helped him get into Harriet's where he started in the taproom and helping with distribution. He learned from the ground up from Jason and then took the reins when he was ready. The brewers try to stay true to the styles with the proper ingredients, and the German equipment helps. Jason's artist friend Jesse Brödd (jessebrodd. com) displays his art in the brewery and designed the beer labels. He also is in charge of booking the bands.

The taproom is partly an art gallery. Picnic tables and regular tables sit in front of the stage and a lollipop-shaped bar juts out from the wall separating the music from the serving area. Along a side wall is an impressive vinyl collection. A stuffed mountain lion above the door looks down on the taproom. A chain-link fence, previously an enclosure for the garbage outside, separates the taproom from the brewing area. The small bar is portable. Garage doors along the back wall of the building open in the summer to a patio and tent. The entrance is in the back of the building and there is a large parking lot there.

WiFi. Facebook.com/harrietbrewing and Twitter @harrietbrewing

Stumbling Distance: *Hymie's Vintage Records* (3820 E Lake St, 612-729-8890, hymiesrecords.com) is a mecca for vinyl junkies. *Minnehaha Falls Park* (4801 S Minnehaha Park Dr, 612-230-6400, minneapolisparks.org) a nice place to visit. *Sea Salt Seafood Eatery* (4825 Minnehaha Ave, 612-721-8990, seasalteatery.wordpress.com) is only open in the summer but a delicious. *Gandhi Mahal Restaurant* (3009 27th Ave S, 612-729-5222, gandhimahal.com) serves some of the best Indian food in the Twin Cities.

The Herkimer

Opened: December 1999
Brewers: Blake Richardson, Matt Asay, Ben Salyards, and Randy Ust
Address: 2922 Lyndale Avenue S • Minneapolis, MN 55408
Phone: 612-821-0101
Web Site: www.theherkimer.com
Annual Production: 1,000 barrels
Number of Beers: 7 on tap (one on nitro)

Beers:

- A57N ALT Bier
- A57S Kölsch
- Baltic porter
- Bock
- Czech Pilsner
- Daily Pils
- Dortmunder
- Eva Cöttbusser
- Glitchen Rye
- Gose Speziell Weizen
- Handy's Lager
- High Point Dunkel
- Jeffrey Kream Ale
- The Lutz IPA
- Maibock
- Minnesota IP 'eh
- Oktoberfest
- Red Flyer Marzen
- Schwarz Bier
- Sky Pilot Kellerbier
- Slushbox Pale IPA
- Tomorrow Doppel Pils
- Toolers Weiss
- Waggelwater Belgian Pale Ale
- …plus the Small Batch Series

Most Popular Brew: Eva Cöttbusser and The Lutz IPA

Samples: Yes, four tasters for about $9.

Brewmaster's Fave: Eva Cöttbusser

Best Time to Go: Open daily 10AM–2AM. Happy hour is 3–6PM daily and Sun–Thu from 10PM–2AM. Watch for trivia night.

Where can you buy it? Only here over the bar. No growlers.

Got food? Yes, soups and salads, burgers and sandwiches, plus bar appetizers such as cheese curds, wings, and nachos, plus a full bar. Entrees include a buffalo pork chop and chicken & waffles, plus a Friday fish fry.

Tours? By appointment.

Special Offer: Not participating at this time.

Directions: Coming from the east on I-94, take Exit 231B for Hennepin Ave toward Lyndale Ave, and keep right until the road turns left to merge into Lyndale Ave. Go 1.2 miles and the brewery is on the right. From the north on I-94, Exit 231A-231B is a long ramp to Lyndale Ave, stay left on 231B when they split, and continue to follow signs for Lyndale. Continue about 1.6 miles and the brewery is on the right.

Cyclists: About 400 feet south of the Midtown Greenway at Lyndale Ave.

The Beer Buzz: Founder and brewer Blake Richardson had been brewing for a while and decided to go to Siebel. Soon after in 1999 he opened this brewpub with an impressively long list of beers rotating in and out of the menu. The small batches allow the brewers to move many styles through the lineup each year. Herkimer is a modified spelling of an old German slang word. It's what his friend was called by his German grandmother.

While Blake is the owner and perhaps technically the head brewer, this is definitely a team-brewing effort. They brew with the more labor and time intensive **decoction mashing.** All of them are first level Cicerones, and Matt is a BJCP beer judge. Matt is also a Certified Sake Professional (Level I) while Blake has the advanced Level II certification. They both brew the sake over at sister restaurant *moto-i* just down the street.

The brew system is behind glass on the left as you walk in. The room shows columns with mosaic tiles, booths and tall cocktail tables for seating, and a sort of u-shaped bar at the center with a pressed tin ceiling above it. In

addition to the eight TVs around the bar, there is also trivia and board games to pass the time. Parking is on the street which is metered during the day. There is a VIP club for both the brewpub and *moto-i* down the block. Members earn points on what they spend at each place and it translates into credit for future visits.

ATM on site. WiFi. Facebook.com/theherkimer,
Twitter @TheHerkimerPub, Instagram theherkimerpub

Stumbling Distance: Check out The Herkimer's sister restaurant—also a sake brewery!—*moto-i* (2940 Lyndale Ave S, 612-821-6262, moto-i.com) serving Japanese food and Minnesota beers just down the block. *Jungle Theater* (2951 Lyndale Ave S, 612-822-7063, jungletheater.com) is right across the street. *LynLake Brewery* is just a few steps away, same side of the street.

Indeed Brewing Co.

Founded: 2011
Brewmaster: Josh Bischoff
Address: 711 15th Avenue NE • Minneapolis, MN 55413
Phone: 612-843-5090
Web Site: www.indeedbrewing.com
Annual Production: 11,000 barrels
Number of Beers: 10 on tap, plus two casks

Staple Beers:
- » Day Tripper American Pale Ale
- » Midnight Ryder American Black Ale

Seasonal Beers:
- » Let It Ride IPA (spring)
- » Shenanigans Summer Ale (summer)
- » Sweet Yamma Jamma Ale (fall)
- » Stir Crazy Winter Ale (winter)

Specialty Beers:
- » Burr Grinder Beer Coffee Ale
- » Double Day Tripper Double Pale Ale
- » Fresh Hop Pale Ale
- » Haywire Double American Black Ale
- » Hot Box Imperial Smoked Pepper Porter
- » L.S.D. Honey Ale
- » Mexican Honey Imperial Lager
- » Old Friend Holiday Ale
- » plus "Derailed Series" beers, sour beers, and barrel aging.

Most Popular Brew: Day Tripper Pale Ale

Samples: Yes

Brewmaster's Fave: L.S.D.

Best Time to Go: Open Wed–Fri 3–11pm, Sat 12–11pm, Sun 12pm–close. Happy hour Wed–Fri 3–6pm.

Where can you buy it? Here in 10-, 16-, and 20-oz. pours, plus growlers and 750s to go. Distributed in cans and on draft throughout Minnesota and just creeping into western Wisconsin. There's a beer finder on their website.

Got food? No, but food friendly and food trucks often park outside.

Tours? Free, 60–75 minutes. Each tour is limited to 40 guests and only online registrations are accepted.

Special Offer: A free Indeed Brewing sticker with your book signature.

Directions: From I-94 take Exit 229 and turn east on Broadway Ave (from the south at Exit 229 you need to take Washington north to Broadway first) and after 1.6 miles, turn left (north) on Quincy St. Drive 0.3 mile and you will go straight into the parking lot. From the east side, I-35W Exit 21A will get you onto County Road 88/New Brighton Blvd. Go south and turn right (west) on Broadway and it's 0.8 mile to Quincy, turn right, and follow it to the brewery.

The Beer Buzz: Working for the school newspaper might look good on your resume someday, but in this case it brought together three friends who would one day open a brewery together. Rachel Anderson, Nathan Berndt, and Tom Whisenand were roommates and worked as photographers for their college newspaper. When the time was right, they searched for and found the critical head brewer, Josh Bischoff. Josh used to work at the Green Mill, a former brewpub, and during that time he took up homebrewing. Ron Flett, the head brewer invited him to come in on his days off to job shadow him a bit. Some time later, the head brewer at Great Waters left the position and an assistant brewer over at Town Hall Brewery left to take it. Flett heard about the change and suggested Josh look into it if he was serious about going professional. He applied and got the job and spent 7 years at Town Hall Brewery working with Mike Hoops. Rachel, Nathan, and Tom picked up Josh and he began working on beers for their new brewery. Josh developed the flagship beers on a homebrew system in Tom's garage. Josh is most proud of his L.S.D. Honey Ale, a brew he said

took years to develop from concept to getting the recipe just right, earned him a silver medal at the Great American Beer Festival.

The brewery is located inside the Solar Arts Building, a former tire factory right next to the railroad tracks. There's a small patio near the side door where you enter the taproom. Plenty of bike racks and a fixed tire pump. Parking is in a narrow lot beside the building. The taproom has a concrete floor and a long handsome varnished wood bar with a train rail for your feet. The back bar has some nice woodwork and a collection of the outdoor series of Schmidt cans. A cribbage board is on hand.

Indeed cares about its local community and initiated Indeed We Can, a sort of weekly fundraiser: net profits from Wednesday nights in the taproom go to a nonprofit chosen by an Indeed employee.

ATM on site. WiFi. Facebook.com/IndeedBrewing and Twitter @indeedbrewing

Stumbling Distance: Straight south to Broadway find *Uncle Franky's* (728 Broadway St NE, 612-455-2181, unclefrankys.com) for burgers, Chicago dogs, and malts. *Bauhaus Brew Labs* and *612Brew* are just over the railroad tracks to the east on Broadway, while *Dangerous Man Brewing* is 0.8 mile to the west. Good and cheap Vietnamese food at *Cali's* (648 Broadway St NE, 612-623-4704).

INSIGHT BREWING

Founded: 2014

Brewmaster: Ilan Klages-Mundt   **Head Brewer:** Dan Case

Address: 2821 E Hennepin Ave • Minneapolis, MN 55413

Phone: 612-722-7222

Web Site: www.insightbrewing.com

Annual Production: 3,500 barrels

Number of Beers: 6–8 on tap, plus weekly casks

Staple Beers:
- » CHISWICK PORTER
- » CURIOSITY IPA
- » LAMB & FLAG (English-style pub ale)
- » SAISON DE BLANC
- » YUZU PALE ALE

Rotating Beers:
- » GRAVITY WELL™ IMPERIAL STOUT (aged in Cognac barrels)
- » OLD BAMBERG RAUCHBIER
- » PICCOLO IPA (2.8% ABV)
- » PUMPKIN BAMBERG
- » SAISON DE LA VIE
- » … plus barrel aging and frequent casks

Most Popular Brew: Curiosity IPA and Saison De Blanc

Samples: Yes, four 5-oz. pours for about $8.

Beer Ilan Worked Hardest to Perfect: Lamb & Flag

Best Time to Go: Open Mon–Thu 3–11PM, Fri 3–12AM, Sat 12PM–12AM, Sun 12–11PM. Live music every month.

Where can you buy it? On tap here in 10-, 16-, and 20-oz. pours. Pre-filled or exchanged growlers to go. Bottles and cans will be available starting in 2015, and the beer is on tap in Twin Cities establishments.

Got food? No, but food friendly, and there are food trucks most nights from 4PM and a schedule for them is on the website.

Tours? Yes, by request.

Special Offer: Buy your first pint, get one free during your signature visit (limit one).

Directions: Follow Hennepin Ave east out of downtown and the brewery is just past 27th Ave on the left. From I-35W, take Exit 22 and head south on Industrial Blvd for 1 mile. Turn right on Hennepin Ave and the brewery is 0.1 mile on your right.

City bus routes 30 and 61 stop in front of the brewery

The Beer Buzz: How does a cello player end up brewing in Japan and opening a brewery in Minneapolis? Long story. Ilan studied music at Lawrence University in Wisconsin. During that time, he applied for a grant, the recipient of which would pursue something outside their major, something they were passionate about. As a homebrewer, Ilan settled on beer, culture and brewing. But in the end, he didn't get the grant. So what the hell, he decided to carry out the project anyway. He bought a one-way ticket to London where he began a one-year biking, traveling, and brewing experience. He apprentice-brewed at Fuller's there. He did the same in Denmark, and moved on from there to the land of the rising craft beer scene: Japan. He brewed at Kiuchi Brewing in Naka, makers of Hitachino Nest beers. (Note the yuzu, a Japanese citrus fruit, in one of his pale ales.)

After vagabrewing his way round the world, he moved to Minneapolis where he taught homebrewing classes at Northern Brewer and plotted to start his own brewery. Brian Berge took one of those classes. Brian had a marketing background and had always wanted to build a brand. He learned of Ilan's brewery ambitions and they started chatting. Brian's friend Kevin

Hilliard, a homebrewer friend since college, joined them and they tried Ilan's beer. That sealed the deal. Eric Schmidt, the fourth partner in the endeavor, was also a homebrewer who had previously contacted Northern Brewer for some help with a recipe. NB had passed him an email address of someone they claimed could help him sort it out and his questions are answered. Sometime later, in 2013, Eric read about a brewery in planning and sat down at the computer to email the listed contact—and the address autocompleted in his browser. It was Ilan, that same guy who had helped him with that recipe.

As they got up and running, they added Head Brewer Dan Case, a Michigander who has brewed in several MI breweries including Arbor Brewing, Corner Brewery, and Grizzly Peaks in Ann Arbor.

The brewery occupies a rather expansive brick building painted red with glass-block windows and hop vines growing on the walls. Originally a place that manufactured boilers, the building most recently had been Warren Shade Co. A truck bay from the front of the building had to be filled in and leveled with the rest of the terrazzo floor in the taproom, a well lit space the size of a minor beer hall, with a whole variety of short and tall tables, plus some booths and even a bit of lounge furniture. At the back is a long curving bar and behind that is a cooler and taps protruding from a couple of partial wood barrels sticking out of the wall. A glass garage door and large windows look into the brewhouse to the right of the bar, and through this room is another section of the building that will house their bottling or canning line. The brewhouse lights up blue at night. Two big TVs are mounted behind the bar but are typically only on during an important game or event. There's plenty of parking in the adjacent lot where food trucks come each evening.

WiFi. Find them on Facebook.com/insightbrewing, Twitter @InsightBrewing and Instagram @insightbrewing

Stumbling Distance: *Chindian Café* (1500 E Hennepin Ave, 612-676-1818, chindiancafe.com), as you might guess, serves Chinese and Indian dishes. *Mac's Industrial Sports Bar* (312 Central Ave SE, 612-379-3379, macsindustrial.com) boasts 27 craft beer taps that change almost daily. Not to be outdone, *New Bohemia Wurst & BierHaus* (233 E Hennepin Ave, 612-331-4929, newbohemiausa.com) has 36 plus a cask, and an absurdly large menu of sausages.

LAKES & LEGENDS BREWING CO.

Planned Opening: Summer 2015
Brewmaster: Andrew Dimery
Address: 1368 LaSalle Avenue •
Minneapolis, MN 55403
Phone: TBD
Web Site: www.lakesandlegends.com
Annual Production: 2,000 barrels
Number of Beers: 15–20+ beers each year

Staple Beers:
  » Belgian and farmhouse-style ales

Rotating Beers:
  » Frequent seasonal/specialty releases

Samples: Yes, 4-oz. tasters available for most beers for about $2 each.

Best Time to Go: Check website for current hours. Watch for beer release events.

Where can you buy it? Here on tap and to go in 750ml bottles and growlers. Also on tap in regional bars and restaurants and in stores in 750ml bottles. Check website for additional information.

Got food? No, but food friendly with many food options in the area. Food delivery available, plus occasional food vendors and trucks.

Tours? Check website for current schedule.

Special Offer: Bring in *Minnesota's Best Beer Guide* to Lakes & Legends Brewing Company for a signature from our Head Brewer, one of the original founders, or taproom employee, and have a beer on us. Limit one beer per book. Must show Lakes & Legends Brewing Company page for signature verification. *Please note some beers may not be available for this offer.*

Directions: From its intersection with I-35W, get on I-94 heading west and take Exit 231B for Lyndale Ave north and turn right on Lyndale Ave. Go 0.2 mile, turn right on 15th St, and continue 0.3 mile. Turn left on Willow St, go 800 ft, and turn right onto Grant St. Go 700 ft and turn right onto LaSalle Ave and the brewery is 300 ft on your right. Heading east on I-94, take Exit 231B and get on Lyndale Ave. Go 0.5 mile and turn left onto Dunwoody Blvd. Go 0.4 miles, turn right on 12th St, and go 0.2 mile. Turn right on LaSalle Ave and the brewery is 0.3 mile on your right.

Nicollet Mall Station on the Green Line is 0.9 mile from here.

The Beer Buzz: The brewery is located on the bottom floor of an apartment complex at the heart of Loring Park in downtown Minneapolis, not far from various must-visit attractions such as *Walker Art Center* and *Minneapolis Sculpture Garden*. Co-founder Ethan Applen has worked for Disney and Warner Brothers but his real passion has always been for food and the chance to start a brewery was very appealing. (Beer *is* food; ask a Trappist monk. Liquid bread.) Co-founder Derrick Taylor is a Minnesota native with a marketing and event production background. In the past, he's managed the Red Bull Crashed Ice event in St. Paul (something not to miss in January, by the way). Finally, the all important Head Brewer is Andrew Dimery who comes to Lakes & Legends by way of Bluegrass Brewing Co. in Kentucky and Sun King Brewing Co. in Indiana. His brewing will focus on Belgian and farmhouse style ales, improvising wherever possible, and using local and organic ingredients when available. Frequent releases of seasonal and specialty beers will compliment the line-up.

Nearly a third of their 12,000 sq. ft. brewery will be dedicated to the taproom. The founders intend this place to be a community-minded gathering place for friends, families and organizations.

WiFi. Facebook/lakesandlegendsbrewing
Twitter @lakesandlegends
Instagram @lakesandlegends

Stumbling Distance: *Minneapolis Convention Center* (1301 2nd Ave S, 612-335-6000) is 2 blocks away. Popular counter-service Vietnamese eatery *Lotus Restaurant* (113 W Grant St, 612-870-1218, lotusrestaurant-hub. com) is around the block.

Sisyphus Brewing is a 15-minute walk from here; *Rock Bottom* is 10 minutes.

LynLake Brewery

Founded: October 2014
Head Brewer: Joel Carlson
Address: 2934 Lyndale Ave S • Minneapolis, MN 55408
Phone: 612-224-9682
Web Site: www.lynlakebrewery.com
Annual Production: 2,000 barrels
Number of Beers: 8 on tap, plus 2 casks

Staple Beers:
- » Ponyboy Gold
- » Rubbish Oat Amber
- » Sideburns Milk Stout
- » Take 6 IPA

Rotating Beers:
- » Double IPA
- » Raka-Waka (New Zealand hops pale ale)
- » Rye Saison
- » Scottish Strong
- » Smoky Treat
- » Take IPA series (numbered versions)
- » Tradesman Robust Porter
- » Yea Yea Pale Ale

Most Popular Brew: Take IPA

Samples: Yes, four 4-oz. pours for about $8 (served in a tray fashioned from copper tubing).

Brewmaster's Fave: Depends on the day.

Best Time to Go: Open Wed–Thu 5PM–12AM, Fri 5PM–1AM, Sat 12PM–1AM, Sun 12–10PM.

Where can you buy it? Only here in pints and to go in growlers and 750ml "roadies" but expect area draft accounts soon.

Got food? No, but food friendly. Menus at the tables for delivery—just mention your table number.

Tours? By chance if someone is free.

Special Offer: Not participating at this time.

Directions: Coming from the east on I-94, take Exit 231B for Hennepin Ave toward Lyndale Ave, and keep right until the road turns left to merge into Lyndale Ave. Go 1.2 miles and the brewery is on the right. From the north on I-94, Exit 231A-231B is a long ramp to Lyndale Ave, stay left on 231B when they split, and continue to follow signs for Lyndale. Continue about 1.6 miles and the brewery is on the right.

Cyclists: *About 400 feet south of the Midtown Greenway at Lyndale Ave.*

The Beer Buzz: You'll recognize this brewery by its old-school theater marquee over the sidewalk that lights up like opening night. In 1914 this was the Lyndale Theatre, one of the original movie houses. Co-founders Mark Anderson and Paul Cossette had worked together on other buildings, mostly high-rises in the Twin Cities area. But give a couple of construction guys some beer—Surly, in this case, apparently—and next thing you know they are building a brewery. They partnered with Brewer Joel and renovated this historical building. The historic Lyn-Lake neighborhood was actually a suburb back in the day, but had gotten a little rough over the years as the city grew. Gentrification has turned this into a nice area for younger families.

During the remodel, they found stadium seats under the original floor. Note the crown moldings, which have been restored. They found the plaster had horse hair in it as reinforcement, an old building technique.

This is a huge space with high ceilings and lots of light. There are concrete floors, exposed light brick, tall wood tables, and at center a square island bar—built with reclaimed barn wood and tin—with a couple dozen bike wheel rims hanging like chandeliers above. Toward the back is the open 10-barrel brewhouse set apart only by a velvet cordon and some kegs waiting to be filled. Black metal staircases rise up on either side of the taproom and there's even a rooftop patio with fireball fireplaces made from metal by a local artist. Rogue Citizen, a local art group, did the first floor mural, and a couple high school kids from Minnetonka who won a talent show did the 2nd floor mural.

Brewer Joel is from northern Minnesota and got into homebrewing in 2004 (lured there by Summit and Bell's craft beer). In 2007 he went pro and has worked at Boathouse Brewing, Great Waters Brewing, and Town Hall Brewery. Assistant brewer Justin Skyberg was a longtime homebrewer and used to bring his brews to family holiday gatherings until his uncle asked him how he felt about opening a brewery. Of course he liked the idea and soon he was having a long chat with Mark and Paul.

WiFi. Facebook.com/lynlakebrewery,
Twitter @LynLakeBrewery, Instagram @lynlakebrewery

Stumbling Distance: *It's Greek to Me* (626 W Lake St, 612-825-9922, itsgreektomemn.com) across the street is one of the oldest eateries in the hood and highly regarded for... Greek food. Bet you didn't see that coming. *Galactic Pizza* (2917 Lyndale Ave S, 612-824-9100, galacticpizza.com) has great locally sourced pies (vegan and GF available), plus superheroes delivering them. *Muddy Waters* (2933 Lyndale Ave S, 612-872-2232, muddywatersmpls.com) has burgers, pot roast sliders, and a great beer list. Worth a little extra walking, *Hola Arepa* (3501 Nicollet Ave S, 612-345-5583, holaarepa.com) is highly regarded for this delicious Venezuelan street food both at their restaurant and food truck. *The Herkimer* brewpub is just a few steps away, same side of the street.

TWIN CITIES CULINARY CLASSIC: THE JUCY LUCY

Think molten cheese. The Jucy Lucy is a Twin Cities classic and a dining experience you shouldn't miss. The concept is simple and genius: take your cheese and build your burger around it. Sealed inside the ground beef, the hamburger is fried until the cheese melts. Just don't burn yourself when you take that first bite, for cryin' out loud.

The spelling is as sloppy as the burger. *Matt's Bar* is often said to be the original, though *5-8 Club* begs to differ (and in differing adds that missing i to "juicy"). But rather than rounding up the trademark lawyers, there is a cheerful rivalry and a whole series of playful variations of the simple cheeseburger original exist around both cities.

If one had the urge and safe cholesterol levels to go on a tour of the best Jucy Lucys (Lucies?) in town, here's where you should go:

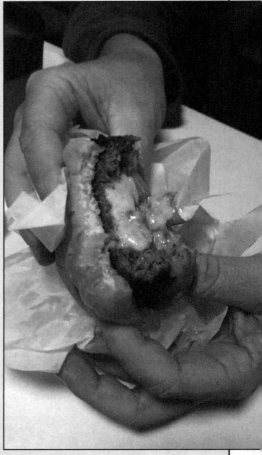

PHOTO COURTESY OF DAVID HIGGINS

Matt's Bar
3500 Cedar Ave S, Minneapolis | 612-722-7072
mattsbar.com
The original

5-8 Club
5800 Cedar Ave S., Minneapolis | 612-823-5858
5-8club.com
The other original

Crooked Pint Ale House
501 S Washington Ave, Minneapolis | 612-877-6900
crookedpint.com
Cerrano peppers and habanero jack? That's a Hot Lips Lucy

The Blue Door Pub
1811 Selby Ave, St Paul | 651-493-1865
thebluedoorpubmn.com
Several options, including Juicy Blucy with bleu cheese

Casper's & Runyon's Nook
492 Hamline Ave S, St. Paul | 651-698-4347
crnook.com
Juicy Nookie with variations such as The Spanish Fly (chorizo burger with queso) and another with bacon and pepper jack

Groveland Tap
1834 St. Clair Ave, St. Paul | 651-699-5058
grovelandtap.com
Offers a Cajun Lucy

Tin Cup
1220 Rice Street, St Paul | 651-487-7967
Six variations, notably Eggcellent Lucy with Swiss and bacon, topped with cheese and an egg

FOR THE VEGETARIANS:

Sapor Café
428 Washington Ave N, Minneapolis | 612-375-1971
saporcafe.com
Black Bean Juicy Lucy stuffed with Chihuahua cheese on a tostada with mojo picante, avocado, queso fresco, cilantro, and slaw. No one's judging.

Minneapolis Town Hall Brewery

Founded: October 1997
Brewmaster: Michael Hoops
Address: 1430 Washington Ave S • Minneapolis, MN 55454
Phone: 612-339-8696
Web Site: www.townhallbrewery.com
Annual Production: 2,200 barrels
Number of Beers: 17 on tap, 9 guests, 10 ciders, 3 casks; 50+ beers per year

Staple Beers:
- » Black H$_2$O Oatmeal
- » Dortmunder Local
- » Hope and King Scotch Ale
- » Masala Mama IPA
- » West Bank Pale Ale

Rotating Beers:
- » Amber Falcon
- » Buffalo Bock (Weizenbock in Buffalo Trace barrels)
- » Center Sky
- » Czar Jack (Russian Imperial Stout in Jack Daniels barrels)
- » ...plus rotating infusions and casks, barrel-aging, lagers, nitro taps

Most Popular Brew: Masala Mama IPA

Samples: Yes, flights of five 5-oz. core beers ($9) or seasonals ($11), or even ciders, whiskey, or nitro pours.

Best Time to Go: Open Mon–Thu 11–1AM, Fri–Sat 11–2AM, Sun 11–12AM. Watch for their anniversary season in October, and Barrel Age Week in February.

Where can you buy it? Here on tap and to go in pre-filled growlers, and on draft at sister establishments Town Hall Tap (4810 Chicago Ave S, 612-767-7307, townhalltap.com) and Town Hall Lanes (5019 S 34th Ave, 612-767-3354, thlanes.com)

Got food? Yes, scheduled first Saturday of the month or by appointment for groups.

Tours? By appointment.

Special Offer: $2 off a flight of Town Hall Brewery beers at Washington Ave location during your signature visit.

Directions: Coming from the north on I-35W take Exit 17C and turn left (east) on Washington Ave. The brewery is 0.1 mile on the left. From the south take Exit 17C also, but then keep left to continue to Washington Ave. Follow signs for U of M West Bank and turn right on Washington. The brewery is 250 feet on your left.

West Bank Station on the Green Line is just over a block south of here.

Cyclists: *Just a couple blocks south of the Bluff Street Bikeway, which crosses the river on Northern Pacific Bridge No. 9. A connecting trail bridges the elevation difference from the Bluff Street path to the West River Parkway path.*

The Beer Buzz: Pete Rifakes and Scot McClure have known each other since middle school where they grew up in Middleton, Wisconsin. They played little league baseball together at the local town hall and that memory stuck with them and inspired the brewpub's name. Pete worked for Northwest Airlines, but he did his thesis for a Masters in Finance on starting a brewpub. He quit his job and started putting that thesis to work.

Situated in an area of Minneapolis known as Seven Corners, Town Hall is highly esteemed and one of the veteran brewpubs in the industry. "The advantage of a brewpub," Brewer Mike Hoops notes, "is you have control from brew kettle to the glass." Mike started up the brewing program at another notable brewpub back in the 90s, *Fitger's Brewhouse* in Duluth, which he left in his brother's hands three years later when he came to get Town Hall going. Mike's interest in brewing was piqued when his college roommate got a brew kit. He was in San Francisco when he first homebrewed with a friend and made "undrinkable beer." But he stuck with it, did a lot of reading, some volunteering for brewers, and ended up getting the Fitger's gig. His formal training was done at Brewlab at the University of Sunderland near Newcastle in the UK.

Mike has a lot of freedom at this brewery giving him a vast creative outlet which he says explains his longevity here. They've been barrel-aging beers since the end of the 90s. They've won the most Great American Beer Festival medals in the state, 15 as of 2014.

Originally, this was three different buildings: a trolley station, a tavern in the 1950s, and a theater. Wrapped into one now, the brewpub has two dining areas, exposed brick, pressed tin ceilings, and rough-wood floors. A huge recovered clocktower clock greets you at the door, and a couple of murals tout their beers and the brewing process. A few TVs are scattered around the place, and there's a fireplace and lounge furniture in back. In summer, a spacious patio opens up on the walk outside.

ATM on site. WiFi. Facebook.com/townhallbrewery
Twitter @THBrewery

Stumbling Distance: *Acadia Café* (329 Cedar Ave, 612-874-8702, acadiacafe.com) is an awesome beer bar. *Republic* (221 Cedar Ave, 612-338-6146, republicmn.com) is a gastropub with a stellar craft beer list. (Top 100 Beer Bars in America according to Draft Magazine.) *Nomad World Pub* (501 Cedar Ave, 612-338-6424, nomadpub.com) offers beers around the world, soccer on TV, and bocce ball outside. Dog friendly. A great nearby base of operations, *The Commons Hotel* (615 Washington Ave SE, 612-379-8888, commonshotel.com) is a boutique hotel right on the University of Minnesota campus, just 1 mile from the brewery and right at the East Bank Station on the Green Line (one stop from Town Hall's closest stop, West Bank Station). Their signature restaurant *The Beacon Public House* (beaconpublichouse.com) has excellent food, a good happy hour, plus a very nice beer list. *Day Block Brewery* is a 6 minute walk north up Washington Ave.

NORTHBOUND SMOKEHOUSE BREWPUB

Founded: 2012
Brewmaster: Jamie Robinson
Address: 2716 East 38th Street • Minneapolis, MN 55406
Phone: 612-208-1450
Web Site: www.northboundbrewpub.com
Number of Beers: 6 on tap plus 6 guest taps

Staple Beers:
  » BIG JIM MINNESOTA IPA (92 IBU)
  » HONEY WHEAT ALE
  » LIGHT RAIL ALE
  » SMOKEHOUSE PORTER

Rotating Beers:
  » AUBURN NIGHT
  » SNOWMAGEDDON IMPERIAL HONEY BROWN

Samples: Yes, flights of 6 for about $8

Best Time to Go: Open Mon–Thu 11–1AM, Fri–Sat 11–2AM, Sun 10–1AM.

Where can you buy it? Only here on tap and in growlers to go.

Got food? Yes, a full menu, which as the name implies is focused on smoked meats. Beer cheese soup, the 18-hour porketta is popular—an "Iron Range" classic—and the smoked wings are fantastic. A menu oddity, chislic, is a South Dakotan dish of cubed marinated beef with spent-grain-and-parmesan breadsticks.

Tours? On request.

Special Offer: Not participating at this time.

Directions: Heading south from downtown Minneapolis on Hiawatha Ave/MN 55, turn right on 38th St, go 0.2 mile and the brewpub is on the right.

5 blocks west of the 38th Street Station on the Blue Line

Cyclists: *About 5 blocks from the Hiawatha LRT Trail*

The Beer Buzz: With all the clever ways of financing a brewery, especially in the age of Kickstarter, Brewer Jamie's may go down as one of the coolest: free beer for life. Banks said no, as they often do, but Jamie announced to the public: invest $1000 and you drink his beer for the rest of your life for nary a dime. Bam! He had nearly a quarter of million dollars in less than a month, and then the banks were willing to look.

Robinson managed Town Hall Brewery before this, and after taking the Siebel Institute brewing program, he did some brewing at Town Hall with Mike Hoops. Northbound's founding chef, Bryce Strickler also worked there. The two partnered with Amy Johnson as a manager to get this thing up and running. Jason Foster took over the kitchen in 2013. A couple industrial smokers and a smoky menu—even the porter is a smoked malt beer—validates this place as a smokehouse. They smoke everything in house from the meats to cheese and eggs.

CHISLIC

Northbound Smokehouse serves an unusual dish which isn't Minnesotan, but rather South Dakotan. Chislic calls for cubed red meat—typically mutton, but beef or game will do—which is seasoned and then grilled or deep-fried and served on wooden skewers. The name may be derived all the way from Turkish and Arabic origins (*shish kebab*), but its origin here is probably Russian shahslyk. An 1870s Russian immigrant John Hoellwarth gets the credit for the introduction though the sources are slim. This is a rare menu item that few people outside a small circle in South Dakota have ever even heard of.

The bar and dining area show wide plank floors and open duct work ceilings. As a brewpub, they also have a full bar. Some old photos and a map of the old Minneapolis street car system hang on the wall. A couple of TVs pipe in the day's sports or special programs. The brewhouse is visible through windows behind the bar, and another room of tanks can be seen from the street in the next room. It's a good casual restaurant; bar music plays while you dine. The beer list is displayed on a chalkboard. Northbound has been honored as Best Brewpub as well as Best Minneapolis Neighborhood Bar in the City Pages.

ATM on site. WiFi. Facebook.com/NorthboundBrewpub
Twitter @NorthboundBrew

Stumbling Distance: *Matt's Bar* (3500 Cedar Ave, 612-722-7072, mattsbar.com) of Jucy Lucy burger fame is 4 minutes' drive northwest. *Pilgrimage Café* (2403 E 38th St, 612-729-0034, pilgrimagecafe.com) west on 38th a few blocks does brunch and dinner with an eclectic, internationally influenced menu and a few bottled beers. Stellar breakfast, lunch and dinner at *The Tiny Diner* (1024 E 38th St, 612-767-3322, tinydiner.com) plus 16 craft beer taps.

NorthGate Brewing Company

Founded: 2012
Head Brewer: Tuck Carruthers
Address: 783 Harding Street NE • Minneapolis, MN 55413
Phone: 612-354-2858
Web Site: www.northgatebrew.com
Annual Production: 1,500 barrels
Number of Beers: 8–10 on tap, plus a weekly firkin

Staple Beers:
  » Golden SMaSH IPA (single malt, single hop)
  » Maggie's Leap Sweet Stout
  » Parapet ESB
  » Wall's End English Brown

Rotating Beers:
  » Fiddle Smasher Wee Heavy
  » Get Together IPA
  » Last Batch English Wheat Ale
  » Pumpion (pumpkin ale)
  » Red Headed Piper Irish Red Ale
  » Stronghold Robust Porter
  » Winter Soldier Amber Ale

Most Popular Brew: Varies with seasons. Golden SMaSH in warmer times, Maggie's Leap when it's colder. Wall's End leads in growler sales.

Samples: Yes, flights of four 4-oz. pours (flagships or select brews) for about $8.

Brewmaster's Fave: Maggie's Leap on nitro or Parapet ESB

Best Time to Go: Open Thu 4–10PM, Fri 4PM–12AM, Sat 12PM–12AM, Sun 12–6PM. Happy hour Thu–Fri from 4–6PM. Trivia on Thursdays.

Where can you buy it? On tap here in imperial pints and half-pints, and to go in pre-filled growlers. Limited 22-oz. bombers available in Twin Cities metro liquor stores.

Got food? No, but food friendly and food trucks show up most days.

Tours? Yes, free tours on Saturdays between 1 and 5 PM.

Special Offer: $1 off your first imperial pint or 50 cents off one half-pint during your signature visit.

Directions: Coming from the north on I-35W, take Exit 21A and turn left on Stinson Blvd. Go 0.2 mile, turn left on Broadway St, and continue 0.3 mile to Harding St. Turn right, and the brewery is right there on your left. Coming from the south on I-35W, take Exit 21A, keep left for CR 88/New Brighton Blvd, then keep right for I-35W for 0.2 mile to turn right on Stinson Blvd. Go left on Broadway 0.3 mile and turn right on Harding and the brewery is on your left. And Bob's your uncle.

The Beer Buzz: Adam Sjogren and Todd Slininger, homebrewers, founded this brewery, beginning with a plan in early 2012 and finding a small space in an old industrial building in beer-centric Northeast Minneapolis. They sold their first beer to Grumpy's Northeast in January 2013. In just over a year, they had outgrown the space and in October 2014 moved into this much larger location with room for a taproom—but still in that awesome beer 'hood of the city. (Interestingly enough, 56 Brewing bought their old equipment and took over that very same space NorthGate left behind.)

Brewer Tuck trained at Siebel. The name NorthGate was inspired by an English brewery near Stonehenge. Not coincidentally, they focus on English- and Irish-style, malt forward, sessionable ales.

The brewery occupies a former printing shop in the first unit of a longer industrial park building. The taproom is out front and features a long bar plus lots of tables and a few booths. You can see into the brewery behind the bar. There are board games and foosball, and a couple TVs only come on during game days. Parking is in a lot right out front.

WiFi. Facebook.com/northgatebrew and Twitter @northgatebrew

Stumbling Distance: *Zakia Deli* (2412 Kennedy St NE, 612-379-0288, zakiadeli.com) has great Lebanese food and delivers but is only open until 8PM weekdays, 6PM on Sat. *Ramada Plaza Minneapolis* (1330 Industrial Blvd NE, 877-513-4873, ramadaplazampls.com) is about a mile away and makes a good base for hitting all the Northeast Minneapolis breweries. *612Brew, Sociable Cider Werks,* and *Bauhaus Brew Labs* are about 1.3 miles due west of here.

ROCK BOTTOM RESTAURANT & BREWERY

Founded: 1993
Brewmaster: Larry Skellenger
Address: 800 LaSalle Plaza • Minneapolis, MN 55402
Phone: 612-332-2739
Web Site: www.rockbottom/locations/minneapolis
Annual Production: 1,000 barrels
Number of Beers: 10–12 beers
Staple Beers:
  » HENNEPIN MILLS WHEAT
  » HOWLING LOON IPA
  » NORTHERN LIGHTS
  » SKOL VINR! AMBER

Rotating Beers:
  » CATCHER IN THE RYE
  » EVERGREEN RED IPA
  » FALLEN ANGEL DUBBEL
  » FIRE CHIEF RED ALE
  » HONKY TONK LIGHT
  » LA SUPRISE HOUBLON
  » MATES FELLOWSHIP BROWN PORTER
  » PLOUGHBOY STOUT
  » POUND PUPPY
  » SAFE ON THIRD
  » …also offers barrel-aged beers and casks

Samples: Yes, flights of six 5 oz. beers for about $6.

Brewmaster's Fave: Session styles and IPAs

Best Time to Go: Open Sun–Thu 11–1AM, Fri–Sat 11–2AM. Happy hour is weekdays 3–6PM plus Sunday through Thursday from 10PM–close in the bar area only. Watch for tapping parties and Firkin Night. Come for sporting events on TV.

Where can you buy it? Pints for here or growlers and 750 ml bottle-conditioned brews to go.

Got food? Yes, a full menu including soup, sandwich, burgers, and appetizers (beer-battered cheese curds!). The chef and brewer work together to recommend beer pairings for menu items.

Tours? Can be arranged with service staff if time allows. Group tours need to contact the banquet coordinator.

Special Offer: Not participating at this time.

Directions: Get on Hennepin Ave in downtown Minneapolis. The brewery is at street level in the large commercial complex adjacent to the state theater between 9th St and 8th St. Parking is often best nearby ramps. From I-94 to the west of downtown, Exit 231B will connect you to Hennepin and you need to go east toward downtown.

The Beer Buzz: Rock Bottom originated in Denver, Colorado, and in twenty years has come to open 34 other locations including this one in downtown Minneapolis. Despite being part of a larger chain, the brewpub does brew on premises and mills its own grain, and each brewer is allowed to do their own thing.

Listen for the hostess answering the phone: "Hello, you've hit Rock Bottom." The name comes from the original brewpub which was on the ground floor of the Prudential building in Denver. Remember the

Prudential insurance ads? "Get a piece of the rock." Am I dating myself here?

Brewer Larry wasn't even a homebrewer when he left the corporate world in 2006 and took the assistant brewer position at the Rock Bottom in Des Moines, Iowa. He loved craft beer and since 1989 had thought it'd be a cool job. They started him at 10 hours per week gradually adding hours until he was nearly full time. Then he was offered the Head Brewer position here and took over on June 3, 2013.

LaSalle Plaza was originally the site of a famous gay bar, Cloud Nine, which was taken down to build the current complex. The newer building is home to Rock Bottom and also incorporates the State Theatre, restaurants, office space, the original YMCA which was converted to apartments. Enter the plaza building from Hennepin Avenue and Rock Bottom is on your right. The bar area has booths and tall tables and abundant TVs. The brewery is visible through glass windows behind the bar. The dining room has much more seating and in season there are tables outside on the sidewalk.

WiFi. Facebook.com/RockBottomRestaurant,
Twitter @RockBottom and Instagram @rockbottombrewery

Stumbling Distance: *Lakes & Legends Brewing* is a 10 minute walk. *Radisson Blu* (35 S Seventh St, 612-339-4900, radissonblu.com/hotel-minneapolis) is a short walk from here and just a couple blocks from Nicollett Mall Station on the Green Line, making it an excellent home base for a beercation in Minneapolis. Serious eats and serious music at *Dakota Jazz Club & Restaurant* (1010 Nicollet Mall, 612-332-1010, dakotacooks.com), and casual but creative food and bar at *Devil's Advocate* (89 S 10th St, 612-843-2260, devilsadvocatebar.com) with 40 tap beers and a serious wine list.

Sisyphus Brewing Co.

Founded: 2014
Brewmaster: Sam Harriman
Address: 712 Ontario Avenue West • Minneapolis, MN 55403
Phone: 612-321-8324
Web Site: www.sisyphusbrewing.com
Number of Beers: 4 on tap, changing weekly; 25 beers their first 6 months

Rotating Beers: (always changing, but here are some examples)

- » Brett IPA
- » Cascadian Ale
- » Double Rye Ale
- » Double IPA
- » Imperial Brown Ale
- » Milk Stout
- » Oatmeal Stout
- » Winter Warmer
- » …plus some barrel aging

Most Popular Brew: Brett IPA or Oatmeal Pale Ale

Samples: Yes, four 5-oz pours for about $8

Brewmaster's Fave: Brett IPA

Best Time to Go: Open Wed–Thu 3pm–10pm, Fri–Sat noon–1am, but check website. Trivia on Wed, Comedy Showcase once a month featuring 3 local comedians.

Where can you buy it? Only here and in 750ml "growlettes" to go.

Got food? No, but food friendly and food trucks park outside on occasion.

Tours? Only on request for groups.

Special Offer: $1 off your first beer when you get your book signed.

Directions: From downtown Minneapolis, Hennepin Ave heads west, becoming Dunwoody Blvd just before passing under I-94. Pass under and take Aldrich Ave to the right and the brewery is at the next corner, Aldrich and Ontario Ave. Coming from the east on I-94, take Exit 231B and follow signs for Hennepin Ave/Dunwoody Blvd, and turn left on Dunwoody at the light. Follow the Aldrich Ave instructions above. Coming from the west on I-94, take Exit 231A/231B for Lyndale Ave, and stay on 231B following signs for Hennepin/Lyndale. Turn right on Ontario Ave and the brewery is there on the right.

Cyclists: *The brewery is 0.5 mile off the Cedar Lake Trail.*

The Beer Buzz: In Greek mythology, Zeus punished a corrupt king named Sisyphus who was condemned to roll a giant boulder up a mountain. The rock rolled back down just before he got to the top every day and he had to start over. French philosopher Albert Camus wrote an essay comparing the meaninglessness of human existence to this task of Sisyphus. But rather than a depressing, endless, pointless task, he posited that weary worker put meaning into the task and thus into existence. So believe Samuel Harriman and Catherine Cuddy, the husband-and-wife team who founded the brewery believing that their Sisyphus is rolling a barrel up that hill—and loving it. You get to enjoy the fruits of the endless brewing tasks. Harriman's background was pre-med, but he also holds an MBA and degrees in psychology and philosophy (cue Camus). His brewing philosophy is balance—he doesn't want to overwhelm the palate.

Harriman got into homebrewing after an "a-ha" moment on a Samuel Adams brewery tour. Back in Minneapolis he found Four Firkins liquor store and the hobby became habit. Five years later he decided he needed a change, and so he gave up rolling the corporate boulder to go on a month-long *pilsgrimage* to California to visit breweries there and along the way. The couple were convinced and set out in search of a brewery site, ideally, they thought, in St. Louis Park. But they simply couldn't find anything. Then the first place they looked at with a broker in Minneapolis was perfect. An early 20th century brick building, it had manufactured pen parts and then functioned as a machine shop during the World Wars. Dunwoody Technical College across the street had been using it for storage but the only thing ready for business was the floor. Harriman and Cuddy had to build the rest. An old bowling alley became the bar top. A friend who works for Mercury Mosaics did the tile design—a barrel and two hop leaves—behind the long bar. The tap room shows open-beam ceilings, exposed pale brick, and a lot of windows keep the space amply lit. One-third of their space is tap room, another third is the brewhouse, and plans are to add an event space for more comedy and music.

There's a pinball machine, two shuffleboard tables (and a league), some board games (including cribbage, of course). Be sure not to miss the awesome mural on the east side of the building, a Paul Bunyanesque Sisyphus with his barrel burden on a mountain of hops, created by local artists Adam Turman and Jawsh. Street parking is free and the city lot under I-94 is free on Saturdays.

WiFi. Facebook.com/SisyphusBrewing and Twitter @SisyphusBrewing

Stumbling Distance: *Lakes & Legends Brewing* is a 15-minute walk. The 1914 *Basilica of St. Mary* (1600 Hennepin Ave, Minneapolis, 612-333-1381, www.mary.org), the first basilica in North America, is open for self-guided tours and on Sundays, free guided tours after the morning masses. You are quite close to the *Minneapolis Sculpture Garden* (the big spoon and cherry) and the *Walker Art Center* (1750 Hennepin Ave, 612-375-7600, walkerart.org).

THE ART OF BEER

Walker Art Center should be on any visitor's list of things to see here in Minneapolis, but you might want to stop in for some food and drink. The museum features *Gather by D'Amico*, a New American bistro that uses local ingredients to make some edible works of art. But they are only open on Thursdays from 5–9PM.

Check them out for **First Thursdays**, the first Thursday of the month when they invite a guest chef or a local brewer to share their specialties. The tastings are complimentary but will be on the menu for the rest of the month. **Happy Hour** from 5–7PM is another great time to be here, with affordable small plates as well as beer (and wine, cocktail) specials.

Gather by D'Amico / Walker Art Center
1750 Hennepin Ave, Minneapolis | 612-253-3410
gatherbydamico.com | walkerart.org

SOCIABLE CIDER WERKS BREWERY

Founded: 2013
Cidermakers: Jim Watkins & Wade Thompson **Brewer:** Mike Willaford
Address: 1500 Fillmore Street NE • Minneapolis, MN 55413
Phone: 612-758-0105
Web Site: www.sociablecider.com
Annual Production: 250 barrels (cider 3,600 bbls)
Number of Beers: 3–5 beers on tap, 4–6 ciders

Staples:
- » FREEWHEELER DRY APPLE
- » HOP-A-WHEELIE HOPPED APPLE
- » SPOKE WRENCH (Stout Apple)

Rotating Beers & Ciders:
- » BLACK IPAPPLE
- » …endless varieties of small batches

Most Popular Brew: Freewheeler

Samples: Yes, but flights only during happy hour

Best Time to Go: Open Thu–Fri 4–11PM, Sat 12–11PM, Sun 12–6PM. Happy hour 4–6PM Thu–Fri.

Where can you buy it? Here in pints or "swifties" (12 oz.), and to go in growlers. On draft and in cans in the Twin Cities and Duluth areas.

Got food? No, but food friendly and there's a resident food truck: *The Curious Goat* (on Facebook.com/TheCuriousGoatMN)

Tours? Free at 12:30PM on Saturday. Please bring a canned food item.

Special Offer: A free "swifty" size pour and a sticker with your book signature.

Directions: From I-94 take Exit 229 and turn east on Broadway Ave (from the south at Exit 229 you need to take Washington north to Broadway first) and after 2 miles, turn left (north) on Fillmore St. (From the east side, I-35W Exit 21A will get you onto County Road 88/New Brighton Blvd. Go south and turn right (west) on Broadway and its 0.4 mile to Fillmore St, turn north/right.) Take Fillmore St 0.3 mile north to the brewery parking lot entrance on your left. It's set back from the road.

The Beer Buzz: You might wonder what a cidery is doing in a beer book, but this is the first cidery licensed as a brewery. We could merely point out the fact that they do in fact brew beer, but it's more interesting than that. Often in cider one blends in some bitter apples to get a bittering balance, but those are a bit scarce in Minnesota. So the cidery brews in the bitterness using sorghum (gluten-free) and Willamette hops to give the cider nice body and tannins without sweeteners and thus the cider remains dry. This process compelled the tax authority to determine this is not cider (or wine), but beer for tax purposes. So they are able to take advantage of the Surly Bill's creation of legal taprooms for breweries.

Jim and Wade were roommates in college. Wade's father-in-law made French-style cider in his basement for over 20 years, and the two took to cidermaking in the garage. They also traveled over 8,000 miles around the country to check out other cider makers and brewers before they took the big step to open Sociable Cider Werks. The ciders are French-style, not UK style, so they are dry and tart, not at all super sweet like some might expect.

Sociable's mission is to turn people on to the wonders of craft cider, but they also wanted to have great beer, which may draw in a different clientele. This works well for groups of friends who are fans of one or the other; each product stands on its own. Nico Tonks from Fair State Brewing Cooperative helped start the beer program. Brewer Mike took it over. He worked at The Herkimer and was in charge of the cask program at Surly before coming here in 2014. In his first six months he brewed 40 different styles of beer. Sociable once collaborated with Schell's Brewing on a Burn Out Smoked Apple.

Sociable occupies a reclaimed 1922 fabric warehouse, a long low building of cinder-block and some curious fir roof beams. Inside is a long wood bar, a piano by the door, a collection of tables, and a chalkboard menu of what's on offer. Garage doors roll up in season for access to the patio out front. No TVs here, just board games, foosball, and plenty of socializing. Beat the owner in foosball and he'll buy you a pint. Lose, and you buy a stranger a pint.

The cider sources all its apples through Pepin Heights Orchard in Lake City, Minnesota, which either grows them or gathers them from other growers in Minnesota, Wisconsin, and Michigan. They are pressed there and the juice is brought to the cidery. While celiac sufferers won't be inclined to drink the regular beer, many of the cider products are actually naturally gluten-free or otherwise gluten-removed and are marked clearly as such.

As well as being a friendly sounding name, Sociable is also the term for a side-by-side tandem bicycle that fell out of style long ago. You can see one in the taproom.

WiFi. Facebook.com/sociablecider and Twitter @SociableCider Instagram @sociablecider

Stumbling Distance: *Bauhaus Brew Labs* and *612Brew* are about a 10–15 minute walk from here. *Indeed Brewing* is a bit further but still walkable. *Hazel's Northeast* (2859 Johnson Street NE, 612-788-4778, hazelsnortheast.com), a family-owned restaurant, serves excellent, often locally sourced food and serves Sociable products. Another landmark eatery, dating back to 1949, is *The Ideal Diner* (1314 Central Ave NE, 612-789-7630, idealdiner.com), specializing in breakfast. *Tattersall Distilling Company* (1620 Central Ave NE, Ste 150, 773-710-7358, tattersalldistilling.com) is a craft distiller with killer cocktails around the corner. *The Mill* (1851 Central Ave NE, 612-315-2340, themillnortheast.com) has awesome daily brunch and dinner menus plus 12 craft beers on tap.

Surly Brewing Co.

Founded: 2006
Brewmaster: Todd Haug
Address: 520 Malcolm Ave SE • Minneapolis, MN 55414
Phone: 763-999-4040
Web Site: www.surlybrewing.com
Annual Production: For now, about 50,000 bbls here, 30,000 bbls in Brooklyn Center
Number of Beers: up to 20 taps in the Beer Hall, 6+ in distribution plus special/limited releases and seasonals

Staple Beers:
- » BENDER (American oatmeal brown ale)
- » COFFEE BENDER (Bender with Guatemalan coffee)
- » CYNICALE (Belgian-style saison/pale ale)
- » FURIOUS (American IPA/British ESB hybrid)
- » HELL (Munich-style Helles lager)
- » OVERRATED (West Coast IPA)

Rotating Beers:
- » ABRASIVE ALE (Double IPA)
- » ASATOR VIKING IPA
- » BITTER BREWER (in May)
- » BLAKKR (Imperial Black IPA – Mar)
- » CACAO BENDER
- » CULTIVATE (dandelion farmhouse saison)
- » DAMIEN (American Black Ale)

- » DARKNESS (Russian Imperial Stout – Oct)
- » DEVIL'S WORK (robust porter)
- » DOOMTREE
- » DUMPSTER FIRE (smoked IPA with Puya chiles)
- » EL HEFE NEGRO (imperial black wheat weiss-bier)
- » FIERY HELL (Hell Lager with Puya chiles and red oak)
- » MILD (English brown mild – Feb)
- » MISANTHROPE (Belgian-style saison/pale ale)
- » PENTAGRAM (Brett dark ale/sour – Mar)
- » SCHADENFREUDE (German dunkel – Apr)
- » SMOKE (oak-aged smoked Baltic porter – Winter)
- » SURLYFEST (not German-style Oktoberfest – Sep)
- » TODD THE AXE MAN (West Coast IPA)
- » WET (wet-hopped West Coast IPA – Hop harvest time)
- » WITCH'S TOWER (Solstice session brown ale)
- » YOU'RE IN TROUBLE (imperial IPA)
- » …watch for anniversary releases and more

Most Popular Brew: Furious

Samples: Yes

Brewmaster's Fave: Bender

Best Time to Go: Beer Hall hours are Sun–Thu 11AM–11PM, Fri–Sat 11AM–12AM. Be aware that at peak times, Fridays after 5PM, for example, crowds form, and the waits for larger groups for a seat can be a little long.

Where can you buy it? In the beer hall get pints and half pints (or 10 oz. pours of specialty beers). Out in the larger world, Surly is available in 16-oz. cans and 22-oz bottles (and often on tap) throughout Minnesota, Chicagoland, Iowa and Wisconsin. No growler sales here per current Minnesota law for breweries over 25,000 bbls.

Got food? Yes, two menus: Casually elegant dining upstairs, and in the Beer Hall a variety of charcuterie, salads, meat and seafood, some in-house smoked BBQ, and sides. Seasonally changing.

Tours? In planning: likely scheduled and requiring registration. Watch the website, Facebook, or Twitter.

Special Offer: Free bumper sticker and standard pint glass with any purchase in the company store during your signature visit. *Expires 12/31/2015.*

Directions: From I-94 take Exit 236 (MN 280) following signs toward University Ave. Merge onto Cromwell Ave, then turn left on University Ave. Go 0.7 mile, turn right on Malcolm Ave, and go 0.2 mile to the brewery. Turn right on 5th St to reach the parking lot entrance.

Walking distance from the Prospect Park Station of the Green Line and

Cyclists: *Just a block north of the University of Minnesota Transitway / Dinkytown Greenway bike path.*

The Beer Buzz: I don't know who came up with the term "destination brewery," but one can argue that Surly is defining it. Surly sold its first keg on February 1, 2006, finishing off that year with about 800 barrels of production. Before they opened this $30+ million Minneapolis brewery and beer hall in December 2014, they were at just about 40,000 barrels.

That's quite a success story, and while much of it can be credited to exceptional beer and a passionate fan base, founder Omar Ansari also credits a little luck. When Surly Brewing started in 2006, there was just Summit. "No one saw what was coming," he says. He had traveled out west and figured if they can support so many breweries, surely a population of 2 million can support two. Omar had started with a kit from Northern Brewer when he was 23, but the brewery idea came much later in 2004 when he and his wife Becca were looking for a business idea.

Brewer Todd plays speed-metal and back in the late 80s his band toured, opening for other rockers such as Overkill and Blue Oyster Cult. He got into brewing and took part-time work at Summit to learn more. Rock Bottom opened up downtown and he landed the head brewer job. Ironically, Todd met Omar in California. They were both attending a brewers' conference and Todd happened to recognize Omar's name from a post online about grains. Todd told Omar to stop by Rock Bottom back home sometime and he'd buy him a beer. Omar was looking for a brewer, and it seemed like Todd could be it. As it turns out Todd also welds stainless steel. Omar asked him, "Wanna help?" Six month later Todd was on board. He built the system out at

Brooklyn Center, did all the welding himself. Notoriety came quickly; in 2007 they were Best Brewery in the USA on Beer Advocate. In the beginning, Omar went door to door selling it, trying to squeeze in there between Summit and Bell's. "Very few got it except craft beer bars. Now there are 30 handles and 20 other brewers. Now you need to knock the other guy out."

That first brewery—which is still operating but not open to the public—is in Omar's late father's former abrasives factory. A perfect industrial space, but in just a few years they had outgrown it, and Omar wanted to have a taproom. This was something prohibited by law, so just as Mr. Smith went to Washington, Omar went to St. Paul. His lobbying efforts and the public activism from the fan base ("Surly Nation"), led to the introduction of what would be known as the Surly Bill. The Surly Bill passed in May 2011 (see the Introduction) and Surly broke ground for the new brewery in October 2013.

The new brewery started with six 600-barrel fermenters and has room to add perhaps 20 more. Cans are filled at a rate of 180 per minute. Brewer Todd comes up with all the recipes based on his tastes not on research from a marketing team, says Omar. The production scale is quite incredible but the public was most interested in being able to drink the beer on site. The beer hall is huge with long rows of communal tables. There's table service but also a line to order beer at the bar. Linda Haug, the brewer's wife, is Head of Restaurant Operations. Surly hired former Solera chef, Jorge Guzman for the kitchen, and a few months after opening, a menu

of finer fare was added for the upstairs dining room with an open kitchen. An event space holds 175 people.

Attached to the beer hall are a coat check and a large gift shop. There's valet parking most days and a large parking lot, as well as plenty of rack space for bikers (and even a water bottle fill at the drinking fountain inside). The beer hall does not take reservations, and at peak hours there may be a wait for seating (but you can always stand and drink, right?).

ATM on site. WiFi. Facebook.com/surlybrewing
Twitter @SurlyBrewing and @SurlyBeerHall

Stumbling Distance: As noted, you can't get beer to go at the brewery. Your best bet is *Zipp's Liquor* (2618 E Franklin Ave, 612-333-8686, zippsliquors. com) just across the Mississippi River (Franklin Ave Bridge) from here. Zipp's carries all current Surly brews including seasonals and specialty beers, plus a great selection of craft beer in general. Watch for tastings, cheese pairings, special sales, and beer, wine, and liquor classes. Wood-fired Neapolitan pies are served at the casual *Punch Pizza Stadium Village* (802 Washington Ave, 612-331-3122, punchpizza.com). *Urban Growler* and *Bang Brewing* are 6 minutes by car, 25 minutes on foot from here.

A great nearby base of operations, *The Commons Hotel* (615 Washington Ave SE, 612-379-8888, commonshotel.com) is a boutique hotel right on the University of Minnesota campus, just 5 minutes from the brewery and right at the East Bank Station on the Green Line (two stops from Surly's closest stop). Their signature restaurant *The Beacon Public House* (beaconpublichouse.com) has excellent food, a good happy hour, plus a very nice beer list (including Surly).

BAD WEATHER BREWING CO.

Founded: March 2012 | Taproom summer 2015
Brewmaster: Andy Ruhland
Address: 414 7th Street West • Saint Paul, MN
Phone: 612-805-2003
Web Site: www.badweatherbrewery.com
Annual Production: up to 4,000 barrels
Number of Beers: 8–10 on tap; 2 beer engines for casks

Staple Beers:
» WINDVANE Minnesota Red Ale

Rotating Beers:
» FIREFLY A Glimpse of Fall
» MIGRATION Fair Weather Ale
» OMINOUS Midwest Warmer
» STORM CELLAR SERIES: (750 ml/limited draft)
» #1 SCHOKO-WEIZEN (Chocolate Dunkelweizen)
» …many taproom exclusives.

Most Popular Brew: Windvane

Samples: Yes, flights.

Brewmaster's Fave: Windvane

Best Time to Go: Check the website for current hours.

Where can you buy it? By the pint and half pint, and growlers to go. Distributed kegs and 6-pack bottles in the Twin Cities area and as far as Rochester and Mankato. Storm Cellar Series brews come in 750 ml bottles.

Got food? No, but food friendly and menus from local restaurants. Food trucks on occasion.

Tours? Yes, check the website for a schedule.

Special Offer: $1 off your first beer during your signature visit.

Directions: Coming from the south on I-35E take Exit 106B for Kellogg Blvd. Turn right on Kellogg and go 0.1 mile to turn right on 7th St. Drive 0.5 mile and the brewery is on the left. Coming from the west on I-94, take Exit 241B, continue on 5th St, then turn right on 7th St. Coming from the east on I-94, take Exit 241A, merge onto St Anthony Ave, turn left on

Marion St and continue on Kellogg Blvd to turn right on 7th St. (If coming from the north on I-35, be sure to take I-94 to the right at the fork.)

The Beer Buzz: Co-founders Zac Carpenter and Joe Giambruno were both longtime homebrewers and craft beer fans who got connected by Zac's wife and Joe's mother-in-law. The two women were working together and the subject of beer had come up. Joe's mother-in-law said there's this guy, he likes beer, you should get a hold of him. Joe surprised himself by contacting Zac. Turns out they had a lot of similar interest and hit it off and became good friends.

Joe had gotten into brewing when his wife (then girlfriend) bought him a brewing kit. When he finished college, he thought about doing something with this passion. He worried he might regret it later if he didn't give it a try, so instead of going on to grad school he completed the World Brewing Academy Associate in Brewing Technology program at Siebel Institute in 2011. Grad school didn't stand a chance. Zac worked in the finance world and but also took up brewing, studied, and graduated from the American Brewer's Guild program in 2012. The only sensible thing to do at this point was to partner up and open a brewery.

Joe and Zac had heard about Lucid Brewing in Minnetonka inviting other breweries into their brewery as a sort of equipment sharing scheme. For Bad Weather this was a great way to start with minimum investment up front but still with the ability to brew what they wanted. Distribution followed. Two years on they had run out of space and needed to move on so they could brew more beer and a bigger variety of brews. They found a vacant tire shop with big garage doors and a lot of open space, and they started their build out. When they were ready to start brewing, they hired Andy Ruhland, who had been brewing with Lucid but decided to come along for the ride.

Oxidized steel and reclaimed wood highlight the entry. The taproom is spacious with a large concrete bar at the center, and a mix of tall tables and regular tables. The brewhouse is plainly visible. The two garage doors were replaced with glass doors which can be opened to grant seasonal access to the patio outside. An overflow room offers more space for busy nights or special or private events. The large mural is by artist Lucas Gluesenkamp (lucasgluesenkamp.com) who also did the labels and six-pack art for their lineup. Some TVs show the big games, while there are board games, arcade games, and, of course, cribbage to be played. Parking is in the adjacent lot or in the street.

WiFi. Facebook/badweatherbrewing and Twitter @BadweatherBrew

Stumbling Distance: *Xcel Energy Center* (199 W Kellogg Blvd, 651-265-4800, xcelenergycenter.com), home of Minnesota Wild hockey, is just two blocks away. *DeGidio's Italian* (425 7th St W, 651-291-7105, degidios. com) has good, reasonably priced eats plus a good local tap list. Not a pizza joint. *Mancini's Char House* (531 7th St W, 651-224-7345, mancinis. com) in an institution for steak and lobster. *Burger Moe's* (242 7th St W, 651-222-3100, burgermoes.com) offers decent burgers and a good tap list in a sports bar setting.

BEST TWIN CITIES BOTTLE SHOPS

Most brewery taprooms—other than big producers such as Summit or Surly—can sell growlers to go. But if you want to buy a six-pack or the like, you're going to have to go to the local liquor store. Fortunately, Minneapolis and St. Paul are loaded with them. Here are just a few of the all-stars with the brewers they are closest to.

MINNEAPOLIS

Elevated Beer, Wine & Spirits
4135 Hiawatha Ave, Minneapolis | 612-208-0973
Near Harriet Brewing, Northbound Smokehouse Brewpub

The Four Firkins
5630 W 36th St, Minneapolis | 952-938-2847
thefourfirkins.com
Near Steel Toe Brewing
East side location:
8338 3rd St North, Oakdale | 651-414-6216

Lake Wine and Spirits
404 W Lake St, Minneapolis | 612-354-7194
lakewinespirits.com
Near LynLake Brewery, The Herkimer

Stinson Wine, Beer & Spirits
2315 18th Ave NE, Minneapolis | 612-789-0678
stinsonwbs.com
East end of the Northeast Minneapolis neighbrewhood, closest to NorthGate

Surdyk's Liquor & Cheese Shop Wine
303 E Hennepin Ave, Minneapolis | 612-379-3232
surdyks.com
Just south of the Northeast Minneapolis neighbrewhood

Zipp's Liquor
2618 E Franklin Ave, Minneapolis | 612-333-8686
zippsliquors.com
They carry all current Surly brews including seasonals and specialty beers. Watch for tastings, cheese pairings, and beer, wine and liquor classes. Near Surly, Urban Growler, Bang Brewing, Harriet, Northbound, Minneapolis Town Hall, Day Block

ST. PAUL

Party Time Liquor
1835 Larpenteur Ave E, St Paul | 651-770-1447
partytimeliquor.com
Closest to St. Paul's Flat Earth Brewing, Sidhe Brewery

Thomas Liquor
1941 Grand Ave, St Paul | 651-699-1860
thomasliquor.com
Near Burning Brothers Brewing, Lake Monster Brewing, Urban Growler, Bang Brewing

The Wine Thief & Ale Jail
1787 Saint Clair Avenue, Saint Paul | 651-698-9463
winethief.net
Near Summit, Vine Park, Bad Weather, Lake Monster, Burning Brothers

Bang Brewing

Founded: September 2013
Brewmaster: Jay and Sandy Boss Febbo
Address: 2320 Capp Road • St. Paul, MN 55114
Phone: 651-243-2264
Web Site: www.bangbrewing.com
Annual Production: 500 barrels
Number of Beers: 4 on tap, all organic

Staple Beers:
  » Neat – Sparkling Bitter
  » Minn – American Mild
  » Nice – STP Dark Ale

Rotating Beers:
  » Good – German Style Session
  » Loop – Session Stout
  » Nice Coffee (Nice with cold-pressed coffee)
  » Time – Malty Strong Ale (fall)
  » Variations on Minn

Most Popular Brew: They're selling all about even!

Samples: Yes, but not flights.

Best Time to Go: Fri 4–10pm, Sat 2–8pm, but check the website.

Where can you buy it? Half and full pints, and in pre-filled growlers, and limited 750s. Look for some local draft accounts.

Got food? No, but food friendly, and the occasional food truck stops in.

Tours? Not really—you can see everything from a bar stool, and while the owners may chat with you about it, things get wicked busy during their limited tap room hours.

Special Offer: Not participating at this time.

Directions: From I-94 take Exit 236 toward University Ave. Merge onto Cromwell Ave, then turn right on Territorial Rd. Go 0.5 mile, turn left on Hampden Ave and continue 0.4 mile as it becomes Hersey St. Turn left on Capp Rd and the brewery is on your left.

Walking distance (0.7 mile) from the Raymond Avenue Station of the Green Line.

Cyclists: *Half mile east of the University of Minnesota Transitway /Dinkytown Greenway bike path.*

The Beer Buzz: At first glance you might think you've come to the wrong place. "Nothing here but this shiny grain bin." Yep, that's the brewery. Back in 1993, Jay and Sandy were housesitting for her great uncle and found he had a commercial stove in his kitchen. Jay eyed it and said, "I could brew beer on that." And so they did. They got a kit from Northern Brewing and thus were hooked. In 2005 they remodeled their kitchen for brewing. Eventually they figured it was time to go beyond the kitchen batches.

They searched for a good St. Paul site to redevelop for two years, but in the end they decided to build. The city had to rewrite the corridor code to allow this to go forward. Sustainability is important to them so they really hadn't wanted to build something, and so decided to keep it simple and small. They ran through ideas: a custom build? Maybe a pole barn? Neither appealed to them but then they thought, how about something

round? "Grain bin" was thrown out there as a joke, but the happy accident became the plan. Since opening, they've been brewing like crazy and at least for now, tap hours are limited and thus the place is busy during that time. But the two have yet to quit their day jobs. Sandy is an ad agency producer and Jay is a software engineer. (The name Bang is programmer speak for an exclamation point.)

The floor is concrete, the bin is corrugated sheets of metal, and much of the interiors are reclaimed from somewhere: a cedar fence from a neighbor, for example. The sidewalks down by the Mill City Museum are made of wood as they were back in the day. So was the road, but that was pulled out and put out on the market by Wood From the Hood. Jay and Sandy used to commute to work on that road, and now that wood is here, refashioned into steps and the tables and benches out on the patio outside the glass garage door in front. Inside is a very small bar, a few chairs, but mostly some standing room, and the brewhouse is roped off along the curving wall leaving customers in the middle of the magic circle. Most everything is on wheels and can be moved around the rather tight quarters, and that includes the bar, which doubles as a production table. Everything they make is organic. And there's a cribbage board.

Parking is on the street and in a lot shared with Urban Growler, and bicyclists have St. Paul's first bike corral out on the street as well.

Facebook.com/Bang-Brewing and Twitter @bangbrewing

Stumbling Distance: Try the organic-leaning *Foxy Falafel* (791 Raymond Ave, St Paul, 651-888-2255, foxyfalafel.com) for shawarma, meze, cocktails, and its namesake dish. Check Twitter @FoxyFalafel for their food truck location. *The Dubliner Pub* (2162 University Ave W, St Paul, 651-646-5551, thedublinerpub.com) has Bang brews on tap plus live music and dance. *Kopplin's Coffee* (2038 Marshall Ave, St Paul, 651-698-0457, kopplinscoffe.com) roasts its own and serves baked goods.

Burning Brothers Brewing

Established: 2011
Brewmaster: Dane Breimhorst
Address: 1750 W Thomas Ave • St. Paul, MN 55104
Phone: 651-444-8882
Web Site: www.burnbrosbrew.com
Annual Production: up to 4,000 barrels
Number of Beers: 5 on tap

Staple Beers:
» Pyro American Pale Ale (all sorghum, in cans)
» Roasted Coffee Ale (in cans)
» Belgian Saison (all millet)
» Imperial Stout (buckwheat)
» Spiced Brown Ale (buckwheat, sorghum, and millet)

Rotating Beers:
» English Mild
» IPA
» Lime Shandy (summer)
» infused versions of Pyro (orange blossom and honey, cranberry in winter)

Most Popular Brew: Pyro American Pale Ale

Samples: Yes, build your own flight.

Brewmaster's Fave: Pyro American Pale Ale

Best Time to Go: Open Thu–Fri 4–9pm, Sat 2–8pm. Watch for Thirsty Thursday specials. Also, *GetKnit* organizes a Rails and Ales brewery crawl in fall using the light rail.

Where can you buy it? Here on tap in imperial pints (20 oz.) and half pints, or growlers and "grumblers" (750ml) to go. They do NOT fill other people's growlers due to gluten contamination risk. Also available in 4-packs of 16-oz. cans throughout MN, plus ND, SD, and WI.

Got food? Only some gluten-free snacks but GF food trucks may park outside.

Tours? Yes, usually scheduled the first Saturday of the month. Check website.

Special Offer: Buy one beer, get one free during your signature visit.

Directions: Coming from the east on I-94 take Exit 238 for MN 51/ Snelling Ave. Merge onto St Anthony Ave and turn right on Snelling Ave. (Coming from the west, take the same exit but turn left (north) on Snelling.) Go 0.5 mile north, and turn left on Thomas Ave. Go 0.4 mile more and turn left on Wheeler and the brewery front door is on the left.

Two blocks from the Fairview Avenue stop on the Green Line.

The Beer Buzz: It's not often you get to meet a fire eater. Brewer/co-founder Dane used to perform with business partner Thom Foss (not his brother) at the Renaissance Fair. Where does a person learn to eat fire? When Dane was 18, a magician taught him—poorly, as it turned out. One of life's painful lessons perhaps, but then he met an old pro from Barnum & Bailey's. He still performs once or twice a year.

Dane's flame-eating "brother" Thom Foss got a homebrew kit from his wife, and the two of them started brewing. They loved it and were in the process of planning a Brew on Premise business in 2009 when Dane discovered he had celiac disease. Beer brewed normally contains gluten and suddenly he found he could no longer drink it. For a time, they scrapped the idea, and Dane tried to find a gluten-free beer he could

drink, but nothing satisfied. So the two got back together and spent three years, brewing twice a week, trying to come up with the ultimate gluten-free beer recipes. When they were ready, they opened this brewery in a former stone cutter's building. Dane brewed his first commercial batch on December 15, 2013, and opened the taproom in April 2014.

Dane acknowledges there is a process to *remove* gluten using an enzyme that breaks up the protein, but celiac sufferers still report becoming sick from such products. This beer is not *gluten-removed*—one couldn't legally call it gluten-free if it were—but rather these brews are made with ingredients already naturally gluten-free: sorghum, millet, and buckwheat. The process affects the brewery, of course. For example, sorghum beers ferment a bit warmer at around 75 degrees. If you have celiac disease or know someone who does, you realize just how sensitive a person is to even trace amounts of gluten. For this reason no gluten is allowed in the building at all to avoid the risk of contamination. Growlers from other sources will not be filled either.

The taproom is a brightly lit space with a wood bar, cement floors and some tall tables. Some board games are on hand. Not everyone who comes here has celiac. Dane estimates his patrons are divided into thirds: those with celiac, drinkers from the neighborhood, and taproom enthusiasts (probably like yourself). This place is good news for all beer drinkers, but especially those who can no longer drink beer with gluten in it. As the brewery advertises: "Don't fear the beer!"

Facebook.com/BurnBrosBrew and Twitter @BurnBrosBrew

Stumbling Distance: *The Turf Club* (1601 University Ave W, 651-647-0486, turfclub.net) is a popular bar and prefect place to see some local bands. The full menu includes GF items. Nearby restaurants with really good gluten-free options: *The Red Cow* (393 Selby Ave, 651-789-0545, redcowmn.com), *French Meadow Café* (1662 Grand Ave, 651-789-8870, frenchmeadowcafe.com), *Brasa Rotisserie* (777 Grand Ave, 651-224-1302, brasa.us), and *Pizza Luce* (1183 Selby Ave, 651-288-0186, pizzaluce.com). *Urban Growler, Bang Brewing* and *Lake Monster* are close.

HISTORIC ST PAUL WALKING/BIKING TOURS

Minnesota's capital city is loaded with history from fur traders and brewers to gangsters and giants of industry, and the various neighborhoods have plenty of stories to tell. **Historic Saint Paul** is an organization dedicated to preserving the history and culture in these places, from those stories to the structures, and using that mission to also promote community and economic development. They also have an educational mission: Historic Saint Paul has created *Saint Paul Historical* (saintpaulhistorical.org), a free iOS and Android app with 35 self-guided tours throughout the city, complete with clickable GPS points that link to stories and photos. Brewing history tours include Dayton's Bluff: Hamm's Heritage as well as West Side: Yoerg's Heritage, about St. Paul's first brewer Anthony Yoerg. But there is much more beyond the beer heritage. Well suited for walking or biking, the tours are informative, fascinating, and free!

Also available are *Tour Saint Paul Neighborhood Guides.* These booklets are available as PDF downloads, and they are even converting some of them to *downloadable audio tours*. On the Historic Saint Paul website, click on "Tour Saint Paul."

They also host a lecture series called Preservation Talks led by architects, historians, and others; see their events section on the site at the "Newsroom" link. The head office is located in the Landmark Center where you can get paper copies of these neighborhood guides.

Historic Saint Paul
400 Landmark Center
75 West 5th Street, St Paul
651-222-3049 | HistoricSaintPaul.org

IMAGES COURTESY OF HISTORIC SAINT PAUL

GREAT WATERS BREWING CO.

Founded: March 1997
Brewmaster: Tony Digatano
Address: 426 Saint Peter St. • St. Paul, MN 55102
Phone: 651-224-2739
Web Site: www.greatwatersbc.com
Annual Production: 700 barrels
Number of Beers: 10–12 on tap; infinite casks

Staple Beers:
  » BROWN TROUT BROWN ALE
  » GOLDEN PRAIRIE BLOND ALE
  » O'BYRNE'S IRISH RED
  » SAINT PETER PALE ALE

Rotating Beers:
  » THE BLACK WATCH OAT STOUT
  » IMPERIAL STOUT
  » OKTOBERFEST
  » ST. ANDREW'S CROSS SCOTCH ALE
  » TRIPLE A AMERICAN AMBER ALE
  » … various IPAs rotate in

Most Popular Brew: Saint Peter Pale Ale

Samples: Yes, they serve sample flights.

Best Time to Go: Open daily 11–2AM. Happy hour Mon–Fri from 3–6PM. Growler hours are Mon–Thu 11AM–8PM, Fri–Sat 11AM–10PM.

Where can you buy it? Only here on tap and in their own growlers to go.

Got food? Yes, a full menu and a full bar with a fine list of single-malt scotch.

Tours? Yes, on request.

Special Offer: Get Happy Hour beer prices for the book owner only during the signature visit.

Directions: Coming from the south on I-35E, take Exit 106C and turn right on St Peter St. Go 0.3 mile and the brewery is on the left. From the north on I-35E, take Exit 107A on the left, turn right on 10th, and 0.2

mile later, turn left on Jackson. Turn right on 7th St and take it 0.4 mile to St Peter St where you turn left and the brewery is 400 feet down on your left. From the east on I-94, take Exit 242A, turn left on Jackson, then right on 7th St to turn left on St Peter St. From the west on I-94, take Exit 241B onto 10th St. Turn right on St Peter St, go 0.2 mile, and the brewery is on the left.

Three to five blocks from Central Station and 10th Street Station on the Metro Green Line.

The Beer Buzz: Here you've got some beer history. Great Waters was the first brewpub and the second oldest brewery in St. Paul. Owner Sean O'Byrne spent 19 years in medical sales and his business travels took him to the West Coast and Denver area where he became a big fan of craft beer. Downsizing loomed and Sean took a gamble on opening a brewpub, maybe in downtown St. Paul. The Hamm Building, on the National Historic Registry and still owned by the family, would seem a natural fit, and there were office and retail spaces being opened up at the time. He stopped in and chatted with a plumber working on the building that day. The man was getting ready to cap the well. "There's a well???" Sean called the city to confirm this, but they had no record of a well in that building since 1919. He had the water tested and it came back clean. Now the brewpub uses the same hard water aquifer that the Schmidt Brewery once used.

The cask program here is huge, the largest in the Midwest, and the cask beer sales account for 35% of the total beer sold. There may be 78 casks waiting in line at one time. Each beer is released in two or three firkins so the rotation is rather quick, with few beers lasting longer than a week. They are Campaign for Real Ale (CAMRA) compliant and maintain a 52-degree cellar. Why casks? They just decided to do something different, and the owner was inspired by the now defunct but often lovingly recalled real ale brewery Sherlock's Home out in Minnetonka.

The brewpub occupies the first floor corner of the building along the Seventh Place pedestrian mall. Inside are two dining rooms, each with its own bar. The patio along the pedestrian mall becomes an ice patio in winter with a wood fireplace.

WiFi. Facebook.com/GreatWatersBrewingCo and Twitter @greatwatersbc

Stumbling Distance: Check out the Hamm's bear monument outside. Peanuts character statues—creator Charles M. Schulz was a local—occupy the tiny green space across the street, and beyond that is *Landmark Center* (75 W 5th St, 651-292-3225, landmarkcenter.org). *DoubleTree by Hilton* (411 Minnesota St, 651-291-8800, doubletree3.hilton.com) is a short walk from here and a good base of operations.

CAMPAIGN FOR REAL ALE

We have a few Brits to thank for the revival of real ales. Real ale or cask ale was a common way to serve British beer: unfiltered, unpasteurized, and conditioned—left to its secondary fermentation—in the vessel it would be served in. As fewer and fewer brewers in the UK were producing them by the 1960s and 70s, four fellows—Michael Hardman, Graham Lees, Jim Makin and Bill Mellor—founded CAMRA (camra.org.uk) in March 1971, a consumer organization calling for the preservation of the method: the Campaign for the Revitalisation of Ale, which became Campaign for Real Ale two years later. It has over 164,000 members today. Some brewers now feature these beers, and big beer festivals may have a dedicated section of them.

LANDMARK CENTER

The lovely pink granite building across the street from Great Waters Brewpub and the Hamm Building, is Landmark Center. Originally the Federal Courts building, the 1902 Romanesque Revival structure is an eye-catcher with turrets, corner towers, and a prominent clock tower. Dillinger's girlfriend and gangsters such as Alvin "Creepy" Karpis and Arthur "Doc" Barker and went before the judge here. (Barker and Karpis were part of the notorious Barker-Karpis gang which kidnapped William Hamm, Jr., President of Hamm's Brewing for ransom in June 1933.)

Today Landmark Center is an arts and cultural center, with live performances in the 5-story atrium and various museum exhibits including the American Association of Woodturners Gallery, "Uncle Sam Worked Here" (an interactive museum about fed work here, including Prohibition), and Landmark Gallery—a lower level exhibit of the various historical characters who were part of the history of the iconic building.

Beer fans will recognize one of the former occupants: Andrew Volstead, Mr. Prohibition himself. The infamous congressman lends his name to the Volstead Act, properly known as the National Prohibition Enforcement Act of 1919, and kept an office on the 5th floor as head of the local Prohibition Bureau.

The Feds moved out in the late 60s and the building was restored and reopened in 1978. The museums and galleries are open during business hours, and lunchtime performances are common. *Anita's Café* serves food, but visitors can also bring a bag lunch. Check the website for a schedule of events.

75 West 5th Street, St. Paul
651-292-3225 | www.landmarkcenter.org
Hours: Mon–Fri 8AM–5PM; Thu 8AM–8PM; Sun 12PM–5PM

See the Peanuts statues in the plaza in front of Landmark Center.

Cartoonist / creator Charles M. Schulz was born in Minneapolis and grew up in St. Paul.

HAMM'S BEAR

"From the Land of Sky Blue Waters," Hamm's was the "beer refreshing" and had a whole song to go with it including a beat like a Native American drum. But more memorable than that is perhaps Sascha, the cartoon bear mascot of the beer. Originally just a sketch on a cocktail napkin, you can still find Sascha around town in a couple places: Right outside the front door of Great Waters Brewpub in downtown St. Paul, and a statue of the jolly bear way up on the hill in front of the **William Hamm and Marie Scheffer Residence** at 668 Greenbrier Street, St. Paul, overlooking Swede Hollow, an area in the Phalen Creek ravine whose name came from an influx of Swedish immigrants who started settling there in the 1860s. The two houses next door also were owned by Hamm family members.

While Hamm's is still brewed by Miller Brewing (owned by SABMiller), you won't see hide nor hair of Sascha in current marketing. Such a lovable cartoon figure appeared to be marketing toward children, said critics, and so the bear was dropped.

Lake Monster Brewing Co.

Opening: Fall 2015
Brewmaster: Matt Lange
Address: 550 Vandalia St. • St. Paul, MN 55114
Phone: TBD
Web Site: www.lakemonsterbrewing.com
Annual Production: 2,500 barrels
Number of Beers: 4–8 on tap

Staple Beers:
  » Calhoun Claw Pilsener
  » Empty Rowboat IPA

Rotating Beers:
  » Chocolate Porter
  » Loonatick Fresh Hop IPA

Most Popular Brew: Empty Rowboat IPA

Samples: Yes, flights available.

Brewmaster's Fave: Calhoun Claw Pilsener

Best Time to Go: Planning to be open daily. Check website for current times.

Where can you buy it? Here on tap and to go in growlers, and in distribution in 6-pack bottles throughout the Twin Cities Metro area.

Got food? No, but food friendly and food trucks are likely.

Tours? Yes.

Special Offer: A free beer with your book signature.

Directions: From I-94 take Exit 237 and head north on Cretin Ave. Cretin becomes Vandalia and the brewery is on your right.

Walking distance to the Raymond Avenue stop on the Green Line.

The Beer Buzz: Matt Zanetti's father used to work as a vineyard manager, and when Matt decided he had had enough of his job, his father suggested alcohol. As a job, I mean. But rather than wine, he recommended going the beer route. Matt's brother-in-law Jeremy Maynor is a finance guy, so Matt got him on board. All they needed now was a head brewer. Brewer

Matt Lange had brewed for two years at Madison, Wisconsin's famed Ale Asylum. He also used to do Beer Talk Today on the campus radio station at University of Wisconsin-Madison. He has an English lit and journalism degree. What does one do with that? Brew beer, of course. And so there it was: a complete team to make a brewery happen. They started cautiously by getting a couple recipes together and then contract brewing with Sand Creek Brewing in Black River Falls, Wisconsin, to get the beer into the market. Once they got some sales, they could comfortably start setting up their own brewhouse. Sales actually took off for them, and suddenly they were waiting patiently/impatiently for all the paperwork and permits to go through so they could start expanding on their own schedule.

The brewery is in a repurposed industrial zone and is sharing the space with other businesses. To start they have 10,000 sq ft for the brewhouse and taproom.

WiFi. Facebook.com/lakemonsterbrewing
Twitter @LakeMonsterBrew

Stumbling Distance: *Burning Brothers* is the closest brewery, but this is also not far from *Surly, Urban Growler* and *Bang Brewing.*

CREATIVE BEER EVENTS: GETKNIT

GetKnit is an event coordinator, though some may think of them as a tour company since some of the events include them providing transportation. But their mission is to collaborate with local (Minnesota) businesses to bring people together and to bring those people to experience what makes those businesses special. Yoga at the Brewery. A North Shore brewery tour. Curling and Craft Beer. Rails & Ales: Light Rail Brewery Crawl in Minneapolis. Now these are just a few examples of beer-centric events; of course they do other things (fall color tours, kayaking or snowshoeing, a Jucy Lucy cooking class), but it should also be noted they are members of the Minnesota Craft Brewers Guild. These are some very creative and fun activities, plus, ya know, beer! Follow them on Twitter @GetKnitEvents and Facebook.com/getknitevents so you don't miss anything.

GetKnit
855-333-5648 | getknitevents.com

Saint Paul's Flat Earth Brewing Co.

Founded: 2007
Brewmaster: Bob Roepke
Address: 688 Minnehaha Ave East • St. Paul, MN 55106
Phone: 651-698-1945
Web Site: www.flatearthbrewing.com
Annual Production: 1,400 barrels
Number of Beers: 10–12 on tap; 14 beers per year plus many infusions of them

Staple Beers:
- » Angry Planet Pale Ale
- » Belgian-Style Pale Ale
- » Cygnus X-1 Porter (named for a black hole)
- » Northwest Passage IPA

Rotating Beers:
- » Bermuda Triangle Tripel
- » Black Helicopter Coffee Stout (with Dunn Bros. coffee)
- » Eastside Double IPA
- » Element 115 Lager
- » Hep Cat Blonde Ale
- » The Livid Planet Pale Ale (hopped-up Angry Planet)
- » Mummy Train (pumpkin ale)
- » Ovni Ale (bier de garde – spring)
- » Red Cape Ale
- » Winter Warlock (golden English barleywine)
- » … plus many infusions of the various beers, especially the porter

Most Popular Brew: Angry Planet Pale Ale

Samples: Yes, free sips for decision making, flights for sale.

Best Time to Go: At time of printing, growler sales were Mon–Sat 12–6:30PM, but taproom hours will likely go later and may even happen on Sundays. Best to check the website or call first. Watch for Porter Fest in July and after November 1 (see below).

Where can you buy it? In the taproom by the pint or to go in pre-filled growlers. Some beers, especially infusions, are only found in the taproom. Distributed locally to most Twin Cities liquor stores in cans and 22-oz. bombers.

Got food? No, but food friendly.

Tours? Yes, usually scheduled on Tuesdays and Saturdays. Check the website. Please bring a nonperishable item for the food shelf.

Special Offer: Buy your first pint, get one free plus a Saint Paul's Flat Earth Brewing Co. sticker during your signature visit.

Directions: From I-94, take Exit 243 and follow signs to get on Mounds Blvd. Once you are heading north on Mounds Blvd, turn left on 7th St, and just 500 feet later, turn right on Payne Ave. Go 0.6 mile and turn right on Minnehaha Ave. The brewery entrance just ahead on your right.

The Beer Buzz: In 1865, Theodore Hamm received the Excelsior Brewery from his business associate A.F. Keller and went on to build a beer empire. What you see today were the remains of that empire when it closed its

doors as a Stroh's Brewery in 1997. It stood, vacant and abandoned for more than a decade, and the 1864 carpentry building was left in ruins by a fire in 2005. But a community-driven St. Paul craft brewery saw more than ruins. With its perch overlooking Swede Hollow, the old brewery sat in the middle of a neighborhood that had seen better days.

Enter Saint Paul's Flat Earth Brewing, which opened in 2007 in a cramped space in the Highland area at 2035 Benson Ave. New owners took it over in 2010 and were soon looking for a larger space but also looking for a way to add to the St. Paul community by creating jobs, bringing people together, and giving back. The Hamm's Brewery would put them in the right position. Taking over the brick giant was no easy task, and the brewery staff and a goodly number of their friends worked on it over a year to make it into a functioning brewery once again. The building had no electricity, no windows, and had fallen into great disrepair. The project began in December 2012, and finally, on April 22, 2014, after over a year of backbreaking work, Saint Paul's Flat Earth Brewing opened to the public in its new home.

Walk in and the first big public space is an interesting blend between old-school brewery design—barreled brick ceilings, brick walls, and iron columns—and someone's casual hangout with concrete floors, some furniture, and beer-barrel tables. There are books lying around, some board games, and Rock'em Sock'em Robots. This is where folks pick up growlers at a cooler on the right as you enter. Through this large space and to the left is the taproom, a long public space that ends with a window looking into the brewhouse. In summer, the outdoor patio, built into the ruins of the 1864 carpentry building, opens up. All public spaces allow dogs.

The brewery really celebrates its Cygnus X-1 Porter, doing as many as 15 infusions (e.g. chocolate, orange, chocolate-cherry cheesecake, etc.) with it throughout the year. In fact, they have two "Porter Fests" each year: the first is five weeks starting in July. Patrons vote in June on what will be five weekly infusions of the porter. The second fest starts from November 1; the brewery runs nine weeks with nine different porter infusions. Watch for many other events posted on their website.

Brewer Bob used to work for Northwest Airlines out at the airport for 15 years. During that time he had the opportunity to travel to Europe a lot. This led to the discovery of some great beer, and upon returning to the States, he found there weren't many options—only Surly and Summit at the time. He took up homebrewing and when Saint Paul's Flat Earth opened in 2007, he volunteered to help (and learn). Soon he moved up to assistant brewer, and when the head brewer moved on in 2012, Bob found himself running the show.

Facebook.com/Flat-Earth-Brewing-Company
Twitter @flatearthbrew

Stumbling Distance: *Ward 6* (858 Payne Ave, 651-348-8181, ward6stpaul. com) a gastropub offers creative pub food plus 20 primarily Minnesota craft beers on tap. Plus milk shakes with booze. *The Strip Club Meat & Fish* (378 Maria Ave, 651-793-6247, domeats.com) offers a really fine foodie dinner plus the brunch on weekends. *Yarusso-Bros. Italian Restaurant* (635 Payne Ave, 651-776-4848, yarussos.com) has been open since 1933 and serves Saint Paul's Flat Earth beer.

SÍDHE BREWING CO. ("SHEE")

Opened: 2015
Head Brewer: Kathleen Culhane
Address: 990 Payne Ave • St. Paul, MN 55130
Phone: 612-424-1534
Web Site: www.SidheBrewing.com
Annual Production: 200–300 barrels
Number of Beers: 8 on tap

Staple Beers:
  » BARKING CAT TRAPPIST (Belgian Golden Strong)
  » BAST KISSED (cream ale)
  » DARK MOON RISING (dry Irish stout)
  » GREENMAN'S HARVEST (American nut brown ale)

Most Popular Brew: Too soon to tell!

Samples: Yes, flights available.

Brewmaster's Fave: Dark Moon Rising Stout

Best Time to Go: Open 4–11PM Thu–Sat, plus Sunday afternoon. Confirm on website. Live music planned.

Where can you buy it? On draft and growlers to go. Draft accounts in the neighborhood.

Got food? No, but food friendly, and restaurants in the same building.

Tours? Yes, by chance or appointment.

Special Offer: A free beer with the signing of your book.

Directions: From I-94, take Exit 243 and follow signs to get on Mounds Blvd. Once you are heading north on Mounds Blvd, turn left on 7th St, and just 500 feet later, turn right on Payne Ave. Go 1.1 miles and the brewery is on your right at the corner of Payne and Jenks Ave. The main door is on Jenks.

The Beer Buzz: For many, this place may be a bit of an anomaly: An all female and LBGT-owned brewery with Wiccan elements. But for the brewing geeks out there, perhaps the laminar flow hood is more of a surprise. Brewer Kathleen worked at 3M as a researcher in renewable energy, and is a trained chemist with a microbiology background. This piece of

lab equipment prevents contamination when she's growing her own fresh yeast.

Why the Wiccan theme? Besides the owners all practicing the pagan religion, Kathleen likes to say "All beer is magically produced." (Trappist monks, before they knew what yeast was, referred to the magic as "god-is-good" after all.) The brewery's logo shows the four elements of beer which are matched by the four cardinal directions, the four owners (Erica, Kathleen, Robin, Rosemary) and the four elements (earth, air, fire, and water, which combined make the 5th element of spirit, just as grain, water, yeast and hops combine to make beer). Additionally, Kathleen is Irish, and *sidhe* is a Gaelic word for "fairy"—as in the magical creature—and it is pronounced like the female pronoun "she." So you can see there's also a lot going on there with the name.

Kathleen started homebrewing in 1995 when she couldn't find good beer other than the still modestly growing craft beer industry's offerings which were a bit expensive. And like many brewers, the hobby got out of hand. Kathleen credits Allyson Rolph, the brewer at Thirsty Pagan in Superior, Wisconsin, with a bit of mentoring and for allowing her to guest brew there. Her passion sent her on a *pils-grimage* to Ireland where she visited establishments such as Dingle Brewery and Galway Bay Brewing in search of inspiration.

Kathleen likes to build stuff, and she put together much of the brew system, including the welding, and broke the concrete for the drains. She even hung all the sheet rock for the tap room. However, the 10x20 walk-in cooler, amazingly, was already there. An angled bar is set right in front of the cooler wall where the tap lines come out. Her two-barrel system uses an on-demand hot water heater and she employs two massive reclaimed soy sauce containers ("totes"—about four feet tall, cubic) to recycle the water used by the heat exchanger in the brewing process.

But this is all about the beer, right? Kathleen may have an IPA on for the market's demands, but she does not consider herself a hophead. She aims to appeal to the average beer drinker and considers many of her brews to be "gateway" beers, sessionable and balanced.

The neighborhood had a rough reputation in the not-so-distant past but is on the rise as more and more restaurants open up. You can't miss the big brick Plaza del Sol building as it is painted bright yellow with blue trim. Inside is a collection of great food: *Senor Sol's* with its lunchtime AYCE taco bar, *Tazmal Pupuseria*, and So you need not go far to find food to bring into the brewery in the back of the building. You can enter from the market area or use a side door on Jenks Ave. (The street slopes up so stairs make the Payne Avenue-level brewery seem like a basement, but you wouldn't think so once you are inside.)

WiFi. Facebook/sidhebrewingcompany and Twitter @SidheBrewing

Stumbling Distance: *Ward 6* (858 Payne Ave, 651-348-8181, ward6st-paul.com) has reasonably priced finer eats for lunch and dinner, a dedicated Food For Drinking menu, and 12 local brews on tap. *Xtravagant Events & Sweet Treats* (951 Payne Ave, 651-771-1824, xtravagantsweets.com) across the street has some killer cupcakes. Eat sustainable/humane and delicious dinner (and brunch on weekends) at *Tongue in Cheek* (989 Payne Ave, 651-888-6148, tongueincheek.biz). A bit farther away, but close to the Hamm's residences for your bear photo op, is *Swede Hollow Café* (725 7th St E, St Paul, swedehollowcafe.com). Good coffee, breakfast or lunch, including hash-brown pie, stellar caramel rolls, daily quiche.

SUMMIT BREWING CO.

Founded: 1986
Brewmaster: Mark Stutrud **Head Brewer:** Damian McConn
Address: 910 Montreal Circle • St. Paul, MN 55102
Phone: 651-265-7800
Web Site: www.summitbrewing.com
Annual Production: 133,000 barrels
Number of Beers: 8 year round, 15 annually; 10 on tap plus a cask on a beer engine in the Beer Hall

Staple Beers:
>> EPA (EXTRA PALE ALE)
>> GREAT NORTHERN PORTER
>> HOPVALE ORGANIC ALE
>> HORIZON RED IPA
>> OATMEAL STOUT (draft only)
>> PILSENER
>> SÁGA IPA
>> TRUE BRIT IPA

Rotating Beers:
>> FROST LINE RYE (winter)
>> MAIBOCK (spring)
>> OKTOBERFEST
>> SUMMER ALE (Kölsch-style)
>> WINTER ALE
>> UNCHAINED SERIES (3 per year):
>> Hop Silo Double IPA
>> Herkulean Woods (lager with maple syrup, spruce tips)
>> UNION SERIES (1–2 per year)
>> 3X Mild, etc.

Most Popular Brew: EPA but Saga IPA is growing like crazy

Samples: Yes, flights of four 7-oz. pours for about $7.

Best Time to Go: Beer Hall hours: Fri–Sat 4–9PM Gift shop hours: Tue–Thu 2–5PM, Fri 2–9PM, Sat 10AM–9PM. Always check website for current times! Watch for September's "Backyard Bash" when 2,000+ people gather to celebrate the brewery's anniversary with live music and a fundraiser for the Minnesota Music Coalition (mnmusiccoalition.org).

Where can you buy it? No growlers or carryouts in the Beer Hall, but on draft in 7-oz. and 16-oz. pours. Distributed in kegs, 12- and 16-oz. cans, and 12-oz. bottles across 18 states, including Minnesota, Arkansas, Florida, Illinois, Indiana, Iowa, Kansas, Kentucky, Michigan, Missouri, Nebraska, New Jersey, North Dakota, Ohio, Pennsylvania, South Dakota, Texas, and Wisconsin.

Got food? No, but food friendly in the Beer Hall, plus food trucks are common outside and are scheduled on the website. 1919 Root Beer on tap in the Beer Hall.

Tours? Yes, the 90-minute tour is free, but bring a canned or boxed food donation. You must make a reservation online. Times are typically Tue–Fri 3PM, Sat 10AM, 12:30PM, and 3PM, and tours are limited in size and may fill up fast. Check the website to confirm the tour schedule. No sandals or open-toed shoes on the tour.

Special Offer: Buy 1 beer, get 1 free during your signature visit. (Limit 1 per customer.)

Directions: From I-35E take Exit 103B for MN-5/7th St. Turn east onto 7th St, go 0.2 mile, then turn right on Montreal Way. Go another 0.2 mile and turn left on Montreal Circle and the brewery is on the left.

The Beer Buzz: Summit is the elder statesman of Minnesota craft breweries—the Godfather, if you will. Founder and brewmaster Mark Stutrud is the son of two school teachers and hails from a farming region in South Dakota. In fact, his family grows barley for his Pilsener. Mark has a degree in social work and used to work as a family therapist; he spent 8.5 years working with substance abuse patients. He had considered medical school and a psychotherapy specialization, but a passion for brewing took over. His last two years working at a hospital were spent repurposing himself. He apprenticed with some small brewers in 1982 and 1983, and took courses at Siebel Institute. It took him two years to write up his business plan, and when he wrote of his intentions in a letter to the Brewers' Association of America, he received a discouraging reply from the Executive Secretary: "Please know that I am not encouraging you to do so, because it is a long and hard road that you are planning to go down." Needless to say, Mark ignored the warning. That letter is on the wall in the Beer Hall.

With financial help from 20 friend investors, Mark opened his brewery in an auto parts warehouse on University Avenue. By the end of his first year

in business, Mark had 5 full-time and 3 part-time employees and had produced about 3,000 barrels of beer. Today, the employees exceed 90 and their production ranks them in the top 50 breweries in the US. In 1987, Great Northern Porter took gold at the Great American Beer Festival and caught the notice of The Beer Hunter, Michael Jackson, who placed it on the cover of his 1988 *New World Guide to Beer*. In 1998, Summit's production topped 34,000 barrels. Bursting at the seams, the brewery made the move to the facility right here—the first newly built brewery in Minnesota in 75 years.

As one might expect, Summit has a large-scale, state-of-the-art system. At the time of writing, they had twenty-four 438-barrel and twelve 800-barrel fermenters manufactured by DCI, Inc. out of St. Cloud, MN. Through the window outside and from the Beer Hall, you can see 1971 copper Hürnerbraü Ansbach brew kettles. (In fact, the system they started with back on University Ave dated back to 1938!) A tile and marble business next door became the canning and packaging facility. A new canning line was added in 2014. (The Summit cans are produced locally.) Check out the Beer Pipeline that connects it to the brewery. Requests to connect such a pipeline to my home were politely ignored.

The cask ale program here is strong. A pilot system is used to make some limited beers only available in the Beer Hall. The Unchained Series started in 2009 and features various Summit brewers trying something of their own creation. The Union Series allows Head Brewer Damian to bring together new ingredients from around the world, sometimes tweaking an otherwise traditional recipe.

Summit Brewing remains very involved with the community that has supported it all these years, and their anniversary party each year is actually a charitable benefit. Twice a week the brewery offers the Beer Hall as free meeting and event space for nonprofit organizations. Additionally, Mark is highly respected within the brewing community for being approachable and generous with his time and knowledge.

The Beer Hall is rather large with high ceilings and rows of picnic tables. Banners for the beers and medals from competitions adorn the walls. Beer is served at a big wooden bar in the corner. In season, a patio overlooking the bluff opens. Leashed pets are allowed there.

ATM on site. WiFi. Facebook.com/summitbrewingcompany
Twitter @summitbeer

Stumbling Distance: Don't miss *The Beer Dabbler Store* (1095 7th St W, 651-528-8752, store.thebeerdabbler.com) where you can get merch from all your favorite craft breweries, plus a variety of glassware, art, gear, clothing and more. These are also the folks behind the monthly magazine *The Growler*—go pick up a copy. Two of the best craft beer bars in St. Paul are about 10 minutes from Summit: *The Muddy Pig* (162 Dale St N, 651-254-1030, themuddypig.com) and *The Happy Gnome* (498 Selby Ave, 651-287-2018, thehappygnome.com).

THE BEER DABBLER STORE

Be sure to check out this store created by the folks that bring you The Beer Dabbler beer festivals each year and the monthly magazine *The Growler*. This retail outlet makes shopping for branded beer paraphernalia easy. They've got glassware with your favorite brewery's logo, assorted growlers, a whole variety of clothing, books, trinkets, sampler platters/paddles, tap handles, beer soap and candles, and more. You can also pick up a copy of *The Growler*, a free magazine dedicated to Minnesota's craft beer scene. Look for the old barn-wood building on the west side of the street with a colorful mural on the side of the building and a barrel hanging above the front door. Be sure to watch for their awesome annual Beer Dabbler beer festivals, too.

The closest breweries are *Summit Brewing*, *Vine Park Brewing*, and *Bad Weather* as well as downtown St. Paul brewers *Great Waters* and *Tin Whiskers*.

The Beer Dabbler Beer Store
1095 7th St W, St Paul
651-528-8752　|　beerdabbler.com

Tin Whiskers Brewing Co.

Opened: May, 2014

Brewmaster: Jake Johnson & Jeff Moriarty **Head Brewer**: Derek Brown

Address: 125 E 9th Street, Unit 127 • St. Paul, MN 55101

Phone: 651-330-4734

Web Site: www.twbrewing.com

Annual Production: 1,200 barrels

Number of Beers: 8 on tap plus a cask

Staple Beers:
- » Ampere Amber
- » Flip Switch IPA
- » Short Circuit Sweet Stout
- » Wheatstone Bridge

Rotating Beers:
- » Barrel Shifter Porter (winter)
- » Parity Pilsner (summer)
- » Schottky Pumpkin Ale (fall)
- » …plus many pilot batches and infusions

Most Popular Brew: Wheatstone Bridge

Samples: Yes, four 4-oz. pours for about $8.

Brewmaster's Fave: Jeff: Flip Switch IPA

Best Time to Go: Open Wed–Thu 4–10pm, Fr 3–11pm, Sat 12–11pm, Sun 12–5pm.

Where can you buy it? Here on tap and to go in pre-filled or swapped out growlers. Also available in Twin Cities area liquor stores in 22-oz. bombers and on tap in a number of Twin Cities bars.

Got food? No, but food friendly and there are several neighborhood restaurants.

Tours? Yes, by appointment.

Special Offer: Buy one beer, get one free during your signature visit.

Directions: Coming from the north into downtown St. Paul on I-35E, take Exit 107A on the left for 10th St/Wacouta St. Follow this straight onto Wacouta and turn right on 9th St. At 0.2 mile, the brewery is on your right. Coming from the south on I-35E, take Exit 106C for 11th St and continue onto 11th St for about 0.3 mile. Turn right on Robert St and right after that, turn left onto 9th St and the brewery is on the left. From the east on I-94, take Exit 242A, turn left on Jackson, then right on 9th. From the west on I-94, take Exit 242C, turn right on 7th St, another right on the curve into Jackson, and then left onto 9th St.

Three blocks from 10th Street Station on the Metro Green Line.

The Beer Buzz: If this downtown St. Paul brewery gives off a bit of a science nerd vibe, that's because the three founders are electrical engineers. Jake Johnson and Jeff Moriarty met at University of Minnesota where they were studying engineering. After graduation they got into home-brewing, whipping up brews over at Jake's mother's house in Roseville. They fell in love with the science and the art. Another engineer friend George Kellerman joined them. They toured Flat Earth and Surly and were inspired by the success stories of the two breweries, and the decision was made. For four years they worked on recipes over in Roseville. They searched for a location where they could have an inviting taproom and be near food, art, and, of course, people. They looked at 50 places before they found this place, and it was love at first sight. They were concerned about what effect the water at the new location would have on the beers, but St. Paul, it turns out, sells Roseville its water.

The building dates back to 1911 when it was a munitions factory, but after World War I, it produced shoes. Developers turned it into artist studios and condos but left the first floor and basement for commercial space. The taproom has high ceilings, a polished concrete floor, and large front windows letting in lots of light. Patrons drink at long communal tables, and a wide variety of board games are lying about. The walls are exposed brick and there's a mural of a giant beer-drinking robot greeting you as you walk in. The long bar is of polished black concrete with stainless steel. There is a large TV, and the place is good and loud when a festive crowd

THE GROWLER MAGAZINE

Picking up a Growler can mean a couple things in Minnesota: either a jug of your favorite beer or this awesome free magazine for beer lovers. Odds are good you'll find them in the same place: your closest Minnesota brewery.

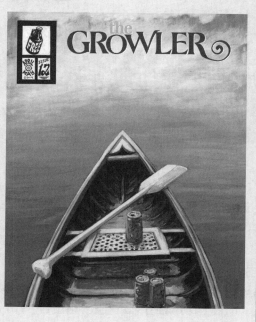

First published in 2012, *The Growler* is a fantastic publication dedicated to craft beer, and produced by the folks of The Beer Dabbler, an organizer of craft beer festivals and an awesome store for the beer lover.

Pick up a copy of *The Growler* (growlermag.com) and keep up to date not only with all things craft beer, but also food, spirits, arts, and various related events. Articles include beer education, interviews with brewers, recent news about breweries, and advance warning of new breweries on the horizon. This monthly magazine is available for free in most breweries, brewpubs, and bars, or you can sign up online and have the e-version delivered to your inbox each month. Follow them on Twitter @GrowlerMag and Facebook.com/GrowlerMag.

THE GROWLER COVER ARTWORK BY DAVID WITT – DWITT.COM

is in the house. The brewhouse is right behind the bar, open to the room and separated from it by a chain.

The brewery name comes from electrical engineering terminology. Pure tin can form little hair-like projections and when this phenomenon occurs between two pins on integrated circuits on a printed circuit board, it can result in a short circuit. Plus, as Jeff says, "It's a really cool sounding name." A piece of Space Shuttle Endeavor on site has tin whiskers on it.

Head Brewer Derek joined the team before they opened. Jake and Jeff put out an ad for a brewer while they were still in the financing phase, and Derek replied. He had no experience at the time, but was getting an associate degree at Siebel. They met for a beer and soon Derek was in their basement helping out for free for a year. His great attention to detail assured them they had the right guy. Derek worked six months over at Town Hall Brewing and came over.

WiFi. Facebook.com/TinWhiskersBrewingCo
Twitter @TinWhiskersBrew Instagram @tinwhiskersbrew

Stumbling Distance: *Black Sheep Coal Fired Pizza* (512 Robert St N, 651-227-4337, blacksheeppizza.com) lies around the corner and delivers. *Sawatdee* (486 Robert St N, 651-528-7106, sawatdeesaintpaul.com) has been voted best Thai food in the Twin Cities, and has craft beer on tap. Do carryout and bring it to the brewery (or they will deliver it for you while you drink). *Embassy Suites* (175 E 10th St, 651-224-5400, embassysuites3. hilton.com) is just a block away, perfect for a base of brew tour operations.

URBAN GROWLER™ BREWING COMPANY

Opened: July 30, 2014
Brewmaster: Deb Loch
Address: 2325 Endicott Street • St. Paul, MN 55114
Phone: 651-340-5793
Web Site: www.urbangrowlerbrewing.com
Annual Production: up to 1,350 barrels
Number of Beers: 8 on tap plus a weekly cask

Staple Beers:

>   » BIG BOOT™ RYE IPA
>   » CITY DAY™ ALE
>   » COWBELL CREAM ALE ™
>   » GRAFFITI IPA
>   » OATMEAL STOUT
>   » WHITE IPA

Rotating Beers:

>   » AMBER SKYLINE™
>   » DE-LOVELY™ PORTER
>   » IMPERIAL SMOKED CHIPOTLE PORTER
>   » PLOW TO PINT® SERIES BEERS

Most Popular Brew: CowBell Cream Ale™

Samples: Yes, flights of six 5-oz. pours for about $12.

Brewmaster's Fave: "Depends on my mood."

Best Time to Go: Open Tue–Thu 3–10PM, Fri–Sat 12–11PM, Sun 12–8PM. Table for Twosday for a food/beer/pretzel package. Cask releases on Thursdays. On Sundays they spice CowBell like a Bloody Mary.

Where can you buy it? On tap here in pints and half pints and to go in pre-filled growlers. Also on tap in a few places around town.

Got food? Yes, nachos, sandwiches, carnitas, desserts (De-Lovely™ Brownies).

Tours? By chance or appointment.

Special Offer: A free taster of a Plow to Pint beer during your signature visit.

Directions: From I-94 take Exit 236 toward University Ave. Merge onto Cromwell Ave, then turn right on Territorial Rd. Go 0.5 mile, turn left on Hampden Ave and continue 0.4 mile as it becomes Hersey St. The brewery is on the left just before you reach Capp Rd.

Walking distance (0.7 mile) from the Raymond Avenue Station of the Green Line.

Cyclists: *About a half mile east of the University of Minnesota Transitway / Dinkytown Greenway bike path.*

The Beer Buzz: "Reinheitsgebot, Shmeinheitsgebot! I like to make beer out of anything," says brewer/owner Deb. And indeed she does. Candy Corn Imperial Pale Ale? A brew with 300 lbs of Wisconsin cranberries? She takes a lot of her inspiration from cooking, another passion of hers. For the Plow to Pint Series, Deb uses local farm-fresh ingredients—rhubarb, pumpkin, Thai seasonings—for unique specialty batches. But her beers are balanced and even the pale ales are sessionable and "not off the charts" hoppy. Before she turned pro, she won a silver medal at the National Homebrew Competition for her Imperial Smoked Chipotle Porter.

Urban Growler was Minnesota's first women-owned brewery—and with a woman brewmaster to boot. Deb Loch and Jill Pavlak planned this place for six years before finally opening the doors in 2014. Both had corporate jobs and found they wanted to do something different. Two co-workers they knew had died young, a sober reminder that "someday" should be now. Jill racked up 35,000-plus miles a year in sales work, while Deb worked in the medical device industry. Deb wanted to follow her passion and so asked for a leave of absence. She put in time at Minocqua Brewing in Wisconsin,

but soon that leave became permanent. She worked at Northern Brewer on weekends, took Master Brewers Program classes from University of California-Davis, and worked various positions for the venerable Mark Stutrud at Summit. She worked on the business plan while working full-time at Northern Brewery. Jill's sales and PR experience serves the brewery as well as Deb's technical experience guides the brewing.

The light-brick building dates back to the late 19th century when the City of St. Paul kept its horses here. Thereafter manufacturers produced carriages and skis or simply used it as a warehouse. Upstairs is a crane from when this was a machine shop, and the "hayloft" there is now their event space.

The taproom has high ceilings, and exposed brick and ductwork. The bar curves like a half-hexagon and the brewhouse stands behind the back bar. Reclaimed barn wood from Jill's cousin's farm and a friend in Iowa give the taproom a "warm industrial" feel, and patrons have a mix of tall and short tables for seating. This is one of the few (for now) taprooms with a kitchen. (Nearby *Surly Brewing* was notably the first since the law changed.) They have a parking lot.

WiFi. Facebook/UrbanGrowlerBrewingCompany
Twitter @UrbanGrowlerMN

Stumbling Distance: *Bang Brewing* is right across the parking lot. For some housemade pasta and other Italian fare, try *Caffe Biaggio* (2356 University Ave W, 651-917-7997, caffebiaggio.com).

A RATHSKELLER IN THE STATE CAPITOL

Methinks there was a time when some drinking went on here. Set on a hill near downtown with a view to downtown and surrounding park and monuments, the Minnesota State Capitol was built in 1905. Third time's a charm—there were two others before it. Designed by architect Cass Gilbert, it is modeled after Saint Peter's in Rome. But what lies in the basement may surprise some: a bona fide German-style rathskeller. Back during the Capitol's construction, Germans made up the largest immigrant population in Minnesota. According to tradition, a rathskeller had 29 mottoes in German painted along the walls, but they didn't last long. The first World War was the beginning of some rather negative nationwide feelings toward all things German. In 1917, Governor Burnquist had them painted over. Thirteen years later Governor Theodore Christianson had them restored, a cheeky move during Prohibition, I'd say. However, "Temperance is a virtue of men"

clearly was not exactly German tradition. This was one of three modifications forced to be made by temperance society pressure. The original in this case was "Better be tipsy than feverish"—good advice if you wanted trouble with the Feds.

Despite the end of Prohibition, the rathskeller was more a cafeteria by the end of the 30s and remodeling lost the German drinking phrases and eventually all the German character altogether. But now you can see the rathskeller in its original glory. Restorations undertaken in 1999 were guided by years of careful research using an old photograph, careful scalpel removal of 22 layers of paint, and chemical analysis of paint chips. Murals of animals and grape vines were rediscovered and the mottoes had been long forgotten.

While there is still no beer here, the Rathskeller Café serves food—but it is only open when the legislature is in session, and then only Mon–Thu 8AM–3:30PM and Fri 8AM–2PM.

Notice: *Capitol Restoration work is expected to be complete in 2017. Until then, Capitol tours are suspended.*

Minnesota State Capitol
75 Rev. Martin Luther King Jr. Blvd.
St. Paul, MN 55155
Tour info: 651-296-2881 | mn.gov/admin/citizen | www.mnhs.org
Hours: Mon-Fri 7AM–5PM, Sat 10AM–3PM, Sun 1PM–4PM

Tin Whiskers Brewing and *Great Waters Brewing* are the closest breweries, each less than a mile or 20 minute walk.

VINE PARK BREWING

Founded: 1995
Brewmaster: Andy Grage
Address: 1254 West 7th Street • St. Paul, MN 55102
Phone: 651-228-1355
Web Site: www.vinepark.com
Annual Production: 150 barrels
Number of Beers: Growlers only. 60 recipes, 6 at any one time

Staple Beers:
- » STUMP JUMPER AMBER ALE
- » WALNUT BROWN ALE
- » at least one IPA

Rotating Beers:
- » Rotating IPAs, nothing imperial

Most Popular Brew: Stump Jumper

Samples: Only of the house root beer.

Brewmaster's Fave: Root beer

Best Time to Go: Tue–Thu 12–8PM, Fri 12–9PM, Sat 9AM–5PM.

Where can you buy it? Only here in growlers; there is no taproom. They sell discount punch cards for a frequent growler buyer or as something you could give as a gift to one.

Got food? No.

Tours? Not really, but if you came in to see what it's all about, Andy will show you.

Special Offer: A free pint glass with your signature visit

Directions: From I-35E take Exit 103B for MN-5/7th St. Turn east onto 7th St, go about 0.7 mile, and the brewery is on the right.

The Beer Buzz: While this is not a taproom or really a place to hang out with friends, you still may want to stop and pick up a growler. While growler sales make up about 10% of Andy Grage's business, the primary mission here is Brew on Premise. You want to do some homebrewing but you don't want to make the equipment investment or you want a larger batch than your stovetop allows? This may be your solution. Make an appointment and come brew a 12.5-gallon batch of one of 60 recipes.

Summit Extra Pale Ale was the beer that made Andy want to be a brewer. He took up homebrewing in 1990 and helped at Northern Brewer when Chris Farley opened it in 1993. In 1995 he began managing Vine Park, eventually taking it over in 2004. This is the oldest brew on premise in the US. Despite all the DIY brewing, Andy brews a 3-barrel batch each week and the growlers sell well. Brewing has been used as a corporate team building activity, and on Tuesdays, Vine Park hosts brewing parties for up to 18 people. They make 6 batches and two weeks later walk away with two mixed cases. Smaller groups of 12 do the same on Wednesdays.

Facebook.com/Vine-Park-Brewery and Twitter @Vine_Park_Brew

Stumbling Distance: *Grand Ole Creamery & Grand Pizzeria* (750 Grand Ave, 651-293-1655, icecreamstpaulmn.com) is a nearby classic. For craft beer swag, gifts, and glassware, *The Beer Dabbler* (1095 7th St W, 651-528-8752, beerdabbler.com) should not be missed just up the street.

Wabasha Brewing Co.

Opened: 26 February 2015
Brewmaster: Brett Erickson
Address: 429 Wabasha Street S • Saint Paul, MN 55107
Phone: 651-224-2102
Web Site: www.wabashabrewing.com
Annual Production: 700 barrels
Number of Beers: 6 on tap; 9 per year

Staple Beers:
» Amber
» Son of Eric Cream Ale
» P.I.A. Double IPA
» Implosion IPA

Rotating Beers:
» Imperial Stout
» Kölsch (summer)
» Oktoberfest
» Pilsner
» Snowblower Robust Porter (winter)

Most Popular Brew: IPA

Samples: Yes, flights of four 5-oz. pours for about $8.

Brewmaster's Fave: Cream Ale

Best Time to Go: Open Thu–Fri 2–10pm, Sat 12pm–10pm.

Where can you buy it? Here on tap and in growlers to go. Also on tap at a few local establishments in St. Paul.

Got food? No, but food friendly. Food trucks show up on occasion and menus of nearby restaurants are on site.

Tours? Not really, you can see everything from a bar stool!

Special Offer: $1 off your first pint during your signature visit.

Directions: From I-94 just east of its juncture with I-35E in downtown St. Paul, take Exit 242D south on US 52 for 1.7 miles. Take the Concord St exit and turn right on Cesar Chavez St. Go 0.7 mile, turn left on Congress St, and turn right at Wabasha, the first cross street. The brewery is on the left at the corner of Wabasha and Isabel. From downtown St. Paul, just take Robert St south across the Mississippi River, turn right on Fillmore, then left on Wabasha. Go 0.5 mile and turn right to stay on Wabasha and the brewery is 400 feet up on your right.

The Beer Buzz: Brett Erickson, Josh Tischleder, and Chris Kolve might have had a few beers in them ("eight beers in") when they decided it was a good idea to open a brewery. They were in Brett's garage after a homebrew session when inspiration struck. Chris and Brett brewed together on a 1-barrel system and decided to take the plunge. Josh and Brett used to bowl together, and he had a background in beer buying and distribution as well as tap line cleaning—a perfect third partner. It took three years to plan and get the brewery up and running, but now St. Paul's West Side has its own brewery.

Back in 1865, this building was a tin shop. Sometime in the 1920s–40s the portion that now houses the brewery was added. They renovated that space and now you have beer to drink. On a historical note, this is less than a mile from the site of the old Yoerg Brewery which opened near the river in 1849. They used to use the nearby caves for lagering.

The taproom opened tucked up right against the brewing space, but by the time you read this it will be out front. The bar uses reclaimed bowling lane wood and the old pressed tin ceiling is restored. They have their own parking lot and will open a patio seasonally. (Check out the old Schmidt sign painted on the brick building next door!)

Facebook/pages/Wabasha-Brewing-Company

Stumbling Distance: Take a great historical tour of the *Wabasha Street Caves* (215 Wabasha St S, 651-224-1191, wabashastreetcaves.com) or stop in on Thursday nights for some swing dancing. *El Burrito Mercado* (175 Cesar Chavez St #2, 651-227-2192, elburritomercado.com) gets raves for their food, sit-down or express, plus offer a deli, bakery, and groceries. *Boca Chica* (11 Cesar Chavez St, 651-222-8499, bocachicarestaurant.com) makes some fine Mexican and delivers to the brewery. Downtown St. Paul and its breweries and attractions are just across the river from here.

WABASHA STREET CAVES

Carved out of the sandstone bluffs along the Mississippi River Valley, various caves served a variety of purposes over the years, from cold storage (such as lagering beer) to growing mushrooms and aging cheese. Originally in the 1800s, however, the caves were dug out as mines for silica to make glass. But there was also a time their purpose was entertainment. During Prohibition, some served as speakeasies. But in 1933, within the 7 caves that make up what is now the Wabasha Street Caves, William and Josie Lehmann opened Castle Royal Night Club. Cab Calloway and Tommy Dorsey took the stage to play here during the club's seven year run. Years later, Anheuser Busch put a bar in here, and in the late 1970s it served as a discotheque. What still remains are a load of great stories and perhaps a couple of ghosts.

The original stage from Castle Royal is also still here, and each week it gets some use: You can relive the club days on Thursday nights when the caves open to the public for Swing Night with a big band. Kick up your heels on the dance floor and arrive early for lessons. Check their website for the speakeasy password.

Tour the caves year round on Thursdays at 5PM, and Sat–Sun at 11AM with a well trained and humorous guide, but don't miss out on the other tours: The Saint Paul Gangster tours are by bus and depart from here at noon on Saturdays year round but add a Sunday tour from June through September. Plus, there's a Lost Souls Tour the last Sunday of each month and every Sunday in October that focuses on the, um, spiritual aspects of the caves. Other special tours may appear on their website as well.

Wabasha Street Caves
215 Wabasha St. S., St Paul
651-224-1191 | wabashastreetcaves.com

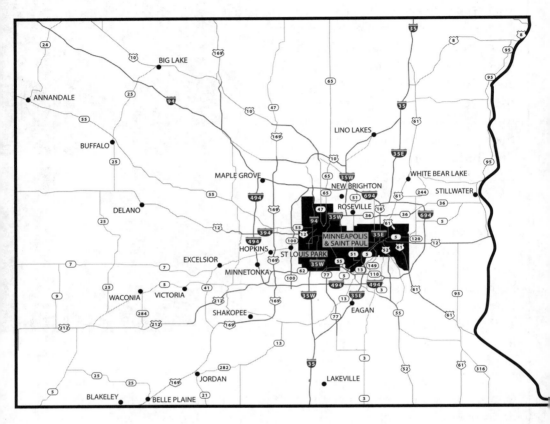

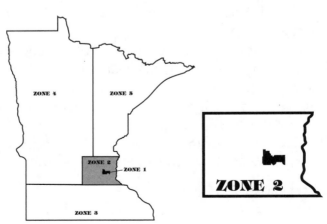

ZONE 2

ZONE 2
Twin Cities Greater Metro

Spilled Grain Brewhouse. . . . . Annandale
Lupulin Brewing Co . . . . Big Lake
u4ic Brewing, Inc. . . . . Blakeley
Hayes' Public House . . . . Buffalo
Lupine Brewing Co. . . . . Delano
South Fork Brewing . . . . Delano
Granite City Food and Brewery . . . . .Eagan
Excelsior Brewing Co. . . . . Excelsior
LTD Brewing . . . . .Hopkins
Roets Jordan Brewing Co. . . . . Jordan
Angry Inch Brewing . . . . Lakeville
HammerHeart Brewing Co. . . . . .Lino Lakes
Granite City Food and Brewery . . . . Maple Grove
Lucid Brewing Co. . . . . .Minnetonka
Barley John's Brew Pub . . . . New Brighton
Bent Brewstillery. . . . . .Roseville
Granite City Food and Brewery . . . . .Roseville
Badger Hill Brewing Co. . . . . Shakopee
Granite City Food and Brewery . . . . St. Louis Park
Steel Toe Brewing Co. . . . . St. Louis Park
Lift Bridge Brewery. . . . . Stillwater
Maple Island Brewery . . . . Stillwater
St. Croix Brewing Co. . . . . Stillwater
ENKI Brewing . . . . Victoria
Schram Vineyard and Brewery . . . . .Waconia
Waconia Brewing Co. . . . . .Waconia
Big Wood Brewery . . . . White Bear Lake

Spilled Grain Brewhouse

Opened: 2015
Brewers: Jacob Schnabel and Dan Seaberg
Address: 300 Elm Street • Annandale, MN 55302
Phone: 612-743-5224
Web Site: www.spilledgrainbrewhouse.com
Annual Production: 150 barrels
Number of Beers: 6 taps, 3 staples

Staple Beers:
   » Extra Special/Strong Bitter (English Pale Ale)
   » India Pale Ale
   » Stout

Rotating Beers:
   » Oktoberfest, bocks, IPAs, stouts, some ciders, sky's the limit

Most Popular Brew: Extra Special Bitter.

Samples: Yes, tasters and flights.

Brewmaster's Fave: Dan: IPAs | Jacob: Stouts

Best Time to Go: Open Fri–Sat (maybe Thu in summer) 5–10pm. Check the web site to be sure.

Where can you buy it? Only here on tap and to go in growlers.

Got food? Just some snacks maybe. Food friendly and the occasional random food truck.

Tours? Yes, if someone's available. It's a small system.

Special Offer: Half off your first beer and a highly prized trinket with your book signature

Directions: MN 55 passes right through Annandale. The brewery is right on the north side of the highway between Poplar Ave to the east and Myrtle Ave to the west.

The Beer Buzz: Brewer Dan playing around with grain isn't something new. Much like this brewhouse, Dan's childhood home was near the railroad tracks. Back in the summer of 1980, he was already climbing piles of it. It was August 28 and he was 7 years old, playing outside, when there was a bang heard round the town. A cloud of dust crept through the yards on the summer breeze and everyone came running to see what had happened. The dust, it turned out, rose from a massive grain spill, and the thundering noise was the derailment of seven Soo Line grain cars.

Years later Dan went off to school, got a job, got married, but decided the best place to raise a family would be back in his hometown. His wife Nik bought him a homebrewing kit for Father's Day, and grain spilled back into his life. He brewed some batches, thought it was awesome and figured, "Boy it'd be kind of cool to make beer and sell it." He and Nik started looking at some available spaces around town, but they seemed expensive. But then Nik met some others in town who turned out to be interested: Dave Hartley, a cabinet maker, and his wife Reyna. Dave's first craft beer experience was at Castle Danger Brewery up in Two Harbors. The couple owned a building that Dave once used as his shop and had also functioned as storage and the storefront for a local HVAC guy. It needed some renovation, but it would cut the expense of rent. Another piece fell into place.

Brewer Jake Schnabel wasn't too impressed by the usual beer in college, but after graduating from North Dakota State with an engineering degree in 2006, he discovered craft brews and started making it himself. It wasn't long before he started winning medals in homebrew competitions. He knew Dan from a homebrew club, and so Jake and his wife Anastacia joined the partnership, and soon after, Josh and Anna Hart rounded off the group, and the project really took off. They are starting with a 3.5 barrel system, but for now are keeping their day jobs.

The bar, made of dark stained mahogany gives the space an old tavern touch, and the rough-cut wood ceiling beams and concrete floor create a wide open space with tables and couches, a low key, low-volume music sort of place, good for conversation. There are dark doors with tiny speak easy style windows look to them. The theme of the decoration is Annandale history and, of course, trains. Board games and cribbage are on hand. The tap room has no TVs (though a projector can be hauled out for big games).

Facebook/spilledgrainbrewhouse

Stumbling Distance: Check out *In Hot Water Coffee-Tea House* (25 Cedar St East, 320-274-6828, inhotwatercoffee.com) for coffee and a scone. *Café Jules* (20 Cedar St East, 320-274-7477, cafejulesmn.com) offers finer dining for breakfast, lunch and dinner, plus a good wine list. *Hayes' Public House Brewery & Taproom* is 14 miles/18 minutes east in Buffalo.

Lupulin Brewing Co.

Opened: April 2015
Brewmaster: Matt Schiller
Address: 570 Humboldt Drive, Suite 107 • Big Lake, MN 55309
Phone: 763-263-9549
Web Site: www.lupulinbrewing.com
Annual Production: 500–1,000 barrels
Number of Beers: 8 on tap; 20+ beers per year

Staple Beers:
- » Belgian Blonde
- » Into the Black American Stout
- » Resin Rapture Red IPA

Rotating Beers:
- » Belgian Dubbel (blue ribbon winner at State Fair competition)
- » Belgian Tripel
- » Pumpplefest (fall – a cross between Oktoberfest/English Brown/ American Pumpkin spiced beer)
- » WIPA Wheat IPA (summer – with Citra and Centennial hops)
- » Spud Fest Beer (with potatoes)
- » …sour program in planning

Most Popular Brew: Too early to tell

Samples: Yes, flights of 2-oz. pours.

Brewmaster's Fave: Resin Rapture Red IPA if forced to choose

Best Time to Go: Open Thu 4–9, Fri 4–11pm, Sat 2–11pm, Sundays likely. Check website. Watch for occasional live music. Big Lake Spud Fest (biglakespudfest.com) in late June.

Where can you buy it? For starters only here in the taproom by the glass or to go in growlers. 750 ml bottles are in planning.

Got food? No, but food friendly, plus there are menus for local delivery, and the occasional food truck.

Tours? Yes, by chance, but this is a small place and is tour-able from the bar stool.

Special Offer: A free glass of their beer during your signature visit.

Directions: From I-94 heading west from Minneapolis, take Exit 193 and turn right on MN 25 North. Go 3.6 miles and turn right on Jefferson Blvd. Just 0.2 mile later, turn right on Eagle Lake Rd and take the next left on Humboldt Dr. The brewery is on your right.

The Beer Buzz: I've always said, beer brings people together. Jeff Zierdt is a University of Minnesota graduate, a Chemical Engineer by trade whose work in the pulp and paper industry took him to Wisconsin Rapids, WI, Matt Schiller's hometown. They met in a homebrew club in Wisconsin Rapids, hit it off, and one day said, Let's just start a brewery. Between the two of them they had 23 awards from homebrew competitions, so why not? In March 2012 they started writing a business plan. The front corner of a 22,000 square foot industrial warehouse here in Big Lake was completely empty when they moved in. There was a retail area, but it had 24-foot

LUPULIN BREWING

ceilings and a cement floor. The build-out started in October 2014 on Halloween and they started brewing in March 2015. A 10-barrel system is for starters, but they have plenty of room to expand.

The brewery is just off US 10 on a frontage road which makes it a great strategic location: Highway 10 is a major artery feeding traffic north to the Brainerd Lakes area. It's bumper to bumper or, as Matt calls it, "growler traffic" in summer time. Big Lake likes small business, so there are not really any big box stores and local support is certain. It is a growing community at the end of the North Star Rail line commuter rail into Minneapolis. The walk to the central station is less than a half mile, so this makes for a nice rails-to-ales experience from the Twin Cities.

The bar has a mocha-stained hickory bar top from a northern Minnesota cabin furniture maker and a sort of canopy of rough cut wood. Charging ports under the front of the bar are for cell phones. The names of the people who helped them start—through crowdfunding and donated time—are proudly displayed. A chalkboard displays the current beer menu. A look-through double-sided fireplace is also in the taproom. A roped off area of the parking lot serves as a patio in summer. Men will find an interesting oddity in the restroom—a keg urinal. Some games and cribbage are around for entertainment, but there are no TVs for now.

WiFi. On Facebook.

Stumbling Distance: *Russell's on the Lake* (111 Jefferson Blvd, 763-263-6111, russellsonthelake.com) offers a sort of casual fine-dining supper-club experience. *Raymie's Pizza* (651 Rose Dr, 763-207-8670, raymiespizza.com) delivers to the taproom, as does *Pizza Pub* (726 Martin Ave, 763-262-2224, mypizzapub.com).

LUPULIN BREWING

u4ic Brewing, Inc.

Founded: 2015
Head Brewers: Jeff and Dave Luskey
Address: 23436 Union Trail, Suite 1 • Blakeley, MN 56011
Phone: 952-873-3303
Web Site: www.u4icbrewing.com
Annual Production: 2,000 barrels
Number of Beers: 50+ per year, up to 20 on tap

Staple Beers:
- » Borough Pils
- » Car Show American Ale
- » Old Corn Crib American IPA
- » Vanity Rye Pale Ale

Rotating Beers:
- » Chernilla Cherry Vanilla Stout (on nitro)
- » Many others plus barrel aging and sour beers planned

Most Popular Brew: Old Corn Crib American IPA

Samples: Yes, a flight of any 6 beers.

Brewmaster's Fave: Old Corn Crib or Two Step Viper Russian Imperial Stout (with vanilla and locally roasted coffee, 11% abv)

Best Time to Go: Call to confirm! Thu 4–8, Fri 4–12, Sat noon–12. Summers add Tue 4–8.

Where can you buy it? Very locally on draft or in 6-pack bottles and 22 oz. bombers. Their own growlers are available and exchangeable.

Got food? No, but food friendly and area deliveries available. Plus they make Patrick's Honey Pot Root Beer.

Tours? Nothing concrete yet, but usually Saturdays, or by chance.

Special Offer: A free bottle opener or other equally prized trinket.

Directions: Following US 169 southwest away from the Cities, turn right (west) on 250th St and follow it a 2.6 miles, as it becomes Union Trail, and the brewery is on the left on a curve in the road.

The Beer Buzz: The Village of Blakeley may have a population of about 200 these days, but it once was a river town with the railroad running through as well. In the 1930s this building you see was originally a creamery, but it was purchased by an animal pharmaceutical company in the 1970s. Now it's going to be making beer.

Jeff Luskey has homebrewed since 1989. For years he and his brother Dave have dreamed of opening a brewery. But it wasn't just dreams: Jeff has been purchasing equipment for 14 years, including a 30-barrel brewhouse from Anderson Valley. When they opened in 2015, he started with a more modest 6-barrel operation (with a hot liquor tank converted to a boil kettle), with a 10-barrel waiting in the wings for when they get rolling. A third partner, Kurt Fossen, joined them and the serious search for a location started in 2012.

They found the creamery and started the long process of getting approvals. The biggest problem was the creamery needed its own wastewater treatment as it is not on a city system. That alone took two years, and they drove to North Carolina to dismantle one and ship it north. On June 19, 2014, a devastating downpour sent mudslides from the bluffs through Blakeley. People lost homes and the lower part of Blakeley was evacuated. Power was out for several days, but the brewery escaped with a fine coating of mud on the floor. A major load of work, but fortunately fixable.

They got approval to brew in March 2015, and thus Blakeley has beer. In addition to the taproom, an outdoor patio with a fire pit will offer a place to imbibe and enjoy the river valley.

Free WiFi. Find them on Facebook.com/u4icBrewingIncorporated

Stumbling Distance: Plenty to do along the 287-mile *Minnesota River Valley National Scenic Byway* (888-463-9856, mnrivervalley.com) which passes down the opposite side of the river from the brewery. Also across the river, *Kerfoot Canopy Tour* (30200 Scenic Byway Road, Henderson, 952-873-3901, kerfootcanopytour.com) offers 14 zip lines and a 170-foot suspension bridge for a different view of the river valley. Get a bite to eat and some entertainment at *Henderson Road Haus* (510 Main St, Henderson, 507-248-3691, hendersonroadhaus.com). *Minnesota Valley State Recreation Area* (19825 Park Blvd, Jordan, 651-259-5774, dnr. state.mn.us/state_parks) is just up the road in Jordan and the multi-use *Minnesota Valley State Trail* runs from Shakopee to nearby Belle Plaine. Watch for *Belle Plaine German Days* often the 3rd weekend in June.

HAYES' PUBLIC HOUSE

Opened: 29 November 2013
Brewmaster: Pugs Hayes
Address: 112 1st Street South • Buffalo, MN 55313
Phone: 763-746-6389
Web Site: www.hayespublichouse.com
Annual Production: 240 barrels
Number of Beers: 6 on tap plus a beer engine

Staple Beers:
- » HAYES IRISH STOUT
- » O'RUAIDHRI IRISH RED

Rotating Beers:
- » DAIKER'S WEE HEAVY
- » THE DULLAHAN (coffee porter)
- » IMPERIAL IPA
- » SGT. STELLA'S PALE ALE
- » …plus nitro taps, casks, and barrel-aged brews

Samples: Yes, flights of 5 oz. pours

Brewmaster's Fave: Irish Stout, the first homebrew he ever did.

Best Time to Go: Open Wed–Thu 5–10PM, Fri–Sat 3–10PM. Closed Sun–Tue.

Where can you buy it? Only here in 5 oz., 12 oz., pints, or growlers to go.

Got food? No, just some snacks, but the place is food friendly.

Tours? Yes, but by chance.

Special Offer: A free sticker with your book signature.

Directions: Highway 55 goes right through Buffalo. Watch for 2nd St and take it west into town 0.8 mile and it becomes 1st St. The brewery is on the left.

The Beer Buzz: A lot of great ideas happen when someone is drinking beer, and this one is no different. A buddy got Pug a brew kit for Christmas. One thing led to another. A certified welder, he went to school for business management. His goal had always been to open an Irish pub but then the state regulations changed (the "Surly Bill") to allow breweries to have a taproom, and so he figured why not an Irish brewery instead? This is the end product of seven years of planning.

Why Buffalo? Pugs loves his community. Buffalo has a unique downtown, he says, but it needed something, and when it opened, locals latched onto it quickly. "It's not just mine; it's the community's." Local regulars bring in outside guests and are proud of their local brewery. "This is ours." His passion for community comes out in Gaelic: Written on the bar top (and Pug's matching tattoo) is the phrase "Ni neart go cur le chéile" (nee nyart guh curr leh kay-leh)—There is no strength without unity. The name of the red ale, O'Ruaidhri, is Gaelic for "Rogers," the name of a friend who helped build the brewery.

The taproom is about coffee-shop sized, and functions socially as such, with no TVs, but some small round tables and one big table. Board games are available. The bar has a rail and dark wood accents, and beyond it is a pressed tin backdrop for the taps and a chalkboard beer menu above. The brewhouse is through a door behind the bar. Irish music plays in the background and sometimes there are live performances.

The Holy Corner has a church pew and a collection of musical instruments that patrons can just pick up and play if they'd like. Above the fake fireplace is a portrait of Andrew Jackson Hayes, the owner's great grandfather, an Irish immigrant farmer and beekeeper who after a stint in Shenandoah Valley, moved up to Minnesota. Being close to the lake is nice and there's a good water view from the outdoor patio. It's also a good location due to the road traffic and the abundance of events held in the neighborhood.

WiFi. Facebook.com./pages/Hayes-Public-House
Twitter @hayespublichous

Stumbling Distance: Just east of town is *Norm's Wayside Bar & Grill* (2448 Carling Ave SE, 763-684-0300, normswayside.com) with some great pub grub plus Detroit-style pizza. *Buffalo Books & Coffee* (6 Division St E, 763-682-3147) is a great indie bookstore with great coffee—they supply the coffee for the porter. *South Fork Brewing* is about 12 miles/16 minutes south in Delano, and *Spilled Grain Brewhouse* is 14 miles/18 minutes west in Annandale.

LUPINE BREWING COMPANY

Founded: 2013
Brewmaster: Grant Aldrich
Taproom Address: 248 River Street North • Delano MN 55328
Phone: 763-333-1033
Web Site: www.lupinebrewing.com
Annual Production: 800 barrels
Number of Beers: 6–8 on tap

Staple Beers:
- » IPA
- » OATMEAL CRANBERRY STOUT
- » PALE ALE
- » ROUT BROWN ALE

Rotating Beers:
- » CHOCOLATE CAYENNE STOUT
- » HEFEWEIZEN
- » O'PHELAN IRISH ALE
- » …variations on the Oatmeal Stout

Samples: Yes, flights available.

Best Time to Go: Open Wed–Fri 4–10PM, 4–12AM Fri 1–12 Sat. Call or confirm on website.

Where can you buy it? St Cloud area and the Twin Cities draft accounts and growler and howler (750 ml) fills.

Got food? No, but food friendly, vendors and food trucks are likely.

Tours? Yes, by chance or by appointment.

Special Offer: $1 off your first beer during the signature visit.

Directions: US 12 passes right through Delano as Babcock Blvd. On the west side of the river, it connects with Bridge Ave. Go east here, cross the river, and take the first left (north) on River St and it's on your right halfway up the first block.

The Beer Buzz: Founders James Anderle, Eric Sargent, and Mike Dumas put this brewery together, taking over a space that had once been the brewpub O'Hara's and McCann's Food & Brew. James had been in the healthcare industry for 20 years when he decided to take this leap, but the others still work their day jobs—for now. James had been homebrewing and the first beers they brewed when they opened in late 2014 were his best recipes. In January 2015, they hired Grant as head brewer and started looking for a taproom location. Grant Aldrich got his first professional experience with Brau Brothers.

They found the brewing space first and started making beer in St. Cloud where they also did growler fills, but the taproom is in a separate location altogether, not even the same town.

Facebook/pages Luoine-Brewing-Company and Twitter @LupineBrewing

Stumbling Distance: Check out *South Fork Brewing* across the alley. *Dave's Town Club* (136 N River St, 763-972-6815) offers some really cheap but good bar food, burgers and the like in a family atmosphere. *Hayes' Public House Brewery & Taproom* is about 12 miles/16 minutes north in Buffalo.

South Fork Brewing Co.

Founded: 2015
Brewmaster: Guy Schmaedeke
Address: 221 2nd Street N • Delano, MN 55328
Phone: TBD
Web Site: www.southforkbrewingcompany.com
Annual Production: 500 barrels
Number of Beers: 8 on tap

Staple Beers:
- » Chocolate Porter
- » Honey Basil Golden Ale
- » IPA

Rotating Beers:
- » Maibock
- » Stout — a sort of re-creation of Beamish Irish Stout (Sara Beamish has family ties to Beamish in County Cork)

Most Popular Brew: Too soon to tell!

Samples: Yes, flights available.

Brewmaster's Fave: He likes darker beers

Best Time to Go: Open Fri–Sat 4–10PM. Sun 11–10PM is likely as well. Check the website.

Where can you buy it? On tap and to go in growlers. Some area establishments have them on tap.

Got food? No, but possibly some beer snacks. This place is food friendly and food trucks show up from time to time.

Tours? All is visible from a bar stool and they love to chat beer.

Special Offer: A free flight of four tasters during your signature visit.

Directions: US 12 passes right through Delano as Babcock Blvd. On the west side of the river, it connects with Bridge Ave. Go east here, cross the river, and take the second left (north) on 2nd St and it's on your left halfway up the first block.

The Beer Buzz: In 2012, Sara Beamish (co-owner who met her husband Ken over Oktoberfest beer) owned The Bohemian Wine Bar and Pub (right here) where she ran rotating taps trying to expose her customers to as many Minnesota craft beers as possible, but she wanted to take it to a different level and actually create the beer for them. She enlisted Karen Zimmerman as a partner and decided, let's just get a brewery. Brewer Guy had been homebrewing 20 years but also got into BBQ competitions. Some folks in Delano knew him for his awesome BBQ and had sampled the brews he brought along to the competitions. They raved about them to Sara and Ken; soon they had enlisted him as the brewer for South Fork. Guy did his professional training at Siebel and finished the program in Germany.

What was originally purchased as a restaurant in downtown Delano is now a taproom with 14-foot ceilings of pine and tile floors. The 1890s building, a block off the South Fork of the Crow River, was a commercial laundromat until the mid-1900s when it became a heating and plumbing business. A massive boiler from the laundry days still sits in the basement. The wood bar has a stone front to it. A projector TV shows games or other events from time to time on the wall. Live music is featured on a movable stage, and for other entertainment there are board games, adult-sized Jenga, and, logically, cribbage. Outdoor seating is huge—1000 square feet —and features a fire pit, which, combined with radiant heat, extends the beer garden season into October and November.

WiFi. Facebook.com/southforkbrewingcompany

Stumbling Distance: Check out *Lupine Brewing* across the alley. *El Molcajete Mexican Restaurant & Cantina* (45 Babcock Blvd., el-molcajete. com) serves fantastic Mexican food. *Hayes' Public House Brewery & Taproom* is about 12 miles/16 minutes north in Buffalo.

GRANITE CITY FOOD AND BREWERY

Founded: June 1999
Brewmaster: Cory O'Neel
Address: 3330 Pilot Knob Rd. • Eagan, MN 55121
Phone: 651-452-4600
Web Site: www.gcfb.net
Annual Production: 700 barrels
Number of Beers: 5

Staple Beers:
> » BATCH 1000 DOUBLE IPA
> » BROAD AXE STOUT
> » BROTHER BENEDICT'S BOCK
> » DUKE OF WELLINGTON IPA
> » NORTHERN LIGHT LAGER

Samples: A tray for about $4.95 for eight 3-oz. samples.

Best Time to Go: Open daily; Mon–Thu 11AM–1AM, Fri–Sat 11AM–2AM, Sun 9AM–10PM. Happy hour runs weekdays 3–6PM, Sat–Sun noon–5PM, and every night 9PM–close.

Where can you buy it? Growlers on site (or any of the other 34 Granite City locations in 14 states)!

Got food? Yes, flatbread pizzas, soups and salads, seafood, pasta, burgers, steaks and monthly specials. There are also a gluten-free and kids' menus.

Special Offer: Not participating.

Directions: Coming from the north on I-35E, take exit 97B for Yankee Doodle Rd and turn right. Take the next right on Pilot Knob Rd and go 0.2 mile and the brewery is on the right. From the south take exit 97A-B for Pilot Knob Rd. Turn left onto Pilot Knob Rd, go 0.5 mile north and the brewery is on the right.

The Beer Buzz: This brewpub franchise was first founded in 1999 in St. Cloud, Minnesota, but has since expanded throughout the Midwest. Part of their ease of expansion was streamlining the brewing process and eliminating some of the need for equipment at each location. One of the co-founders was a bit of a legend in the craft brewing scene in the Twin Cities: Bill Burdick was the guy behind Sherlock's Home Restaurant Pub and Brewery, which made a lasting impression on brewers and beer drinkers during its run from 1989 to 2002. At Granite City, Burdick developed a process they called Fermentus Interruptus™. The wort is actually prepared in their central brewing facility—a brewhouse in Ellsworth, Iowa—and then shipped to each location where it is fermented. The result is consistent staple beers and less investment in multiple brewhouses. The Granite City name comes from the 19th century industry that built St. Cloud: quarrying granite.

Granite City offers a Mug Club loyalty program wherein you receive points for what you spend at the brewpub and discounts on food purchases.

The restaurant is a stand-alone building not far off the interstate. Plenty of parking.

Stumbling Distance: *Mall of America* (60 E Broadway, Bloomington, 952-883-8800, mallofamerica.com) is about 10 minutes away to the west on I-494. It's about 16 miles/22 minutes south to *Angry Inch Brewing* (20841 Holyoke Ave, Lakeville).

Excelsior Brewing Co.

Founded: 1 July 2012
Head Brewer: Niles Lewin
Address: 421 3rd Street • Excelsior, MN 55331
Phone: 952-474-7837
Web Site: www.excelsiorbrew.com
Annual Production: 8,000 barrels
Number of Beers: 16 taps

Staple Beers:
- » Big Island Blond
- » Bitteschlappe Brown Ale
- » Bridge Jumper IPA
- » XLCR American Pale Ale

Rotating Beers:
- » Biscuit Pants Session Pale Ale
- » Helius Hefeweizen
- » Mr. Jimmy Baltic Porter
- » Oarlock Oat Stout
- » Offshore Series one-offs
- » Shattered Solstice Ale
- » Milfoil Lakehouse Saison

Most Popular Brew: Big Island Blond

Samples: Yes, four 4-oz. pours for about $7.

Best Time to Go: Open Wed 4–10PM, Thu–Fri 4–11PM, Sat 12–11PM. Watch for special events: Arctic Fat Tire Bike Race (Jan), Maifest (May), the brewery's Beerthday (July), Oktoberfest, and Christkindlsmarkt (weekend after Thanksgiving).

Where can you buy it? Here on tap in 9-oz pours and pints, and in pre-filled growlers to go. Distributed in barrels and six-pack 12-oz. bottles throughout the Twin Cities and St. Cloud metro areas. Seasonals are released in 750-ml bottles.

Got food? Only pretzels, but Excelsior is food friendly.

Tours? Free tours on Saturdays from noon to 2PM. No reservations required.

Special Offer: A free pint of beer with the signature of your book.

Directions: MN 7 passes through Excelsior. From MN 7, turn north on Morse Ave, go 0.1 mile, then turn left on 3rd St. The brewery is on the right. Coming from the west on MN 7, turn left on Oak St, then right on Water St to get to 3rd St. Turn right and the brewery is on the left in the first block.

Cyclists: *The Lake Minnetonka LRT Regional Trail is one block south and passes through Excelsior and connects to Victoria's ENKI Brewing Co.*

The Beer Buzz: Baseball and beer, what could be more American? Owners John Klick, Jon Lewin, and Patrick Foss met in the stands of their sons' little league game, and the idea of a brewery grew out of those conversations. In July 2012, the brewery opened in a smaller space in the back of this building, originally a Ford dealership back in the 1920s, and then moved into the rest of the space in April 2014.

Brewer Niles is the brother of Jon Lewin, one of the owners, and had taken up work under the previous brewer, watching and learning, until he took over in late 2014. In addition to the large batches of their staple beers, a 3.5-barrel pilot system allows the brewer to make smaller one-off batches that can only be found in the taproom. A testament to their creativity and boundary-pushing was their Milfoil Lakehouse Saison. The recipe included hops, honey, and wild rice… and zebra mussel shells and Eurasian milfoil from Lake Minnetonka—two invasive species. A percentage of the profits went to the Freshwater Society (freshwater.org).

The taproom has large storefront windows, letting in lots of light, and a spacious seating area of tables and cocktail tables. Half-growler lamps hang above a stainless steel bar. Board games are on hand. The decoration

MISTER JIMMY

Excelsior Brewing's Baltic porter is named after "Mister Jimmy" Hutmaker, a much beloved local who allegedly ran into Mick Jagger at an Excelsior drugstore while the Rolling Stones were in town for a concert at the local amusement park in 1964. Jimmy, a fan of fountain-made Cherry Coke, had not gotten what he ordered and lamented to Jagger, who had dropped in for a prescription, "You can't always get what you want." The 1969 song mentions Mister Jimmy, along with a prescription, cherry soda, and a drugstore. True story? Who knows? But Mister Jimmy believed it and when someone made him business cards identifying him as the town's "roving ambassador" he also had the song lyrics printed on them.

is a bit eclectic. You can see surfboards, bikes, and skis on the walls and in the rafters, and people are dropping off random things all the time that may work their way into the décor. Live bands play twice a week on a stage in front of the windows in the front corner, and one of the owners himself, John Klick, is in a band called High Trousers.

This place is dog-friendly; not just in the outdoor patio/beer garden, but inside the taproom as well. Parking is in the street or a lot in back.

ATM on site. WiFi. Facebook.com/excelsiorbrew
Twitter @excelsiorbrew

Stumbling Distance: *The Suburban* (342 3rd St, 952-283-1663, thesuburbanmn.com) serves burgers, pizza and Excelsior's beer. Coffee shop *318 Café* (318 Water St, 952-401-7902, three-eighteen.com) does live music at night and serves Excelsior.

LTD Brewing Co.

Founded: 2012 (Grand opening June 7, 2014)
Brewers: Blake Verdon and Jeremy Hale
Address: 8 8th Avenue North • Hopkins, MN 55343
Phone: 952-938-2415
Web Site: www.ltdbrewing.com
Annual Production: 800 barrels
Number of Beers: 7–10 on tap; 30 beers in first 6 months

Staple Styles:
>> A Brown or a Red
>> IPA
>> Something Light
>> Something Dark – Stout or Porter

Rotating Beers: (all of them change constantly)
>> 5 Pepper Cream Ale
>> Nightmare Dry Irish Stout
>> Peppercorn Rye
>> Tripel
>> Wee Heavy
>> (and so on… plus some barrel-aging)

Most Popular Style: IPA

Samples: Yes, flights of five 5-oz. pours for about $10.

Brewmaster's Fave: Jeremy: Nightmare Dry Irish Stout or Double Chocolate Milk Stout | Blake: Triple IPA

Best Time to Go: Open Wed 4–10PM, Thu 3–10PM, Fri 2–12AM, Sat 12PM–12AM, Sun 12PM–7PM. Confirm on website.

Where can you buy it? Here on tap and to go in growlers and howlers (half-growlers) but not your own. Plus on tap in a few establishments in town.

Got food? Just chips and free popcorn. But food friendly and many places deliver here.

Tours? By request or when scheduled on the website.

Special Offer: A free bottle opener or other trinket when you get your book signed.

Directions: US 169 runs north-south through Hopkins. Take the Excelsior Rd exit following signs for Downtown/Hopkins and merge (heading west) onto Excelsior Blvd. Go 0.5 mile and turn right on 8th Ave. Continue 0.2 mile and the brewery is on the left.

The Beer Buzz: Jeremy and Blake, co-owners and co-brewers, met as freshmen at college. They were not old enough to buy beer, so they made it in their dorm rooms. They graduated and got desk jobs, and after a couple of years grew dissatisfied. Blake suggested they start a brewery. Jeremy said it was the dumbest idea he had ever heard. Clearly he didn't stick to his guns on that opinion, however.

After four years of planning, they opened LTD in this simple commercial building, a former flower shop, in downtown Hopkins. They did the demo and construction themselves to modify the space and found used equipment for sale in Ohio: an electric kettle designed for extract brewing. So they added a mash tun and tanks from North Carolina and California.

The brewery name plays on "limited" and "Live the Dream." "Everyone who has brewed at home has thought of someday opening a brewery," says Jeremy. A large chalkboard is emblazoned with the words What's Your Dream? This brewery was theirs; others have written their own dreams and messages around the question on the wall.

Inside the door is a copper-painted dome, above and beyond that a wide space with lots of tables. Taps pour from a pipe that dives down from above the long right-angle copper-top bar sitting at center. The constantly

changing beers are listed on a couple chalkboards there. The brewery is just over a short wall on the left. A couple of TVs project on the wall plus there are board games, and a Nintendo 64 system with a TV surrounded by lounge chairs. Parking is free in the lot outside.

WiFi. Facebook/ltdbrewing and Twitter @ltdbrewing

Stumbling Distance: *Pizza Lucé* (210 Blake Rd N, 952-767-0854, pizzaluce.com) has late-night pizza, craft beer and delivers here. *Hoagie's* (824 Mainstreet, 952-935-2865) offers breakfast anytime. *Aji Contemporary Japanese* (712 Mainstreet, 952-358-3558, ajicj.com) has sushi and grilled dishes.

ROETS JORDAN BREWING CO.

Founded: 2015
Brewmaster: Tim Roets
Address: 230 Broadway Avenue South • Jordan, MN 55352
Phone: 952-406-8865
Web Site: www.roetsjordanbrewery.com
Annual Production: 500–1000 barrels
Number of Beers: up to 10 on tap including root beer, another soda, and cold press coffee

Beers:
- » Always a dark one on and some hoppy beers
- » AMERICAN PALE ALE
- » FRUIT BEERS
- » IPA
- » KÖLSCH
- » OATMEAL MILK STOUT

Samples: Yes, samplers and possibly flights when not busy.

Brewmaster's Fave: Sessionable pale ales and IPAs.

Best Time to Go: Open Fri–Sun. Check website for current hours.

Where can you buy it? Only here in pints and in growlers to go.

Got food? No, but food friendly and possible food trucks.

Tours? Yes, by appointment.

PHOTO COURTESY ROETS JORDAN BREWERY

Special Offer: A free beer during your signature visit.

Directions: Coming into Jordan from Minneapolis on US 169, take the slight right on MN 21/Broadway St N, continue 1 mile, and the brewery is on the right.

The Beer Buzz: A horrible mudslide almost prevented this brewery from happening. Tim Roets was close to moving in his brewing equipment

THE BREWERY THAT ALMOST WAS

The history of brewing in Jordan goes back deep into the 19th century, when Frank Nicolin built his first brewery in 1861. He built another six years later on the site on this street where you can still see a brewery standing. (It's not the same building and the first one is also gone.) He sold that second brewery and it became the largest one in the area. The brewery changed hands but kept on until Prohibition. During that dark period, it was an egg hatchery and the lagering caves provided refrigeration. Prohibition was lifted and Schutz & Hilgers Jordan Brewery burst out of the gates soon distributing Old Style Brew, Natural Product Beer and Jordan Beer in seven states. Grain rationing during World War II made the brewery's grain allotment attractive, and it was bought by one and then another: Mankato Brewing, which closed it due to financial problems in 1949. Fire damaged it in 1954. Gail Andersen bought the building at auction in 1972, cleaned it up a bit, sold it, and years later bought it back again when the city figured to give it the wrecking ball. Gail renovated this time and moved a couple more historic houses here. There were several apartments in here and in 2011, Barbara Lee and Kevin Breeggemann bought it with hopes of bringing in a brewer. These hopes matched Tim Roets and that was just about to happen when Mother Nature put the kibosh on them: a massive downpour triggered a landslide off the backing hill which brought a tree down into the building leaving the structure condemned.

Photo Courtesy Roets Jordan Brewery

when torrential rain triggered a mudslide that sent 30 tons of dirt and a tree through the back of his future brewery (not to mention several resident apartments upstairs). Tim was nearly as devastated as the historic Jordan brewery building, but he carried on and the City of Jordan came back to him with an idea: what about the old bank building? It had been repurposed as a library, but since that closed, it was available as a commercial space. (Turns out Jordan has an inordinate number of buildings on the National Register!)

Tim has been homebrewing since college in the early 80s, and over the years he's won some homebrewing awards. He had a chance to brew with the great Mike Hoops at *Town Hall Brewing*, and Mike once took Tim's beer to the Great American Beer Festival to enter it in the Pro-Am competition. Tim currently manages the cider works and meadery at Minnesota Harvest Orchard Winery as his day job. Having that great historical brewery building as a location is what really got Tim going on the brewery idea, so it was ironic that he lost it and fortunate that another option came up just a block away.

The taproom has a short bar and a combination of high and low tables. Current beers are listed on an old chalkboard from the library, and you can still see a couple old safes from the banking days. You can expect a TV, music playing in the background, and the occasional live performances as well. A small beer garden occupies the back courtyard. Tim works a 3-barrel system with a lot of fermenters. His two adult sons Dylan and P.J. and his wife Steffanie Sanders are also part of the team.

WiFi. Facebook.com/roetsjordanbrewery and Twitter @RoetsBrewery

Stumbling Distance: You can still see the remains of the *Old Jordan Brewery* just down the street on Broadway. *Jim's Apple & Candy Store* (20430 Johnson Memorial Dr, Jordan) is a seasonal place, but something not to be missed. Billing itself as Minnesota's largest candy store, it makes a convincing display, with candy from places all over the world. Also, this is the best selection of root beers you will ever see in your life. *Minnesota Harvest Orchard* (8251 Old Hwy 169 Blvd, 952-492-2785, minnesotaharvest.net) has wagon rides and bonfires from mid-May through December, and apple picking in fall as well as a petting zoo.

Angry Inch Brewing Co.

Opened: Planned July 2015
Brewers: Jon Erickson and Josh Hebzynski
Address: 20841 Holyoke Ave. • Lakeville, MN 55044
Phone: 952-220-7047
Web Site: www.angryinchbrewing.com
Annual Production: 1,000 barrels
Number of Beers: 9 on tap

Staple Beers:
- » Angry inch Pale Ale
- » Daddy's Honey Pot (honey saison)
- » Easy Amber Irish red
- » 42 Short & Portly Porter (aged on cocoa nibs)
- » Four Horsemen IPA
- » Samoan Kisses (on nitro)

Rotating Beers:
- » Resolution Ale (fermented on green grapes)
- » Solar Eclipse (white IPA)
- » Menage a Trois (Belgian tripel)
- » Dubbel Troubbel
- » What's Your Weiss?

Most Popular Brew: Daddy's Honey Pot

Samples: Yes, six 4-oz. pours for about $10.

Brewmaster's Fave: Jon: Tynan Tirim Dry Irish Stout (nitro)
Josh: Angry Inch Pale Ale

Best Time to Go: Planning to be open daily, but check website to confirm current hours.

Where can you buy it? Here on tap and in growlers to go, maybe some local draft accounts.

Got food? No, but food friendly.

Tours? Yes, you can see everything from a perch at the bar.

Special Offer: Buy your first flight and your next beer is free during your signature visit.

Directions: From I-35 south Minneapolis, take Exit 81 and follow County Rd 70 east toward Lakeville/Farmington for 2.9 miles. Turn left on Holyoke Ave, go 0.7 mile, and the brewery is on the left.

The Beer Buzz: Founders Josh and Jon have been friends since kindergarten and they took up homebrewing only a few years ago. Jon was working as a Volkswagen mechanic when a co-worker bought a brew kit, talked about it a lot, but then never got into it. He gave the kit to Jon and he too just set it aside in his garage for about four years. Then one day he and Josh were throwing darts in the garage when Josh noticed it. "What's that? Why are we not making beer?" So in January 2011, on the coldest day of the year, they brewed their first beer in that frozen garage.

They really got into it, but when Daddy's Honey Pot won an award at a Beer Dabbler homebrewing event, they started thinking about a brewery. While they hosted tastings for friends, that beer remained the favorite. Then they co-sponsored a golf tournament and provided some beer, and the next day they got a call from a fan who wanted them to consider a site in Lakeville for a brewery. The second site he showed them was this place, a former Ace Hardware store that had been vacant for several years. They took a portion of the space and split it with a popular food truck that was looking for a street address.

They are running a 7-barrel system with four fermenters and four brite tanks. The six beers listed above are at least for now intended to be year round, while the 7th and 8th taps will pour a six-month and two-month rotational beer. That leaves one more tap line for pilot batches which will fall in the Tap 9 category.

The name Angry Inch came from a game of charades gone terribly wrong. While playing, Jon managed to confuse the children's book *The Very Hungry Caterpillar* with *Hedwig and the Angry Inch*, a rock musical about a rock band fronted by a gay East German male. Hey, it could happen to anyone. But while being razzed about the humorous incident, the light bulb went on. Angry Inch? Great name for a brewery.

Jon works at Northern Brewer, the brew supply store, and Monday is typically his day off. But most breweries are also closed that day, which is frustrating when a guy wants a beer. Their intentions are to be open on Mondays, and even 7 days a week, but that will be decided by the municipality, so check their website. Watch for game nights at the brewery co-hosted with neighbor World of Games. Cribbage is also on hand. The outdoor patio is dog friendly.

WiFi. Facebook/pages/Angry-Inch-Brewing
Twitter @AngryInchBrew

Stumbling Distance: *Mainstreet* (20788 Holyoke Ave, 952-985-7650, mainstreetcoffeecafe.com) is a coffee shop by day, wine bar by night. *World of Games* (20777 Holyoke Ave, 952-469-1830, worldofgamesonline.com) sells a boatload of games and collectibles. *Motley Crews Heavy Metal Grill* (612-310-7266, motleycrews.com) is an awesome food truck and taking on some brick and mortar to share this space with Angry Inch.

CRIBBAGE – THE GAME OF THE NORTH

You'll see them around the bars and taverns, and in just about every taproom and brewpub in this book. A little plank of wood with tiny holes drilled into it. 120 holes, to be exact. At Barley John's in New Brighton, it's even drilled into a table top. This is cribbage and it's fair to say it is a tradition here in Minnesota.

Cribbage dates back to the 1600s in England. Sir John Suckling, a wealthy poet, is presumed the creator. It's a card game, typically for two people—though teams of two can play against each other and a special change in the deal makes three-person cribbage possible as well. Points are awarded for The Deal, the card combinations in dealt hands (plus an extra hand called The Crib which goes to the alternating dealer). But in addition to the luck of the draw, as it were, players try to earn points from The Play. Starting left of the dealer, each player strategically lays down one card at a turn, adding the number value to the previous cards until another card cannot be laid without going over 31. One earns points from arriving at 15 or 31 and for combinations—pairs, runs, three of a kind—made with previously laid cards, or for receiving a "Go" from a player who cannot put a card down without exceeding 31. The players move pegs along the holes in the board in accordance with the score. The end of the line is that 121 mark.

*Author Jordan Wiklund of St. Paul has a fascination with the game and is working on a book about it. His blog is cribbageland.com Forget Giant Jenga: According to Wiklund, Minnesotans have drilled holes in lake ice to play with a giant, outdoor cribbage board.

HammerHeart Brewing Co

Founded: 2013
Brewmaster: Austin Lunn
Address: 7785 Lake Drive • Lino Lakes, MN 55014
Phone: 651-964-2160
Web Site: www.hammerheartbrewing.com
Annual Production: 600 barrels
Number of Beers: 18 on tap, plus casks; 40+ beers their first year

Staple Beer:
  » British Invasion British-style Pale Ale

Common Beers:
  » Åttebeint Hest Northern IPA
  » Bergtatt Juniper Pale Ale
  » Black Cascade Dark Ale
  » Dublin Raid (peat-smoked Irish red ale)
  » FautzRauch Smoked Pale Ale
  » Flaming Longship Scotch Ale
  » Flanary's Brew Smoked Irish stout
  » Hokan's Brown Ale
  » Jörmungandrsblod Rye Pale Ale
  » Loki's Treachery Sour Smoked IPA
  » Olaf the Stout Oak-Aged Rye Stout
  » Peter's Portar peat-smoked porter
  » Steadfast Best Bitter
  » Surtr's Flame Smoked IPA
  » Thor's Smoked Hot Pepper Imperial Porter

Summer Seasonals:
  » Blåtand Blueberry India Pale Ale
  » Brekkefossensvann Amber Ale

Autumn Seasonals:
  » Hail to the Dark Gourd (wheat ale with smoked pumpkin and spices)
  » Herbstklagen (rauchbier)
  » Høst Øl Smoked Harvest Ale

Winter Seasonals:
  » Fimbulvetr Oak Smoked Wheat India Pale Ale

- » Ginnungagap Oatmeal Coffee Stout
- » Imperial Longship Barrel Aged Smoked Scotch Ale
- » Midvinter Øl Black Ale with Spices
- » Sköll och Hati Smoked Chocolate Stout

Most Popular Brew: Flaming Longship

Samples: Yes, four 5.5-oz. pours for about $11.

Brewmaster's Fave: Høst Øl

Best Time to Go: Open Tue–Sat 2–10pm, Sun 12–8pm.

Where can you buy it? Here on tap with a two-tier pricing (four-tiers for growlers) and tulip-glass pours for the highest-gravity beers. Growlers and 750 ml to go, and they will fill outside growlers. Bottling is planned, but for now they self-distributed kegs in the northeast quadrant of Minnesota, from the Twin Cities to Duluth and into Wisconsin up there.

Got food? No, but food friendly and food trucks are common (see website for who is parked there and when).

Tours? Nope.

Special Offer: Not participating at this time.

Directions: From I-35W, take Exit 36 for County Highway 23, go north on Hwy 23 for 0.8 mile and the brewery is on the left.

The Beer Buzz: Co-owners Nathanial Chapman and his brother-in-law Austin Lunn set up this highway-side brewery in a former machine shop that looks more like a Viking lodge. The name comes from an album by Swedish band Bathory, a Viking metal band (where metal and Norse my-

thology meet). Beer names tend to be Norse or Celtic, making them much easier to drink than to pronounce or spell. Every one of them has a story.

Austin got his start homebrewing, so when he and Nathaniel decided to leave their day jobs for something more creative, he at least had a start. To ready himself for commercial brewing, he took an internship under brewer Andreas Riis at Haand Brewery in Norway.

High-gravity is the general rule here which adds a little more meaning to the hammer part of the name. They do a lot of smoked beers, you can see, and at times as many as half the taps are aged in barrels that once held whiskey, brandy, bourbon, rum, rye, or even aquavit.

The taproom shows mostly rustic wood interiors with lots of antlers, deer, and a moose. Antlers function as the front door handle, the chandelier, and the tap handles. A sword is mounted in the window looking into the brewhouse in back, and a shield hangs behind the bar. No TVs here, just beer and some music, sometimes as potent as the beers: metal or traditional Scandinavian folk music. Clientele sit on bar stools around barrel tables and at a couple long tables. The beer flight comes on a replica of a Viking whalebone plaque made of solid maple by Tim Jorgensen who coordinates the Midwest Viking Festival over in Moorhead each June.

No WiFi. Facebook.com and Twitter @HammerHeartBeer

Stumbling Distance: *Chanticlear Pizza* (7771 Lake Dr, 651-786-7022, chanticlearpizza.com) is next door and delivers. *Bistro La Roux* (9372 Lexington Ave N, Circle Pines, 763-717-8288, bistrolaroux.com) 4.5 miles south of here has great Cajun and Creole fare.

GRANITE CITY FOOD AND BREWERY

Founded: June 1999
Brewmaster: Cory O'Neel
Address: 11909 Main St. • Maple Grove, MN 55369
Phone: 763-416-0010
Web Site: www.gcfb.net
Annual Production: 700 barrels
Number of Beers: 5

Staple Beers:
- » BATCH 1000 DOUBLE IPA
- » BROAD AXE STOUT
- » BROTHER BENEDICT'S BOCK
- » DUKE OF WELLINGTON IPA
- » NORTHERN LIGHT LAGER

Samples: A tray for about $4.95 for eight 3-oz. samples.

Best Time to Go: Open daily; Mon–Thu 11AM–1AM, Fri–Sat 11AM–2AM, Sun 9AM–10PM. Happy hour runs weekdays 3–6PM, Sat–Sun noon–5PM, and every night 9PM–close.

Where can you buy it? Growlers on site (or any of the other 34 Granite City locations in 14 states)!

Got food? Yes, flatbread pizzas, soups and salads, seafood, pasta, burgers, steaks and monthly specials. There are also a gluten-free and kids' menus.

Special Offer: Not participating.

Directions: Heading west on I-694 just before meeting I-94, take Exit 28 for Hemlock Ln, cross the intersection onto Main St, and the entrance to the brewery is on the left. Coming from the west off I-94, take I-694 and Exit 28 for Hemlock Ln. Turn right on Hemlock, then left on Main St and the brewery is on the left.

The Beer Buzz: This brewpub franchise was first founded in 1999 in St. Cloud, Minnesota, but has since expanded throughout the Midwest. Part of their ease of expansion was streamlining the brewing process and eliminating some of the need for equipment at each location. One of the co-founders was a bit of a legend in the craft brewing scene in the Twin Cities: Bill Burdick was the guy behind Sherlock's Home Restaurant Pub and Brewery, which made a lasting impression on brewers and beer drinkers during its run from 1989 to 2002. At Granite City, Burdick developed a process they called Fermentus Interruptus™. The wort is actually prepared in their central brewing facility—a brewhouse in Ellsworth, Iowa—and then shipped to each location where it is fermented. The result is consistent staple beers and less investment in multiple brewhouses. The Granite City name comes from the 19th century industry that built St. Cloud: quarrying granite.

Granite City offers a Mug Club loyalty program wherein you receive points for what you spend at the brewpub and discounts on food purchases.

The restaurant is a stand-alone building just off the interstate at Exit 28. Plenty of parking.

Lucid Brewing Co.

Founded: January 2011
Brewmaster: Eric Biermann
Address: 6020 Culligan Way • Minnetonka, MN 55345
Phone: 612-615-8243
Web Site: www.lucidbrewing.com
Number of Beers: 10 taps, some taproom exclusive

Staple Beers:
» Air ("Enlightened Ale")
» Dyno (American Pale Ale)
» Foto (IPA)

Rotating Beers:
» Duce the Imperial Red
» Düo (Double IPA)
» Foto #Fresh (fresh-hopped IPA)
» Goslar (Gose)
» Halucidation Belgian-style (with white grapes)
» Ora (Amber Ale)
» Silo (Saison)
» Surfside
» Sweet Stout

Samples: Yes, up to 5 with a bracelet that has 5 tabs on it.

Best Time to Go: Thu–Fri 5–8pm, Sat 12–5pm.

Where can you buy it? On site, only in growlers available Thu–Fri 5–8pm, Sat 12–5pm, but also in distribution in Minnesota.

Got food? No.

Tours? By appointment only. Sign up when tours are posted on the website. The 45-minute tour includes some sampling. Donations for a local food pantry (money or non-perishable food items) are appreciated.

Special Offer: Not participating at this time.

Directions: Head west on I-494 (or take I-394 to I-494 and head south) to Exit 13 for County Road 62. Go west on CR 62 and turn right on CR 60/Baker Rd. Continue 0.6 mile and turn left onto Culligan Way. The brewery is behind a building on your right. See special directions in The Beer Buzz below.

The Beer Buzz: Lucid is a production brewery with bottling line. But because of an unusual business arrangement, they are also a sort of incubator for some up-and-coming brewers who aren't immediately ready to sink a fortune into a brewhouse. The Alcohol and Tobacco Tax and Trade Bureau (known as the TTB) calls it an "alternating proprietorship," an arrangement in which two or more brewers or brewing companies take turns using a physical brewery. Usually there's a host—in this case Lucid Brewing—and tenant brewers. At the time of writing, that includes Pryes Brewing, but prior to this both Badger Hill Brewing and Bad Weather Brewing operated here as tenants. It's a clever and beneficial arrangement for all parties. Founders Eric Biermann and Jon Messier left the corporate world to pursue this dream back in 2011. And yes, Eric's name really is Bier Man.

Special Directions: Lucid Brewing may be a tricky one to find. When you come to the building that, based on the numbers, should contain 6020 Culligan Way, you are in the right place. (Minnetonka Brewing and Equipment is at 6022 in this same building.) However, you need to

go to the end of the building (if it's on your right) and there is a driveway that takes you down the hill to the right, *behind* the building on Culligan Way. Once back there you will see the brewery across the lot all the way to the left.

Inside is pretty much what you'd expect an industrial brewing space to look like, but a portable bar is rolled out of the corner to serve as a taproom. No pints are served: It's only samples and growler fills. People do, however, enjoy hanging out. In summer, they roll up the utility door for some outside air.

Homebrewers watch for Big Brew Day: In 1988, Congress named May 7 as National Homebrew Day and Lucid makes an annual practice of celebrating, the first Saturday in May, by inviting homebrewers to bring their own equipment and brew together here. Hot and cold water provided, and perhaps some beer as well. The brewery also has a B.F.D.— Brewer for the Day competition. The winning homebrew ends up on tap at the brewery and entered in the Pro-Am Competition at the Great American Beer Festival where professional brewers and amateurs team up.

Facebook/lucidbrewing, Twitter @Lucidbrewing, Instagram @LucidBrewing

Stumbling Distance: *LTD Brewing* is in nearby Hopkins, about 7 minutes away.

BARLEY JOHN'S BREW PUB

Opened: March 16, 2000
Head Brewer: JT Dalton
Address: 781 Old Highway 8 SW • New Brighton, MN 55112
Phone: 651-636-4670
Web Site: www.barleyjohns.com
Annual Production: 300 barrels
Number of Beers: 16 on tap with a few guest beers, beer engine and nitro taps

Staple Beers:
- » LITTLE BARLEY BITTER
- » OLD 8 PORTER
- » STOCKYARD IPA
- » WILD BRUNETTE WILD RICE BROWN ALE

Rotating Beers:
- » ANNIVERSARY ALE (a strong Irish Red – March 16)
- » COBBLEPOT'S DUNKELWEIZEN DOPPELBOCK
- » DARK KNIGHT (barrel-aged Old 8)
- » DARK KNIGHT RETURNS (barrel-aged Old 8, second batch in the barrel)
- » IMPERIAL BROWN ALE
- » JUMP START COFFEE STOUT
- » MAIBOCK
- » OKTOBERFEST
- » OYSTER STOUT
- » ROSIE'S OLD ALE
- » 3 PEPPER BLONDE (ghost and habanero peppers)
- » TWO FACE (double-decocted double IPA – 176 IBUS 10.9% ABV)
- » …plus casks, barrel-aging, and sours

Most Popular Brew: IPA and Wild Brunette

Samples: Yes, four 5-oz. pours

Best Time to Go: Open Mon–Sat 11AM–1AM. Happy Hours: Mon 4PM–12AM, Tue–Sat 4–6PM, Tue–Thu 10PM–12AM. Closed Sundays. Cask releases on Wednesdays.

Where can you buy it? Only here on tap and to go in growlers (64 oz. and 750 ml). Watch for Barley John's in New Richmond, Wisconsin as well.

Got food? Yes, a full menu and full bar with wine and good whiskey selection. Highlights: Little Barley Beer Brat, beer-battered catfish, smoked local pork chop, housemade soups, Minnesota hot artichoke dip. Much is from scratch and a 5,000 sq ft garden on the property supplies a lot of the fresh produce. Daily specials.

Tours? Yes, from the bar stool, but only if someone is free.

Special Offer: A free 4-beer sampler flight with your book signature.

Directions: From I-35W, take Exit 25 for County Road D and go west 0.5 mile. The entrance to the parking lot is on the right at the corner just before the intersection with Old Highway 8 (which also has an entrance).

The Beer Buzz: Previously this was an A&W Root Beer joint, so really it's still beer, right?

John and his wife bought a homebrew kit in 1991, the year they were married. He tried it with extracts first but graduated to grain a few months later. He made 5 gallon batches and everyone was drinking it, so he went bigger and bigger. A few boil-overs and a sticky stovetop got him kicked out of the house. John, whose undergrad education was in nutrition, had been working for Pillsbury, but his beer interest took him to NE Minneapolis'

James Page Brewing, one of the earliest craft brewers, founded around the time Summit opened. Their Burly Brown Ale was John's recipe. (That beer is still produced at the Point Brewery in Wisconsin but with an altered recipe it would seem.) He was considering going to graduate school in nutrition but opted to go to Seibel to study brewing instead. When the James Page job ended, there was nothing else available. Stroh's left town for La Crosse and Schmidt was failing, so he wrote the business plan for Barley John's. He bought an old A&W building in 1999 and did the build-out in 2000 here on Old 8.

John favors a Germanic style of brewing, decoction mashing. "This time-intensive way of heating up part of the wort creates a different malt profile that cannot be obtained any other way." Can't argue with the results. They consistently win awards at Winter Fest for Dark Knight, Dark Knight Returns, and Rosie's Old Ale, which is a highly desired brew when it is available.

The brewpub overlooks the highway and has its own parking lot. As you walk in, you enter the small bar area. The bar top and the tables near the bar are made from a sugar maple which was downed in a storm at his grandmother's. The restaurant area is separated from the bar by stained glass made by John's mother. (She also does all the baking at the restaurant.) The bar has only 5 perches and a couple tables, and the rest of the place is like a small diner. The brewhouse is squeezed—impossibly I would say—into a room to the right of the bar. There's no TV but there's cribbage, including a board drilled into a tabletop with a deck of cards at hand. Outside, a patio features a fire in winter and on cool summer nights. Hop vines grow outside and many of the fresh ingredients come from a garden there as well.

WiFi. Facebook.com/BarleyJohns and Twitter @barleyjohns

Stumbling Distance: Not much going on here in New Brighton, but you can get into the Northeast ("Nordeast") Minneapolis brewery zone in about 10 minutes down County Road 88. The closest hotel is *Fairfield Inn & Suites* (3045 Centre Pointe Dr N, Roseville, 651-636-7869, marriott.com). *Bent Brewstillery* in Roseville is about five minutes away to the southeast.

Bent Brewstillery

Founded: January 2014
Head Brewer: Kristen England
Address: 1744 Terrace Drive •
Roseville, MN 55113
Phone: 844-879-2368
Web Site: www.bentbrewstillery.com
Annual Production: less than 1,000 barrels
Number of Beers: 6–8 on tap, 6–7 beers per year

Staple Beers:
- » Moar historical IPA
- » Nordic Blonde
- » Patersbier

Rotating Beers:
- » Brewer's ExperimentALE Series
- » Dark Fatha (December – American Emperial Stout in scotch, rye, bourbon barrels)
- » El Guerrero (Fall – Chilean double stout with honey, coffee and merkén)
- » Lakeside Blonde (Summer)
- » Maroon and Bold (100% Minnesota ingredients double IPA)
- » Über Lüpin
- » …plus sour beers and special taproom only brews

Samples: Yes, flights of four 5-oz. pours for about $8.

Brewmaster's Fave: Nordic Blonde

Best Time to Go: Open Wed–Thu 4–10pm, Fri 2:30–10pm, Sat 12–10pm, Sun 11:30am–8pm. Live music on weekends, including the Bent Brewstillery Band. Watch for trivia nights and other events on the website.

Where can you buy it? Here on tap and in their own glass, stainless steel, or recyclable plastic growlers and 750 ml bottles to go. Available locally at over 170 retailers (map on website). Draft accounts, cans of Nordic Blonde, and 22-oz. bombers or 750 ml bottles of seasonals and special releases.

Got food? Free potato chips or pretzels, plus it's food friendly. Food trucks show up occasionally and menus are on hand to order in. Plus cold pressed coffee on a nitro tap and handmade sodas.

Tours? Yes, randomly scheduled. Sign up for one.

Special Offer: $1 off your first beer during your signature visit.

Directions: Coming from the south on I-35W, take Exit 24 and turn right on Cleveland Ave and go 0.1 mile. Go left on City Centre Dr/ County Road D for 0.5 mile. Then turn left on Fairview Ave, go 0.3 mile, and turn right on Terrace Dr. Continue 0.2 mile and it's the 3rd entrance on the right at the complex numbered 1720-1746. Drive down toward the end and the brewery is on the left. From the north on I-35W, take Exit 24, turn left on Long Lake Rd, go 0.1 mile, and turn left (east) on City Centre Dr/ County Road D. Go 0.8 mile and turn left on Fairview, then Terrace, as indicated above.

The Beer Buzz: Is it a brewery? Is it a distillery? It's both and the first of its kind in Minnesota. Founder Bartley Blume got into homebrewing in 2007 when his wife bought him a Mr. Beer kit. He thought, "This is the best thing ever!" And in 2009 he decided... not to open a brewery. He had started working on a business plan and then Fulton Brewing opened and he thought, forget it, too late. By 2011 there were 20 more and he started to reconsider, but by then he had started reading up on distilling and revised his business plan. An electrical engineer, he has worked for NASA, but that profession never gave him a creative outlet. He loves to cook and felt it was expression, and he figured brewing and distilling would offer that right-brain/left-brain balance. His homebrew was good but not ready, so he started contract brewing with Pour Decisions. His plan had been to own a place small enough to supply a taproom and then contract with a local brewery to distribute larger quantities. He found the second half of the plan before the first and shacked up with Pour Decisions in this space. At the end of 2013, they invited him to merge. They merger took place in 2014 and they continue to brew their beers. Brewer Kristen also brings an enormous number of recipes.

"Brewstillery" combines the brewing and distilling, and Bent reflects "a way of life," says Bartley. His beers didn't fit styles for competition. Creating and merging styles and bending the rules is more his thing. "Taking a hobby and making it your life? That's the American Dream." Small batches are brewed on a 5-barrel pilot system. The distillery is a 500-gallon MegaStill he uses to make whiskey and gin, and a 26-gallon spirit still is for playing around with new recipes or concepts. They distilled a double IPA and dry-hopped it before bottling.

As you enter the parking lot between two long brick industrial buildings, head toward the end on the left where you'll find Bent with a brick patio out front. The taproom features tall tables, a few booths, and a curving stainless steel bar with the tap lines descending from above. A metal fence separates the taproom from the brewhouse and the distillery is visible beyond the bar. An old upright piano stands along one wall, three big TVs show games and such, and there are board games.

WiFi. Facebook.com/bentbrewstillery and Twitter @BentBrewstiller Instagram @bentbrewstillery

Stumbling Distance: *Grumpy's Bar & Grill* (2801 Snelling Ave, Roseville, 651-379-1180, grumpys-bar.com) is nearby for food and some other regional tap beers. *Country Inn & Suites* (2740 Snelling Ave N, 651-628-3500, countryinns.com) is a good nearby place to crash. *Barley John's Brew Pub* in New Brighton is about five minutes away to the northwest and serves food.

GRANITE CITY FOOD AND BREWERY

Founded: June 1999
Brewmaster: Cory O'Neel
Address: 851 Rosedale Center • Roseville, MN 55113
Phone: 651-209-3500
Web Site: www.gcfb.net
Annual Production: 700 barrels
Number of Beers: 5

Staple Beers:
- » BATCH 1000 DOUBLE IPA
- » BROAD AXE STOUT
- » BROTHER BENEDICT'S BOCK
- » DUKE OF WELLINGTON IPA
- » NORTHERN LIGHT LAGER

Samples: A tray for about $4.95 for eight 3-oz. samples.

Best Time to Go: Open daily: Mon–Thu 11AM–1AM, Fri–Sat 11AM–2AM, Sun 9AM–10PM. Happy hour runs weekdays 3–6PM, Sat–Sun noon–5PM, and every night 9PM–close.

Where can you buy it? Growlers on site (or any of the other 34 Granite City locations in 14 states)!

Got food? Yes, flatbread pizzas, soups and salads, seafood, pasta, burgers, steaks and monthly specials. There are also a gluten-free and kids' menus.

Special Offer: Not participating.

Directions: From MN 36, exit onto MN 51/Snelling Ave and almost immediately take the County Rd B2 exit. Turn left into the Rosedale Shopping Center and the brewery is behind the cinema on the left.

The Beer Buzz: This brewpub franchise was first founded in 1999 in St. Cloud, Minnesota, but has since expanded throughout the Midwest. Part of their ease of expansion was streamlining the brewing process and eliminating some of the need for equipment at each location. One of the co-founders was a bit of a legend in the craft brewing scene in the Twin Cities: Bill Burdick was the guy behind Sherlock's Home Restaurant Pub and Brewery, which made a lasting impression on brewers and beer drinkers during its run from 1989 to 2002. At Granite City, Burdick developed a process they called Fermentus Interruptus™. The wort is actually prepared in their central brewing facility—a brewhouse in Ellsworth, Iowa—and then shipped to each location where it is fermented. The result is consistent staple beers and less investment in multiple brewhouses. The Granite City name comes from the 19th century industry that built St. Cloud: quarrying granite.

Granite City offers a Mug Club loyalty program wherein you receive points for what you spend at the brewpub and discounts on food purchases.

The restaurant is at one end of the Rosedale Shopping Center, right across from the AMC Cineplex. Plenty of parking.

Stumbling Distance: *Bent Brewstillery* is about 5 minutes north of here.

RAHR MALTING

Without malt, we wouldn't have beer, but the malting process is no small undertaking. Especially when there is such high demand for so much of it to make a nation's beer. But Minnesota is part of the nation's grain belt and with all the trainloads coming to the Mill City, as Minneapolis was known, there'd be lots of barley. William Rahr, a German immigrant, founded a company in his name in Wisconsin in 1847. In fact, the family still owns the company. As the company expanded over the years, Rahr Malting Co. chose Shakopee, MN as the site of what would become one of the largest single site malting facilities in the world. It is now the company headquarters.

The process has three stages: Steeping, where water is added to the barley for 1.5 to 2 days; Germination, a four-day period allowing the grain to activate enzymes and break down starches into simple sugars; and finally Kilning, 1 to 1.5 days of drying the malt in large containers with perforated floors.

Rahr Malting produces over 380,000 metric tons of malt each year in five malthouses, the first dating back to 1937. One of their subsidiaries, BSG, does the distribution specifically for the craft brewing industry and homebrew supply shops.

800 1st Avenue West, Shakopee
952-445-1431 | rahr.com

BADGER HILL BREWING CO.

Opened: December 2014, but brewing since June 2012
Head Brewer: Michael Koppelman
Address: 4571 Valley Industrial Boulevard S #500 • Shakopee, MN 55379
Phone: 952-230-2739
Web Site: www.badgerhillbrewing.com
Annual Production: up to 4,000 barrels
Number of Beers: 6–8 on tap, plus craft sodas; as many as 20 per year

Staple Beers:
  » FOUNDATION STOUT
  » HIGH ROAD EVERYDAY ALE
  » MSB MINNESOTA SPECIAL BITTER
  » THREE TREE AMERICAN RYE
  » TRAITOR IPA
  » WHITE INDIA PALE ALE

Rotating Beers:
  » WANDERLUST SERIES (many small batch, taproom-only offerings and seasonals, frequent casks)

Most Popular Brew: High Road and Traitor IPA

Samples: Yes, sips for decision-making and flights four 5-oz. pours for about $8.

Brewmaster's Fave: Traitor IPA

Best Time to Go: Open Wed–Thu 3–10PM, Fri 3–11PM, Sat 12–11PM, Sun 12–6PM.

Where can you buy it? On tap here in pints and half-pints, and pre-filled and exchanged growlers to go. Six-pack 12-oz. cans available throughout most of Minnesota.

Got food? No, but food friendly. Delivery menus on hand and food trucks typically on Fridays.

Tours? Yes, scheduled on Saturday afternoons, 2–3 times per month. Check the website to confirm. Sign up online or in the taproom. Free and includes samples.

Special Offer: Not participating at this time.

Directions: US 169 takes you south from Exit 10 on I-494. From US 169, exit at MN 13 for Shakopee. Keep right and merge onto County Road 101. Go 2.4 miles, turn left on Valley Park Dr. Go 0.4 mile, turn right on Valley Industrial Blvd, and the brewery is 0.5 mile farther, on the right.

The Beer Buzz: Badger Hill might seem a random name—and perhaps risqué in Gopher country—but it actually derives from the Gaelic origins of two of the founders' names, brothers Broc and Brent Krekelberg. Broc and Brent meant badger and hill. Broc met his wife Britt over beer and the three of them founded this brewing company focused mainly on English pub style brews. Broc and Brent Krekelberg trace their homebrewing origins back to the days they were living in Colorado during the birth of the craft beer scene there. They decided they had some good recipes they could bring to a production level, brews that were not too aggressive but highly drinkable. Their mission was to build the brand around that.

Brewer Michael is a bit of a Renaissance man. He earned an astronomy degree just for fun. He's a musician and has produced records for Prince and Booker T and the MGs. Michael was helping the Badger Hill team produce their beer when the brewery was still sharing the space out at Lucid Brewing with an Alternating Proprietor arrangement. (Bad Weather was also there at the time, others will follow.) They launched with MSB in June of 2012 and by early 2014 they were looking to move into their own independent brewery.

The 20-barrel brewhouse is situated in a gutted industrial space built out for the brewery and a 110-person capacity taproom. Their industrial park location puts them a couple miles south of Valleyfair and the south metro entertainment district. The taproom has a couple TVs for sports, occasional live music, and background music the rest of the time. It's a family friendly place and you can find board games and cribbage to pass the time. Parking is in the lot outside and a nice patio opens in season.

WiFi. Facebook/BadgerHillBrewing and Twitter @BadgerHillBeer

Stumbling Distance: *Mr. Pigstuff* (1561 1st Ave E, 952-233-7306, mrpigstuff.com) offers some great BBQ nearby. *Taco Loco* (1555 1st Ave E, 952-224-2449, facebook.com/tacolocoshakopee) is the best Mexican in town. *Pizza Man* (479 Marschall Rd, 952-445-5566, pizzaman.biz) has been dealing pies since 1977. All three of them deliver to the taproom. *Mystic Lake Casino* (2400 Mystic Lake Blvd NW, Prior Lake, 952-445-9000, mysticlake.com) is 10 minutes south if you're feeling lucky.

GRANITE CITY FOOD AND BREWERY

Founded: June 1999
Brewmaster: Cory O'Neel
Address: 5500 Excelsior Blvd. • St. Louis Park, MN 55416
Phone: 952-746-9900
Web Site: www.gcfb.net
Annual Production: 700 barrels
Number of Beers: 5

Staple Beers:
- » BATCH 1000 DOUBLE IPA
- » BROAD AXE STOUT
- » BROTHER BENEDICT'S BOCK
- » DUKE OF WELLINGTON IPA
- » NORTHERN LIGHT LAGER

Samples: A tray for about $4.95 for eight 3-oz. samples.

Best Time to Go: Open daily; Mon–Thu 11AM–1AM, Fri–Sat 11AM–2AM, Sun 9AM–10PM. Happy hour runs weekdays 3–6PM, Sat–Sun noon–5PM, and every night 9PM–close.

Where can you buy it? Growlers on site (or any of the other 34 Granite City locations in 14 states)!

Got food? Yes, flatbread pizzas, soups and salads, seafood, pasta, burgers, steaks and monthly specials. There are also a gluten-free and kids' menus.

Special Offer: Not participating.

Directions: Heading south on MN 100 from I-364, take the Excelsior Blvd exit. Turn right on Excelsior Blvd, go 0.2 mile, turn left on Park Center Blvd. The brewery is on the right.

The Beer Buzz: This brewpub franchise was first founded in 1999 in St. Cloud, Minnesota, but has since expanded throughout the Midwest. Part of their ease of expansion was streamlining the brewing process and eliminating some of the need for equipment at each location. One of the co-founders was a bit of a legend in the craft brewing scene in the Twin Cities: Bill Burdick was the guy behind Sherlock's Home Restaurant Pub and Brewery, which made a lasting impression on brewers and beer drinkers during its run from 1989 to 2002. At Granite City, Burdick developed a process they called Fermentus Interruptus™. The wort is actually prepared in their central brewing facility—a brewhouse in Ellsworth, Iowa—and then shipped to each location where it is fermented. The result is consistent staple beers and less investment in multiple brewhouses. The Granite City name comes from the 19th century industry that built St. Cloud: quarrying granite.

Granite City offers a Mug Club loyalty program wherein you receive points for what you spend at the brewpub and discounts on food purchases.

The restaurant is a stand-alone building with plenty of parking.

Stumbling Distance: *The Four Firkins* (5630 W 36th St, Minneapolis, 952-938-2847, thefourfirkins.com) is a stellar liquor store with a good MN craft beer selection. Do not miss *Steel Toe Brewing* less than 5 minutes up the road from here.

STEEL TOE BREWING

Founded: August 2011
Brewmaster: Jason Schoneman
Address: 4848 West 35th Street • St. Louis Park, MN 55416
Phone: 952-955-9965
Web Site: www.steeltoebrewing.com
Annual Production: 2,000 barrels
Number of Beers: up to 8 on tap;

Staple Beers:
- » DISSENT DARK ALE
- » PROVIDER ALE
- » RAINMAKER DOUBLE RED ALE
- » SIZE 7 IPA

Rotating Beers:
- » BEFORE THE DAWN (Barrel-aged Black Barleywine)
- » DOUGLAS (Cascadian Dark Ale)
- » LUNKER (Rye-barrel-aged English Barleywine)
- » SIZE 11 (Double IPA – winter)
- » SOMMER VICE (Bavarian-style hefeweizen – summer)
- » WEE HEAVY SCOTCH ALE
- » ... plus occasional casks

Most Popular Brew: Size 7 IPA

Samples: Yes, flights.

Brewmaster's Fave: Provider Ale

Best Time to Go: Open Wed–Thu 3–8PM, Fri 3–10PM, Sat 12–10PM. Busy most nights, and it's quieter Wednesday afternoons and early on Thursdays.

Where can you buy it? Here in pints, samplers, and growlers and occasional 750s to go. In about 70 Twin Cities area liquor stores in 22 oz. bombers and limited release 750 ml bottles, and on draft in select bars and restaurants in the greater Twin Cities metro area.

Got food? No, but food friendly. Food trucks comes most weekend nights.

Tours? No.

Special Offer: Not participating at this time.

Directions: From MN 100 (which connects heading south from Exit 5 on I-394) take the MN 7 exit for County Rd 25. Turn left/east (opposite if coming from the south) on MN 7/CR 25, about 0.3 mile, then turn right on Beltline Blvd and go 0.4 mile. Turn right on 35th St and the brewery is 400 feet down on your right.

The Beer Buzz: Jason may be the brewers' brewer: Several brewers along this journey recommended a visit here and said it's what they drink if they aren't drinking their own. That's quite an endorsement. Like most, he started as a homebrewer, but when it was clear he should take that next step, he first put in the time learning the trade more seriously. His wife Hannah encouraged and supported him in the endeavor.

In Montana he was a cellarman and then assistant brewer at Lightning Boy Brewery. The next step was coursework at World Brewing Academy where he took a diploma after 3 months in Chicago and Germany. His first job thereafter was in Oregon with Pelican Pub and Brewery where he worked his way up to head brewer and learned much more than just the brewing part of it, but also the business end and community component. At the end of 2009, Jason and Hannah came back to Minnesota. It took them two more years to sort out the many details of opening a brewery, from business plan and site to equipment and marketing. They finally opened their doors in August 2011.

Growth has been slow and steady, but Jason has no intention "to conquer the world." He just really likes beer and takes pride in both producing a high quality product and using local materials. All the brewing equipment is US made.

The building was once manufacturing space and was converted from machine shop to beer shop. The taproom has a simple bar with wire shelves of growlers behind it, and tap lines descending from the ceiling. A simple narrow bar counter runs along the wall opposite. There's a TV, but it's not on very often—just for big games. Music is always playing but not so loud, and it becomes almost unheard on busy nights. It's mostly a gathering place to have good beer with good friends. They expanded the taproom in early 2015. Parking is off-street in a lot right outside.

Jason was a tool maker, and much of the work he's done in his adult life has required him to wear steel-toe work boots, and as brewing is his labor of love, Steel Toe seemed appropriate and representative of hard work ethics.

WiFi. Facebook.com/steeltoebrewing and Twitter @SteelToeBrewing

Stumbling Distance: *McCoy's Public House* (3801 Grand Way, St Louis Park, 952-224-9494, mccoysmn.com)is full menu dining with brick-oven pizza, burgers, entrees, and 24 on tap and a long list of bottles. A serious sports bar with good food *Bunny's Bar & Grill* (5916 Excelsior Blvd, St. Louis Park, 952-922-9515, bunnysbarandgrill.com) has a craft beer cooler and a few on tap including Steel Toe. Highly regarded bottle shop *The Four Firkins* (5630 W 36th Street, Minneapolis, 952-938-2847, thefourfirkins.com) is minutes from here (even walking).

Lift Bridge Brewing Co.

Founded: 2008

Brewmaster: Matt Hall

Address: 1900 Tower Drive W • Stillwater, MN 55082

Phone: 888-430-2337

Web Site: www.liftbridgebrewery.com

Annual Production: 9,000 barrels

Number of Beers: 11 on tap, 16 beers per year, a firkin per week

Staple Beers:
- » Chestnut Hill Brown Ale
- » Crosscut Pale Ale
- » Farm Girl saison
- » Getaway Pilsner
- » Hop Dish IPA
- » Mild Ale

Rotating Beers:
- » Biscotti (with local honey, winter)
- » Commander Barleywine
- » Fresh Hop Ale
- » Irish Coffee Stout (March)
- » Minnesota Tan (Belgian Triple, summer)
- » Russian Imperial Stout (barrel-aged, January)

Most Popular Brew: Farm Girl Saison

Samples: Yes, 6-oz. pours, four for $7, six for $10.

Best Time to Go: Tue–Thu 5–10pm, Fri–Sat 12–10pm, Sun 12–6pm. Watch for event nights: game night on Wednesday (cribbage the 3rd Wed of the month), live music on Thursdays and Fridays.

Where can you buy it? Here on tap in shorties (10 oz.) and pints, and their growlers to go. Six-pack bottles and cans and limited 750 ml special releases in Minnesota, western Wisconsin, and eastern North Dakota. Draft accounts in Minnesota.

Got food? No, but there's free popcorn, plus their own root beer. Also food friendly.

Tours? Yes, free scheduled 45-minute tours on Saturdays (1, 3, 5pm) and Sundays (2pm) with free samples. Confirm times on website.

Special Offer: A free patch or sticker when you get your book signed.

Directions: From I-694, take Exit 52B to get on MN 36 to Stillwater. Go 6.6 miles and turn left on Washington Ave. Go 0.2 mile, turn right on Tower Dr, and the destination is 0.1 mile ahead on the left. From downtown Stillwater, take MN 36 west to Washington, turn right, and follow the rest of the directions above.

The Beer Buzz: You might say the brewery began with a card game. The owners all play poker together: Brad Glynn, Dan Schwarz, Jim Pierson, Trevor Cronk. Two of them were homebrewers and they all got together in Brad's basement to brew and play cards. Soon they were more interested in the beer and started sharing outside the card circle. It was well received so in 2008 they began contract brewing their beers for distribution. By 2010 the success of the brand was enough to move them to open their own brewery right here, inside an old gymnastic studio and dog grooming business.

Matt, a St. Paul native, brewed at Stroh's there, then at Stevens Point Brewery where he served as assistant head brewer. Then he took a job in Hawaii at Keokie (sp) Kauai in 2009, until coming back to the continent to be production manager at Firestone Walker in California. His wife got a job in Minnesota and so they moved back. He met Dan at a beerfest and they worked out a deal that he could be a partner in the brewery. Matt

is very into barrel aging and blending, and recipes can get creative—an example: Almond Joy Silhouette, their Russian Imperial Stout with cocoa nibs, toasted coconut, vanilla beans, and lactose. They have an 1888 wooden fermenter, last used in Stevens Point, WI in 1984.

The taproom features tables made of oak barrels and locally built thick-planked tables. The Adirondack chairs were fashioned from whiskey barrels as well. Board games and cribbage are on hand and there's a jukebox.

The brewery name comes from the lift bridge downtown, a local landmark connecting Stillwater to Wisconsin over the St. Croix River.

WiFi. Facebook.com/LiftBridgeBrewery and Twitter @LiftBridge

Stumbling Distance: *Smalley's Caribbean BBQ* (423 Main St S, 651-439-5375, smalleyscaribbeanbbq.com) has Lift Bridge on tap. Go see *Chateau St. Croix Winery & Vineyards* (6428 Manning Ave N, 651-430-3310, chateaustcroix.com) if you would like some grapes with your grains today.

Maple Island Brewing Co.

Founded: 2014
Brewmaster: Nic Brau
Address: 225 Main Street N • Stillwater, MN 55082
Phone: 651-430-0044
Web Site: www.mapleislandbrewing.com
Annual Production: 920 barrels
Number of Beers: up to 9 on tap, occasional casks; over 50 brews per year

Staple Beers:
- » Burlesque Kölsch
- » Cup of Joe Freak Show Oatmeal Stout
- » Maple Island Bock

Rotating Beers:
- » The Beast IPA
- » Belgian Belly Dancer
- » I Scream Brew
- » Monkey Business Mosaic Wheat
- » Peel Me Wit
- » Roctober Fest
- » Zephyr Steam Engine Ale
- » …always an IPA on, typically West Coast style

Most Popular Brew: Cup of Joe and Bock

Samples: Yes, five 4-oz. pours for about $10.

Best Time to Go: Check website for current hours. Open in Winter Tue–Thu 5–10PM, Fri–Sat 12–10PM, Sun 12–8PM. Live music on weekends. Watch for beer release parties.

Where can you buy it? Here on tap and in house growlers to go. Distribution of Cup of Joe coming soon in four-packs of 16-oz. cans.

Got food? Just free popcorn and some sodas for sale, but also food friendly. Local menus on site, plus a food cart parks outside in summer, and sometimes caters inside in colder seasons.

Tours? Yes, free tours by appointment.

Special Offer: A free Maple Island Brewery sticker with your book signature.

Directions: MN 95 runs north-south right through Stillwater as Main St. The brewery is on the river (east) side of the street, between cross streets Myrtle to the south and Mulberry to the north.

The Beer Buzz: Owner Frank Fabio runs a restoration company out of the upstairs of the building, and he wondered how he might fill the lower space. Frank likes good beer and he decided a brewery would fit quite nicely here in Stillwater. He asked Nic to be the brewer. Nic was hesitant about the big step to commercial brewing, but friends and family, already fans of his homebrew, insisted.

Nic—with his appropriate surname, Brau—has some relatives down in Lycan, and when he was younger, the family would go to visit and do some pheasant hunting. As it turns out, Brau Brothers Brewing's Dustin Brau is his second cousin. At the time Dustin had a smaller bar and restaurant. Nic, then accustomed to mass-market beer, had a bit of his cousin's and was hooked. He took a couple growlers back to the Twin Cities and did his friends the favor of getting them hooked as well. With Lycan a 6-hour roundtrip, he needed an alternative, so he started homebrewing—and got his kids involved too. He recalls soaking 200 Samuel Adams empties in a bathtub so they could peel the labels off. His son Joe helped Nic brew the flagship oatmeal stout here which incorporates cold pressed coffee and a touch of vanilla. For his efforts Joe got naming rights.

Frank puts no restrictions on Nic's brewing leaving him to pursue some nontraditional recipes. Nic doesn't like to conform to seasonal expectations and brews what he wants when he wants. And he isn't too concerned about sticking to style as his half witbier, half pilsner Witner might suggest. I Scream Brew is made with 60 lbs. of local Nelson's Ice Cream.

The brewery occupies a former creamery which was later taken over by Maple Island Hardware. The location is on Stillwater's historical Main Street. Isaac Staples Sawmill, now a converted antique shop, stands just

THE STILLWATER BIERCYCLE

Stillwater is quite scenic—what with the historic downtown, the old buildings, the lift bridge, the bluffs, and the St. Croix River. So why not take an open-air tour of the place for the views and have a couple beers along the way? Climb aboard the BierCycle for a historic tour and pedal your way through Stillwater. It's about a 35-minute loop around town with a brief stop to rest. You are allowed to bring your own beer (or wine) and if you have glass, they will provide you with plastic cups. Space for a couple of coolers is on board as well. They do both public and private tours.

BierCycle Adventures
651-300-2202
biercycleadventures.com

PHOTO COURTESY OF BIERCYCLE ADVENTURES

across the street. Glass garage doors open up to the seasonal patio that wraps around to the back of the building. A large parking lot is right outside. The taproom has open industrial ceilings, a polished concrete floor, and wood-barrel chandeliers. A rare John Deere bicycle is mounted on the wall, and there's a scale from the hardware store days. A long marble bar in front of a cooler lies along one wall, and a growler collection lines up across the top. Brewhouse is up front at the street entrance, while the tables are in back where windows look out at the St. Croix River and the bluffs of Wisconsin beyond. You can see the city's famous lift bridge downstream. A mezzanine area offers extra seating or private event space. A few board games are on hand, plus cribbage, naturally. Beer soap is for sale as is some maple syrup from the Sanderson family in nearby Hastings.

WiFi. Facebook.com/Mapleislandbrewing,
Twitter @mapleislandbrew and Instagram @mapleislandbrew

Stumbling Distance: *Leo's Grill & Malt Shop* (131 Main St S, 651-351-3943) does old-school malts and burgers. Wood-fired *Quick Fire Pizza* (116 Main St S, 651-439-7009, quickfirepizza.com) is the best pizza in town. Get some fine cheeses and charcuterie at *The Wedge & Wheel* (308 Chestnut St E, 651-342-1687, wedgeandwheel.com) cheese bar and shop. *Pub 112* (112 Main St N, 651-342-0836, pub112.com) offers the "perfect pint paired with the perfect bite." *Staples Mill Antiques* (410 Main St N, 651-430-1816, staplesmillantiques.com) has 10,000 square feet of showroom.

St. Croix Brewing Co.

Opening: Mid-summer 2015
Brewmaster: Tod Fyten II
Address: 114 East Chestnut Street • Stillwater, MN 55082
Phone: 651-387-0708
Web Site: www.stcroixbeer.com
Annual Production: 200 barrels
Number of Beers: 6 on tap; casks and kegs

Staple Beers:
- » St Croix Cream Ale
- » St Croix Creamy Brown
- » St Croix Cream Stout

Rotating Beers:
- » A whole variety of cask of Irish, Scottish, and British styles and perhaps a French Bière de Garde

Samples: Yes, flights available.

Best Time to Go: Open Thu 5–9PM, Fri–Sat noon–9PM. Possibly Sun noon–5PM in summer. Check the website.

Where can you buy it? Cask ales only here and perhaps a few local draft accounts; the keg beer is widely distributed, and St Croix bottles in Twin Cities, Twin Ports, and in Wisconsin in Brennan's Market.

Got food? No, but food friendly.

Tours? Yes, by appointment.

Special Offer: A free sample of their beer during your signature visit.

Directions: Coming into Stillwater from the south on MN 95, turn left up the hill on Olive St two blocks, then turn right on 3rd St. Turn right again a block later on Chestnut and the brewery is on the left. If you come into town from the west on Hwy 12/Myrtle St, turn right on 3rd St and take the next left to be right in front of the brewery.

The Beer Buzz: Tod Fyten—the owner of Mantorville Brewing Co. and Fytenburg Brewing—bought the rights to the old St. Croix brand, and gave this brewery as a gift to his wife Madeline on their 25th wedding anniversary. Not a bad gift, eh? So Madeline owns and Tod brews. Tod brews

Stagecoach brand beers in Mantorville, and contract brews bottled St. Croix beers at Lake Superior Brewing in Duluth. The kegged draft beers are brewed off site as well. But what Tod is brewing here in the basement are cask conditioned ales. Prior to the Fytens moving in here, the place was used by a local restaurateur who had tiled the basement and brought it up to kitchen specs—perfect for someone to slip a little brew system in here. A root cel-

MINNESOTA'S FIRST CAPITOL AND ST. CROIX BREWERY

The Capitol in St. Paul was the third structure there to serve as the capitol. But long before that, long before Minnesota was a state (1858) or even a territory (1849), the first capitol building was here in Stillwater. Joseph R. Brown was the first European settler to set up in this river valley and set the plan for the town of Dahcotah. Brown was a member of the Wisconsin Territorial Legislature and brought a bill through to create St. Croix County and Dahcotah was elected as county seat. Brown built Tamarack House as a courthouse and the first capitol in the state. If you follow Main St/MN 95 north out of town you can see an historical marker alongside the road.

Eventually the area became known as Dutchtown and on this same spot, Gerhard Knips founded a brewery in 1858. It ran into hard times and changed hands in 1877, and for less than a year it was St. Croix Brewery before giving up the ghost. Near the Tamarack House sign is an old lagering cave that has been covered over.

While the brewery was soon demolished, many of the other structures from that time still survive in Stillwater. Over 60 homes are Landmark homes, and over 300 are Heirloom homes, all protected for their historical significance and along with the historic downtown make quite an old-school atmosphere here along the waters of the St. Croix. Adding to the charm is an unusual lift bridge (from which another local brewery gets its name) which connects downtown Stillwater to Wisconsin's bluffs on the other side.

PHOTOS COURTESY OF ST CROIX BREWING CO.

lar with 50-degree temperatures was also perfect for his cask mission. So while three taps are occupied consistently by his other beers, the rest will be a constant rotation of whatever gets made for casks on site.

This building is the Brunswick House. Built in 1848 it is the oldest frame structure in Stillwater, and one of the oldest in the state even, yet it is not on the National Historic Register. It's older than the state *and* territory of Minnesota. The original meeting for the Independent Order of Odd Fellows (a benevolent fraternity) took place here in 1849. The Brunswick family purchased it in 1862 and remained there through three generations until 1968. The house survived a mudslide in 1852 which left the east wall bowed a bit, but it still sits here on the hill overlooking the historical downtown of Stillwater and out across the river to the bluffs of Wisconsin. Now it is a tiny brewery with a European pub feel to it. The taproom on the main floor holds perhaps 30 people, and still shows the original fir plank flooring from the St. Croix River Valley. Patrons can enjoy the fireplace room and a four season porch with a bar. In the backyard you will find a beer garden.

WiFi.

Stumbling Distance: You can get a 30-minute tour of the historic *Joseph Wolf Brewery* caves. The caves are not huge, but a good guide can fill the time with a lot of history. This is attached to *Luna Rossa* (402 Main St S, 651-430-0560, lunarossawinebar.com/cavetour.html) where you can dine on Italian fare.

ENKI Brewing

Opened: June 2013
Brewmaster: Jason Davis
Address: 7929 Victoria Dr • Victoria, MN 55386
Phone: 952-300-8408
Web Site: www.enkibrewing.com
Annual Production: 1,000 barrels
Number of Beers: 6–12 on tap

Staple Beers:
- » Auburn Kölsch
- » Journey Pale Ale
- » Tail Feather IPA
- » Victoria's Gold

Rotating Beers: (6–8 seasonals)
- » Cacao Porter
- » Creamery Reserve Line (brews only served in the taproom)

Most Popular Brew: Tail Feather IPA

Samples: Yes, four 5-oz. pours for about $10.

Brewmaster's Fave: Journey Pale Ale

Best Time to Go: Open Wed–Fri 4–10PM, Sat 12–10PM, Sun 12–6PM.

Where can you buy it? Here on tap and to go in growlers, and in over 90 bars and restaurants. 750 ml bottles available in regional liquor stores.

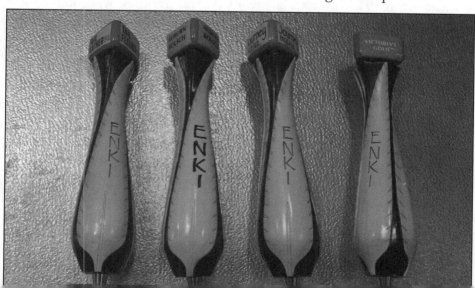

Got food? No, just some peanuts and pretzels for sale, but food friendly.

Tours? Yes, free tours on Saturdays from noon to 4PM, or by appointment.

Special Offer: Not participating at this time.

Directions: MN 5 passes right through Victoria as Arboretum Blvd. Turn north and go 1.5 blocks toward the lake on Victoria Dr and the brewery is a brick building on the right.

Cyclists: *The Lake Minnetonka LRT Regional Trail goes right past the brewery.*

The Beer Buzz: The brewery's motto is "Making the World a Friendlier Place—Two Beers at a Time" but this old brick building covered in vines got its start in 1917 as Victoria Creamery. The city itself was founded just two years before this was built. The creamery lasted until 1947, and a few of the current beer drinkers remember the place. If not for the brewery moving in, this may have ended up demolished and turned into a strip mall.

Owners John Hayes and Dan Norton met each other when they worked together at Nike back in the 80s. They used to run together in their free time, seeking out good beer afterwards. John's biochemistry and biophysics background eventually took him on a different path while Dan continued designing athletic shoes there, many of which were directly picked up by Olympians and World Record holders. Adidas hired Dan and he ended up in Germany where he collected 151 beer steins from as many breweries. In 2012, the two old friends got together and decided it was time to just do it: open a brewery.

Brewer Jason brewed for 12 years in Sioux Falls, South Dakota, and has 4 Great American Beer Festival awards to his credit. His wife took a job in the Twin Cities and they moved here. Jason to a job at Midwest Supplies where John found him. His spent grain goes to a dairy farmer a mile from here, and the cows get pretty thrilled about it.

The name ENKI comes from the Sumerian god of mischief and flowing water; his daughter Ninkasi was the goddess of beer. The oldest known written beer recipe can be found in a poem for Ninkasi etched into stone in the 19th century B.C. (ENKI is also an anagram of Nike. Coincidence?)

The small taproom has an open rafter ceiling and a bar with a corrugated tin front. Their contractor made the bar top as a gift using reclaimed barn floorboards. The brewery's logo is a tweaked version of a Sumerian icon and the feathers carry over to the tap handles. A beer garden outside has a view of Steiger Lake and a fire pit. Look for the faces on the outside of the building which were created by an artist who had been living upstairs. He had planned five but completed only four.

WiFi. Facebook.com/ENKIBrewing and Twitter @enkibrewing

Stumbling Distance: *The Victoria House* (1715 Steiger Lake Ln, 952-443-2858, cuzzys.com) serves ribs, burgers, salads and such. *Waconia Brewing* is just 7 miles west of here.

Schram Vineyards
Winery & Brewery

Opened: 2013 (Brewery: June 2014)
Brewers: Phil Petersen and Aaron Lorenzen
Address: 8785 Airport Road • Waconia, MN 55387
Phone: 612-229-8477
Web Site: www.SchramVineyards.com
Annual Production: 1,000 barrels
Number of Beers: 10–14 on tap but up to 26 possible; more than 20 beers per year

Staple Beers:
- » Blonde Ale
- » Brett and Barrel Sour Saison
- » Mocha Monkey Coffee Ale
- » IPA
- » Red Ale
- » Smoked Porter

Rotating Beers:
- » Bier de Garde
- » Double Barrel IPA
- » English Pub Ale
- » Gentleman Farmer Saison
- » Lucky Lederhosen Wheat

Most Popular Brew: Blonde Ale

Samples: Yes, flights of four 5-oz. beers for about $10. (Wine flights of 3 or 6 for $5/$10 plus a logoed wine glass with the $10 flight.)

Best Time to Go: Open Thu–Sun 11AM–11PM, but at the moment they cannot serve or sell beer on Sunday. That may change, so check website.

Where can you buy it? On draft here and in 750 ml bottles in liquor stores. Growlers likely by summer 2014 after some legal approvals.

Got food? Limited pre-packaged foods, cheese and crackers, and food trucks most days. Food friendly.

Tours? Tasting and tour options vary seasonally. Summer and fall: by reservation only, otherwise watch website for sign ups.

Special Offer: $1 off your first pint during your signature visit.

Directions: MN 5 passes through Waconia and intersects with Main St. Take Main St south (away from the lake and downtown) just 0.1 mile and take the first (possibly unmarked) left on Airport Rd. Go 0.3 miles, turn left to stay on Airport Rd for another 1 mile, and the brewery/vineyard is on the right.

The Beer Buzz: Husband and wife founders Aaron and Ashley Schram met, appropriately enough, in an Oktoberfest tent. Both were working in the Twin Cities corporate world—and still are. But Aaron, who grew up on a farm in Wisconsin, had picked up the hobby of winemaking while he was in college, and that, along with his green acres roots, compelled him to dream of someday starting a vineyard. In fact, on their first date Aaron told Ashley of his ambition and his enthusiasm was infectious. They ended up getting married and found this 12.5-acre farm where they started a family and a vineyard.

Then, because apparently with two kids, two dogs, a full-time job, and winemaking they weren't quite busy enough, they decided to add a brewery. Theirs is the first winery/brewery combo in the state of Minnesota. Though

PHOTO COURTESY SCHRAM VINEYARDS WINERY & BREWERY

they started on a modest 1.5-barrel system in June 2014, by the end of the year they were already looking to step up to a 7-barrel system—so they did.

Brewer Phil has many years of beer brewing experience and works with Aaron at the corporate job, and Aaron brought him in to take charge of the beer. Aaron Lorenzen, a friend of the couple's neighbor, came on to help out Phil.

The rules for wineries and breweries are different and in some cases a bit convoluted. The small white building you see is the brewery. The new building, a rustic-looking wood building completed in October 2014, houses the tasting room, a spacious area for events and even live music, and down below is the wine cellar. The two needed to be separate, and in order to serve beer there, the brewery is actually selling the beer to the winery. If they manage to tweak their small kitchen arrangement, they may soon be able to fill growlers as well. In front of the winery is an open pavilion with a bar, and there are other places to sit and enjoy a drink in green spaces. Windows in the taproom look out over the vineyards and down the hill to Reitz Lake in the distance. Two large bocce ball courts lie just along the vineyards as well.

The winery has a nice Case Club loyalty program and produces several whites, including pinot gris, chardonnay and a couple blends, a rosé, four reds, two honey wines, and a sparkling wine. Friends and family helped them plant over 4,000 vines, and now they produce a third of their own grape juice, while the rest comes from other Minnesota and Washington vineyards (half and half). The brewery partners with local hop growers and the future plans are to grow more ingredients to make this more of a farmhouse brewery.

Find them on Facebook and Twitter @SchramVineyards

Stumbling Distance: Waconia is a nice little tasting destination now, with a second brewery (*Waconia Brewing*) and two other wineries *Sovereign Estate Wine* (9950 N Shore Rd, 952-446-9957, sovereignestatewine.com) and *Parley Lake Winery* (8280 Parley Lake Rd, 952-442-2290, parley-lakewinery.com), also *J. Carver Distillery* (1320 Mill Lane, 952-442-2433, jcarverdistillery.com).

Waconia Brewing Co.

Founded: October 2014

Head Brewer: Tom Schufman

Address: 255 Main Street West • Waconia, MN 55387

Phone: 612-888-2739

Web Site: www.waconiabrewing.com

Annual Production: 600 barrels

Number of Beers: 8–12 on tap; 30+ beers each year

Staple Beers:
- » Carver Co. Kölsch
- » 90K IPA
- » 255 Amber Ale
- » WacTown Wheat

Rotating Beers:
- » Laketown Brown
- » Mo'Winta Milk
- » Single Hop Series IPAs
- » 342
- » Waconia Wit
- » Various seasonals, stouts, wit and such, occasional firkin releases
- » … plus some barrel aging with local J. Carver barrels.

Most Popular Brew: 90K IPA or 255 Amber Ale

Samples: Yes, flight of six 5-oz. pours for about $12

Brewmaster's Fave: Mo'Winta Milk Stout

Best Time to Go: Mon–Tue closed. Open Wed–Thu 2–9PM, Fri 2–10PM, Sat 11–10PM, Sun 11–6PM. Game nights every other Wednesday.

Where can you buy it? On tap or in growlers to go. Some bottling is planned and they have draft accounts in the Waconia area (west of I-494).

Got food? Just free popcorn, menus for ordering in, and food trucks often on weekends. Food friendly. Root beer on tap.

Tours? Yes, by appointment or by chance.

Special Offer: A free pint when you get your book signed.

Directions: MN 5 passes right through Waconia. Follow this into town from either direction and turn north on Olive St (toward the lake). Go 0.5 mile, then turn left on Main St. The brewery is on the left at the corner of Main and Maple, but turn left onto Vine, the block before, to get into the parking lot.

The Beer Buzz: For over a century there hasn't been a brewery in Waconia, not since the original Waconia Brewing Co. closed its doors in 1890. Now there's two. This brewery is a family affair. Owners Peter and Kaye DeLange quit their day jobs to take this on. His brother Bob is COO and Bob's wife Dee runs the taproom. Their brother Kevin owns Dry Dock Brewing in Colorado and gave them advice. All of them got their start homebrewing.

Brewer Tom has worked around a bit, including some time at Summit Brewing, Northern Brewery, and Fulton Brewing. He saw Waconia's ad and came for the head brewer job.

This building was a daycare before this. Now it's an adult daycare. The old playground will become an outdoor patio. The stained concrete floor has a sort of bowling ball look to it. The taproom is large with room for 120. There's a photo of the 19th century Waconia Brewery and the brewery initials on the wall were made with 5,700 screws painstakingly placed there by Bob and Dee's daughter Danielle and Pete and Kaye's son Cody. Reclaimed barn wood on the walls contrasts a concrete bar with sheet metal in front and outlets and purse hangers under the counter. The taproom has an adult coffeehouse vibe with some soft seating, a gas fireplace, board games, cribbage, background music, and a couple of TVs. Musicians perform on occasion, mostly acoustic music.

No ATM on site, but there's one at a bank 1.5 blocks away. WIFI. Find them on Facebook and Twitter @WaconiaBrewing

Stumbling Distance: See also *Schram Vineyards Winery & Brewery*. Besides great coffee *Mocha Monkey* (115 S Olive St, 952-442-2853, themochamonkey.com) has sandwiches and baked goods. Handcrafted and delicious *Laketown Chocolates* (141 W 1st St, 952-442-1063, laketownchocolates.com) merits a visit. Citywide festival *Nickle Dickle Day* (nickledickle.com) is in September. *Enki Brewing* is just 7 miles east of here in Victoria.

Big Wood Brewery

Founded: May 2009
Brewmaster: Ty McBee
Address: 2222 4th Street • White Bear Lake, MN 55110
Phone: 612-360-2986
Web Site: www.bigwoodbrewery.com
Annual Production: 5,000 barrels
Number of Beers: 10 on tap, often one on nitro

Staple Beers:
- » Amigo Grande Mexican Lager
- » Bark Bite IPA
- » Jack Savage American Pale Ale
- » Morning Wood Coffee Stout

Rotating Beers:
- » Bad Axe Imperial IPA
- » Big Black Wolf Black IPA
- » Dubbel Entendre (oak wood-aged double brown)
- » Forest Fire Smoked Imperial Rye
- » Udder Stout (milk stout)
- » Wicked Ex IPA

Most Popular Brew: Jack Savage APA

Samples: Yes, flights of five 5-oz. pours for about $11

Brewmaster's Fave: Bad Axe Double IPA

Best Time to Go: Wed–Fri 3–11PM, Sat 1–11PM.

Where can you buy it? On tap in pints and half pints, and to go in growlers. Distributed in 4-packs of 16 oz. cans in six states: IA, MN, NE, ND, SD, WI.

Got food? No, but food friendly.

Tours? Yes, Saturdays at noon and it's free. Check website calendar to confirm or register.

Special Offer: $1 off your first pint during your signature visit.

Directions: From I-694, take Exit 48 and go north on US 61 for 3.7 miles. Turn right on 4th St, and go 0.1 mile and it's on your right. The entrance is in back, as is a parking lot, so turn right on Cook Ave to get to the back of the building.

The Beer Buzz: Founder Steve Merila's background is in the hardwood flooring business. The recession hit and he started brewing and found he liked it. A license was approved in 2009, and in 2011, Brewer Ty, a self-taught homebrewer came to brew here. No sooner was he hired than his coffee stout won a best beer award at the Autumn Brew Review.

A few steps down from sidewalk level, the taproom features a three-sided square bar, tall tables and chairs—all made out of big, heavy wood. The bar top came from a downed tree, and the reclaimed barn wood on the walls is from around Minnesota. A local sailboat manufacturer razed their old building which the brewery pilfered for the bar rail. The sample flights are served on strips of tongue and groove. The current beers are listed on a slate blackboard from an old schoolhouse. Growlers with the bottoms cut off function as lamp shades above the bar. Add the odd hobbit-like doors and brass knockers and the place leaves quite an impression when you first see it.

Steve explains that the brewery name comes from the abundance of wood in the taproom as well as "12 year old humor." The pint glasses are marked with a ruler that denotes half wood and full wood.

Don't expect TVs, but there is ping pong in another room, and, of course, cribbage. A stage occupies a corner for live music. There's parking on the street in front, but the entrance is in back as is a parking lot.

Tree Chuggers is a sort of Mug Club with an annual membership fee. WiFi. Facebook.com/BigWoodBrewery and Twitter @BigWoodBrewery

Stumbling Distance: *Washington Square Bar & Grill* (4736 Washington Square, 651-407-7162, washingtonsquareonline.net) is good for breakfast thru dinner, and has 20 craft beers on tap, typically including Big Wood. *Donatelli's* (2692 East County Road E, 651-777-9199, donatellis. com) has Italian pizza, pasta and burgers, plus MN beers including Big Wood. *Ban Thai* (2186 3rd St, 651-407-8424, banthaionline.com) is the best for Thai food.

ZONE 3
Southern Minnesota

Oswald Brewing Co. . . . . Blue Earth
F-Town Brewing Co. . . . . .Faribault
Wenonah Brewing Co. . . . . Goodview
Bank Brewing Co. . . . . Hendricks
Mankato Brewery . . . . Mankato
Mantorville Brewing Co. (dba Stagecoach Brewing Co.). . . . . . . Mantorville
Brau Brothers Brewing Co . . . . .Marshall
Montgomery Brewing. . . . . Montgomery
August Schell Brewing Co. . . . . .New Ulm
Reads Landing Brewing Co. . . . . .Reads Landing
Red Wing Brewing . . . . Red Wing
Kinney Creek Brewery . . . . .Rochester
LTS Brewing. . . . . .Rochester
Olvalde Farm and Brewing Co. . . . . .Rollingstone

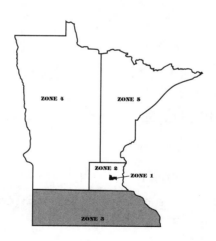

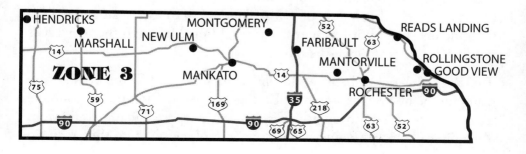

Oswald Brewing Co.

Founded: 2015
Head Brewer: John Oswald
Address: 110 South Main Street • Blue Earth, MN 56013
Phone: 507-526-3101
Web Site: www.oswaldbrewingcompany.com
Annual Production: 300 barrels
Number of Beers: 6–8 on tap

Beers:
- » Berserker NPA (Norwegian pale ale)
- » Eric the Red (amber ale)
- » Fjord Farm Ale (Nordic interpretation of Belgian saison)
- » Odin's Porter
- » Thor's Steam
- » Valkyrie Wheat

Most Popular Brew: Eric the Red

Samples: Yes, sample flights.

Brewmaster's Fave: Berserker NPA

Best Time to Go: Tentatively open Wed–Thu 1–7PM, Fri–Sat 1–10PM. Check the website to confirm.

Where can you buy it? Here on tap and in growlers to go for starters.

Got food? No, but food friendly.

Tours? Yes, informal and by appointment.

Special Offer: 15% off your merchandise purchase (not including the Das Horns) during your signature visit.

Directions: US 169 runs north-south through Blue Earth as Grove St. At a traffic circle in the middle of town take the 7th St exit heading west for 0.6 mile on 7th St until Main St. Turn right on Main and the brewery is on the left 240 feet down the block.

The Beer Buzz: Husband and wife team John and Tami Oswald are bringing the first brewery to Blue Earth since before Prohibition. John is a native son here and moved back for this very purpose. He met Tami from Yuengling Country (Pennsylvania) out in Colorado where they married and started a family. During his 14 years in Colorado, he was surrounded by one of the most serious craft beer scenes in the nation, and unsurprisingly he took up homebrewing. He toured many places, especially small intimate nanobreweries, which is what he is aiming for here.

The Nordic theme of his beer and the longship on the logo are a nod to his Norwegian heritage. Moving back to Blue Earth was good for the family and the brewery offered some craft brew for an under-served community.

The brewery is located in the former First and Farmers National Bank building built back in 1930. The façade is sandstone and marble, and you'll see Art Deco motives throughout including the plaster frieze crown moldings. Terrazzo flooring remains from the bank days as well. The taproom is roomy with a bar in back and tables in the center. Shuffleboard, foosball, and darts are on offer and all are free. It's a family friendly sort of place.

Facebook/Oswald-brewing-company-inc and Twitter @oswaldbrewingco

Stumbling Distance: The menu at *Double Play Bar & Grill* (115 E 6th St, 507-526-3032) includes pizza and other bar food. Blue Earth is the home of a 55.5-foot-tall *Jolly Green Giant*, so don't forget to stop for a photo with the old boy (1126 Giant Drive).

PHOTO COURTESY OF OSWALD BREWING

F-Town Brewing Co.

Opened: July 2015
Brewers: Noah Strouth and Chris Voegele
Address: 22 Fourth Street NE • Faribault, MN 55021
Phone: 507-331-7677
Web Site: www.ftownbeer.com
Annual Production: 2,200 barrels
Number of Beers: up to 16 on tap; 20+ styles per year

Staple Beers:
  » IPAlicious (IPA)
  » #1 American (American pale ale)
  » FLEX Less (craft light lager)
  » FLEX More (craft premium lager)
  » Nutso (nut brown ale)
  » Stout

Most Popular Brews: IPAlicious and Nutso

Samples: Yes, sample flights.

Brewmaster's Fave: Noah: IPAs and Sours | Chris: Stout and IPA

Best Time to Go: Confirm via website once they are open for business! Tentatively open Wed–Fri at 3PM; Sat at noon.

Where can you buy it? Here on tap and in growlers to go, and distributed in cans and kegs in Southern and Central Minnesota and the south Twin Cities Metro Area.

Got food? No, but food friendly. Food trucks at peak times.

Tours? Eventually. Tours will be scheduled and you can sign up on the website.

Special Offer: 15% off any purchase of apparel or merchandise from the taproom during your signature visit.

Directions: Coming south from Minneapolis (about 45 minutes) on I-35, take Exit 56 for MN 60 east toward Faribault. This becomes 4th St. Go 2.4 miles and the brewery is on the left.

The Beer Buzz: Partners Noah Strouth, Chris Voegele, and Travis Temke brought brewing back to Faribault which hasn't had a brewery in 51 years.

But beer history goes back to before statehood: Fleckenstein Brewery was the first of a few Faribault breweries and opened across the river from here in 1856. Family disputes brought it to a close in 1964.

Noah and Chris homebrewed over a decade and built an automated half barrel pilot system. They have created and perfected over 20 recipes in that time, and together with Travis, an experienced entrepreneur and business owner, they sought funding and finally started moving forward in late 2014. The brewery features a 15-barrel brewhouse with four 30-barrel fermenters and an automated canning line. They are committing to using local ingredients for their five flagship beers.

In the 1880s Peterson's Art Furniture manufactured their product here, and you can still see much of the design from the original quarry stone and clay brick building. The taproom is up front with local artists' work displayed on the walls and a number of TVs piping in sports. All the furniture is designed and manufactured by a local wood carver and designer. A patio outside is in development.

Find them on Facebook and Twitter @FTownbeer

Stumbling Distance: *The Cheese Cave* (318 Central Ave N # 6, 507-334-3988 cheesecave.net) is the factory outlet store for the award-winning *Caves of Faribault* (faribaultdairy.com) and shouldn't be missed. Weekly fresh curds. The caves refer to sandstone caverns near the Straight River, and while today they are used to age cheese, back in the mid-1800s, German immigrant brewer Gottfried Fleckenstein lagered his beer here. *Faribault Woolen Mills* (1500 2nd Ave NW, 507-412-5534, faribaultmill.com), making world-famous blankets (and more) since 1865, is the oldest such mill in the US and the oldest existing company in Minnesota. They give tours and have a great factory store.

Photo Courtesy F-Town Brewing

Wenonah Brewing Co.

Opened: October 2013
Brewers: Chris Gardner, Steve Barber, Dave Weinhold, Paul Brown
Address: 4065 6th Street • Goodview, MN 55987
Phone: 507-429-0730
Web Site: www.wenonahbrewingcompany.com
Annual Production: 420 barrels
Number of Beers: 4 on tap

Staple Beers:
  » Nut Brown
  » Pale Ale

Rotating Beers:
  » Bourbon Brown (on occasion)
  » Bragget Mead
  » IPA (with local fresh hops)
  » Kölsch
  » Oatmeal Stout (winter)
  » Wild Rice Ale

Most Popular Brew: 50/50 for Nut Brown and Pale Ale

Samples: Yes, three or four for $5.

Brewmaster's Fave: Pale Ale

Best Time to Go: Open Thu–Fri 4–10PM, Sat 2–10PM, Sun 11:30AM–3PM (Sunday "if the lights are on"). A lot of live music randomly.

Where can you buy it? On tap here, and in growlers to go. 8–10 draft accounts in Wenonah, Rochester, and Stewartville.

Got food? No, maybe pretzels, but food friendly. Also, local deliveries.

Tours? Yes, and you can do it without leaving your seat; you may have to turn your head, however.

Special Offer: $1 off your first pint during your signature visit.

Directions: US 61 along the Mississippi River passes through Goodview/Winona. Coming from the north, turn left on 44th Ave, go 4 blocks, and turn right on 6th St. The brewery is one block down on the right. Coming from the south on US 61, turn right on Pelzer St, go 0.3 mile, and turn left on 5th St. Stay on here 0.5 mile and it magically becomes 6th St and the brewery is on your left at the corner of 41st Ave.

The Beer Buzz: Here's a good place to stop and fill 'er up. What appears to be an abandoned gas station is a different sort of filling station. The four partners—Chris Gardner, Steve Barber, Dave Weinhold, and Paul Brown—collaborate to keep this little place stocked with beer. Chris started homebrewing in the early 90s when the microbrew revolution was on and went on to get his brewer training at Siebel. While selling brewing supplies, he saw an ad for a 1-barrel brew system. So he snatched it up and opened a brewpub in 1995 called Backwater Brewing. This survived until 2011. But he wasn't done with breweries. He and his friend Steve had talked of opening one over 20 years ago while at a rock concert. When Backwater shut down, Steve reminded him and kept badgering him until he relented. They pulled another friend, Dave into the operation, and Paul eventually joined as well.

In the middle of town stood an old grocery store (not a defunct gas station—the pumps and canopy out front had been added later on.) The three original partners looked through the window, saw it was empty, and saw the floor drain. There was space and parking, charm and history, and

the coveted floor drain, which meant no need to bust up concrete to create one for a brewhouse. Additionally, there was an operational cooler and a natural gas line. All the pieces were there. Dave started the paperwork in 2012 and got approval in 2013.

This is all just a part-time gig for them—moonlighting, if you will. They all kept their day jobs and they all share the brewing. Steve has a business and Dave runs a tree service. "We want to make really good beer, something to brag about," says Gardner. With the small system they are constantly juggling to keep up with the distributor and bars and still have variety on hand for taproom patrons.

The brew system is right up in front like a kitchen. The taproom area has some tall tables and a bar along the wall, but this is a small space. Still, you might find the occasional live music and there's a dartboard. No shortage of parking here. There's an ATM at the bank across the street and at *The Bar*.

WiFi. Facebook.com/pages/Wenonah-Brewing-Company

Stumbling Distance: *BoatHouse Restaurant* (2 Johnson St, Winona, 507-474-6550, boathousewinona.com) offer fine dining right on the Mississippi River. *Rocco's Pub & Pizza* (5242 W 6th St, Goodview, 507-454-5911, roocospubandpizza.com) is a local favorite for thin-crust, deep-dish, and Chicago-style pizza, and they deliver to the taproom. *The Bar* (4054 W 6th St, Goodview, 507-454-0128) right across the street has bands every Saturday night.

BREWS BROTHERS

The Trappist monasteries have their brewing monks, but Minnesota has brewing seminarians. You've heard of Minnesota's Brau Brothers Brewing in Marshall, but at St. Thomas Aquinas Seminary in Winona they've got brewing brothers. The students have taken up the art of homebrewing, and since about 2008 or so they have been producing their own beer for monthly gatherings. The grain is donated to the seminary, and the brewing work and its subsequent enjoyment builds community among the brothers. The knowledge of the process is passed down to younger students to keep the tradition alive. The seminary, however, is moving to Virginia in the near future and the tradition will follow.

Bank Brewing Company

Founded: 2009
Brewmasters: Jason Markkula and Richard Drawdy
Address: 216 Main Street • Hendricks, MN 56136
Phone: see website
Web Site: www.bankbeer.com and www.beerforwildlife.com
Annual Production: 500 barrels plus 1,000 bbls contracted in cans
Number of Beers: 10+ beers per year, up to 6 on tap at the tap room.

Staple Beers:

- » 1876 Rye Ale *
- » Hop Bandit
- » Hop Lab
- » Sour Bomb
- » Walleye Chop Lager *
- » Wanted

Rotating Beers:

- » Gulch Rye Ale *
- » Into the Black
- » Rooster Lager (Sep-Dec)*
- » Longbeard Winter Wheat Lager *
- » Smoke Bomb

Beer for Wildlife

Most Popular Brew: Sour Bomb or Hop Bandit

Samples: Yes, $2 each for a build your own flight

Brewmaster's Fave: Walleye Chop Lager

Best Time to Go: Tap room open Fri–Sat 4–8PM.

Where can you buy it? Minnesoa and Dakotas in cans, bottles, 750s and bombers. Pints, samplers, growler fills, and 750s at the tap room.

Got food? Just some snacks, but food friendly and there's a bar next door with food to carry in.

Tours: By appointment and by request.

Special Offer: A free beer when you get your book signed.

Directions: Hendricks lies between I-29 (in South Dakota) and US 75. From the east take County Road 17 west (8 miles from US 75) and follow it through town. It joins Hwy 271 as Division St. Turn left on Garfield St (still CR 17), then the 2nd right (north) is on Main St. Go another block and the taproom is on your right at the first corner and the brewery is on the right at the end of that block. From I-29, take SD 30 east (Exit 140) and it becomes MN 19 over the border. Turn left on MN 271 and it takes you into town to a left on Garfield St as indicated above.

The Beer Buzz: Imagine a 3.5-hour commute to work. That's pretty much what brewer/owner Jason Markkula endures for the love of his beer. But the story here beyond the beer passion is one of preservation—conserving land and wildlife, but also some local history.

Jason started brewing like many: on the kitchen stove until he was kicked out to the garage. Meanwhile he was, and still is, an avid hunter and loves the prairie here for pheasant hunting. As a traveling salesman for power tools, Jason needed to come to Hendricks on business. The local hardware store and lumberyard was one of his visits. They owned the 1900 State Bank of Hendricks building on the short main street, and they kept it only to prevent its demolition. Jason is one part brewer and one part construction worker. He frequently hand-builds gadgets for the brewery and life in general. The self-reliance theme is strong here and in the town as well. It's part of the culture. When Jason expressed interest, they sold it to him.

From the 1940s to the 1970s, Irene's Café occupied the old bank, but after that it was boarded up until 2006. Jason found four feet of water in the basement and the roof had partly collapsed. For the next 2.5 years he came to work on it on the weekends, finally finishing the remodel of what would be his "hunting lodge." But sitting around with some friends there, they came up with the brewing idea. Where once there was a bank vault, now there is a restroom. The former lobby is occupied by a 15-foot oak bar.

In 2009 he started contract brewing what he calls Beer For Wildlife. For every case of these BFW brews (see beers with asterisks above), $1 goes to Build a Wildlife Area, a program put together by Pheasants Forever. Hendricks has its own chapter and the brewery works directly with them. To date, the organization has bought over 11,000 acres of private land just in Lincoln County and converted them to public conservation acreage.

But preservation didn't end with the bank or the prairie. At the other end of the block stood the dilapidated Farmers' Creamery, a brick affair from the early 1900s. After it ceased operations in the late 70s, it stood abandoned until 2011. Jason took that on and again put in 2.5 years of construction before opening it as his brewery in June 2014.

The taproom at the old bank has a bar and some old kitchen cabinets, and a giant Jenga room. "You should hear that thing rattle the floor when that thing goes down. Scares people in the front room." The fenced in backyard functions as a little beer garden with picnic tables.

NB Golf Cars originated in Hendricks and locals license them to drive legally around town. While this town of 700 may seem remote, especially when you try to use your cell phone, agriculture and recreation keep the place alive, and it actually gets busy in summer. And it's got a good brewery, so it's worth the drive.

Facebook.com/BankBrewingCo and Twitter @bankbrewing

Stumbling Distance: *Lake Hendricks* is the center attraction and the park there offers campsites. Play a round at *Hendricks Golf Club* (1037 North Shore Dr, 507-275-3852, hendricksgolfclub.com). *Cedric's on Main* (206 S Main St, 507-275-3586) is your best bet for food. It's 42 minutes to *Brau Brothers* in Marshall to the east and 35 minutes to *Wooden Legs Brewing Co.* (309 5th St, Brookings, SD, 605-692-2337, woodenlegsbrewing.com) to the west if you want to make a hat-trick of your trip to SW Minnesota. It's 69 miles south to *Take 16 Brewing* (509 East Main St, Luverne, 866-663-9986, take16beer.com) which at the moment contract brews with South Shore Brewing in northern Wisconsin.

Travel Warnings: Marshall is the closest place to stay at the moment. Cell phone users: AT&T doesn't work well, Sprint is so-so on one end of town, and Verizon is good.

MANKATO BREWERY

Founded: 2010 (opened January 2012)
Head Brewer: Jacob Hamilton
Address: 1119 Center Street • North Mankato, MN 56003
Phone: 507-386-2337
Web Site: www.mankatobrewery.com
Annual Production: 1,900 barrels
Number of Beers: 4–5 on tap (plus root beer)

Staple Beers:
- » CROOKED ROOK PORTER
- » HAYMAKER IPA
- » ORGAN GRINDER (amber)

Rotating Beers:
- » CERES SUMMER ALE (American wheat ale)
- » DULY NOTED PALE ALE
- » IMPERIAL RED ALE
- » LEAF RAKER NUT BROWN ALE (fall)
- » MANKATO ORIGINAL (Kölsch-style in summer)
- » MINT STOUT (holiday season)
- » STICKÜM (alt in fall or Feb)
- » … plus regular nano-batches and infused versions of their beers

Most Popular Brew: Organ Grinder

Samples: Yes, four 5-oz. pours for about $6.

Best Time to Go: Taproom is open Tue, Thu–Fri 4–7PM, Sat 12–7PM.

Where can you buy it? On tap in the taproom and in growlers to go (but not for nano-batches). Bottles and draft accounts in the Twin Cities area and southern Minnesota.

Got food? Only free popcorn. Sometimes a vendor comes in. Food friendly.

Tours? Often scheduled on Saturdays (check website) or by appointment.

Special Offer: A free pint glass with your book signature.

Directions: From US 169/MN 60, just 0.8 mile south of its juncture with US 14, take Webster Ave west (away from the river), and go 0.3 mile. Turn right on Center St and the brewery is 200 feet down on the left.

The Beer Buzz: Mankato Brewing Co. closed in the 1960s, part of the gradual death of local breweries as the handful of giants either drove them out of business or bought up their labels. But then along came Tony Feuchtenberger and Tim Tupy, a couple of homebrewing friends with entrepreneurial savvy to resurrect the name and bring Mankato its first craft brewery. They created a plan, rounded up investors, and went looking for a head brewer in 2010. Mike Miziorko had spent 5 years brewing at Summit Brewing Co. and took on the challenge of building a brand from the ground up. He spent just over a year at Mankato before Bobby Blasey took the reins. When Bobby moved on, Jacob Hamilton, stepped up to run the show.

The Mankato mission is to keep things local as much as possible. The bottles are from Minnesota as is the cardboard for packaging. Labels are printed locally and were designed by designer/photographer Amy Viland, one of Tony's high school friends.

Beer names often have a story; here is no different. *Organ Grinder* recalls a Mankato organ-box entertainer of long ago who kept a monkey who liked to take a beer now and then. *Duly Noted* refers to Tony listening to remarks and suggestions about other beers and then taking them into account for this beer. It's also dry hopped twice with two different hops

so there is a pun with "dually." *Sticküm* comes from the story of a German brewer who was drinking too much while brewing and lost track of how much malt he added—so he adds even more. His drinkers whisper to each other, "I think he got carried away." According to the brewers, Sticküm means to speak on the sly behind a cupped hand.

The brewery is in a large industrial building and just inside is the tasting area behind a metal railing with picnic tables, some tall tables, and bar stools with a view of production, plus a sort of mezzanine/upper deck with a few more seats and a higher view of the brewhouse. The beers are poured in a corner room with a bar of rough cut wood and corrugated zinc sheets and a gift shop area. An outdoor patio is through a screened utility door. For entertainment you've got giant versions of Connect Four and Jenga, a pool table, foosball, and hammer schlagen, and an MB stage features occasional live performances.

WiFi. Facebook.com/mankatobrewery and Twitter @MankatoBrewery

Stumbling Distance: *Pub 500* (500 S Front St, 507-625-6500, pub500. com) serves several Mankato and other Minnesota beers. Try *Pappageorge Restaurant* (1028 N Riverfront Dr, 507-387-8974, pappageorge.net) for steak and seafood fine dining. *Pagliai's Pizza* (524 S Front St, 507-345-6080, pagliaismankato.com) has the best pie in town, Mankato on tap, and delivers here.

MINNESOTA RIVER VALLEY NATIONAL SCENIC BYWAY

This is a road-trip book, so while you're not drinking, you're going to be doing a lot of driving. And let me tell you, there are a number of great drives in this state. One of them begins only 40 minutes south of downtown Minneapolis near the town of Belle Plaine.

The Minnesota River Valley National Scenic Byway runs from this starting point and heads southwest to Mankato, then northwest across the prairielands to the border of South Dakota at Brown Valley. The 287-mile drive passes through brew cities **Mankato** (*Mankato Brewery*), **Blakeley** (*u4ic Brewing*), and **New Ulm** (*August Schell Brewing*), offering some sudsy stops for the night as you go. (Other worthy brew visits lie south of the last half of that route in **Marshall** (*Brau Brothers*) and **Hendricks** (*Bank Brewing*).

EXPLORE MINNESOTA

The byway offers much natural beauty, various park and protected wildlife areas good for hiking and paddling, historical sites and museums, and friendly communities. Learn some history at **Joseph R. Brown Heritage Society and Minnesota River Center** in Henderson. The **Historic District of St. Peter** has 13 sites on the National Registry. Don't miss a hike to see **Minneopa Falls** in the state park of the same name. See the **Glockenspiel** in New Ulm, visit the **Schell Brewery and Museum**, and stay in a bed and breakfast. Stop at the 1870s **Harkin General Store**, maintained by the state historical society. Learn about **the Dakota** people at several historical sites along the route. See exposed rock from 3.8 million years ago at **Yellow Medicine County Museum** in Granite Falls then pay a visit to **Prohibitionist Andrew Volstead's** 1878 house (163 Ninth Ave, 320-564-3011, gfhistoricalsociety.weebly. com) and take a **Prohibition walking tour** of town. You'll see eagles and a variety of other birds and wildlife along this route, and opportunities for hiking or paddling are many.

Minnesota River Valley National Scenic Byway
888-463-9856 | mnrivervalley.com

MANTORVILLE BREWING CO.
(DBA STAGECOACH BREWING CO.)

Founded: 1996
Brewmaster: Tod Fyten II
Address: 101 East 5th Street • Mantorville, MN 55955
Phone: 651-387-0708
Web Site: www.stagecoachbeer.com
Annual Production: 1,000 barrels
Number of Beers: 3 on tap

Staple Beers:
- » STAGECOACH AMBER
- » STAGECOACH GOLDEN HONEY ALE
- » STAGECOACH SMOKED PORTER

Rotating Beers:
- » RYE WHISKEY ALE (spring)

Most Popular Brew: Stagecoach Amber Ale

Samples: Yes, on the tour.

Brewmaster's Fave: Stagecoach Smoked Porter

Best Time to Go: By appointment only. There are no regular opening hours, but they are planning for Saturday tours eventually. Check the website.

Where can you buy it? Distributed in the Twin Cities and Rochester area, and Brennan's stores in Wisconsin.

Got food? No.

Tours: By appointment only. $5 per person including samples.

Special Offer: A free sample of beer during your signature visit.

Directions: MN 57 runs north-south through town as Main St. At 5th St, turn east and go 400 feet and the brewery is on the right at a curve in the road at the corner of Blanch St.

The Beer Buzz: Tod Fyten's family has been in the beer business since 1869 when his great great grandfather Theodore worked in several St. Paul breweries. His grandfather worked at Jacob Schmidt Brewery. Tod, for his own part, learned about fermentation when he was 10 years old, making wine with his father. He moved on to root beer and sodas, gateway brews, before he started homebrewing beer in college. He went on to work as a rep for Pabst and Leinenkugel's, but started to learn the ropes of professional brewing when he worked at James Page Brewing, one of the original Minnesota craft brewers. He calls Zig Plagens, former brewmaster at Jacob Schmidt Brewery, his mentor. He'd go over there to get yeast for James Page and Zig would chat him up. This was how it was in the early days of craft brewing, says Tod. But Tod eventually moved into publishing; in 2006 Tod and Mike Urseth took over Brewers Digest—the oldest American brewers publication, founded in 1933—from Ron Siebel and Tom Volke. But he never let go of beer. In 1999, he came in as a partner for the brewery in Mantorville, and three years later bought out the others to become the sole owner. In 2003 he bought the St. Croix brand, and he gave the brewery in Stillwater to his wife Madeline as an anniversary gift.

The brewery occupies a former car wash—this may be a first—but sits on the 1857 site of the original Mantorville Brewery. The ruins of that brewery sit across Brewery Creek from here. The brewery isn't typically open to the public, but tours can be arranged by calling Tod. Scheduled Saturday tours may be in the works, however.

Facebook.com/StagecoachBeer and Twitter @stagecoachbeer

Stumbling Distance: *The Hubbell House* (502 N Main St, 507-635-2331, hubbellhouserestaurant.com), a restaurant since 1854, stands right across the street, and though it's a steakhouse, the menu is rather varied. Trivia note: Ulysses S. Grant stayed there.

Brau Brothers Brewing Company

Founded: 2006
Brewmaster: Dustin Brau
Address: 910 East Main Street • Marshall, MN 56258
Phone: 507-747-2337
Web Site: www.braubeer.com
Annual Production: 4,000 barrels
Number of Beers: 12 on tap plus 2 casks; 7–10 in distribution

Staple Beers:
- » Bancreagie Peated Scotch Ale ("bon-cray-gee")
- » Moo Joos Oatmeal Milk Stout
- » Old No. 56 (American light lager)
- » The Ring Neck Braun Ale
- » Sheephead Ale
- » White Cap Crystal Wit Bier

Rotating Beers:
- » Brau Brothers Barrel Aged Belgian Style Quad Ale
- » Hopsession Super Pale Ale
- » 100 Yard Dash Fresh Hopped Ale
- » Ivan the Great Russian Imperial Stout
- » Rye Wyne Ale
- » Strawberry Wheat
- » … plus some barrel aging and sours

Most Popular Brew: Moo Joos Oatmeal Milk Stout

Samples: Yes, sips for decision making and flights of five 5-oz. pours for about $8.

Brewmaster's Fave: Sheephead Ale

Best Time to Go: Mon–Sun 11AM–11PM. Happy hour runs Mon–Fri 4–6PM. Tuesdays growler fills are discounted. Watch for the brewery's Hopfest, normally the first weekend in September, a three-day event with plenty of beer and live polka music in the parking lot.

Where can you buy it? In the taproom on tap and to go in growlers and 750s. Distributed in six-pack bottles, barrels, and occasional 750 ml releases across the upper Midwest: IA, MI, MN, NE, ND, SD, and WI.

Got food? Yes, a full menu of appetizers, salads, burgers and sandwiches, and in-house smoked meats. Local bison, smoked turkey wings, pulled pork. Many items involve beer in the recipes. Friday night fish fries during Lent. Also, ten housemade sodas, including root beer.

Tours: Yes, Saturdays at 2PM or by appointment.

Special Offer: A free pint glass with your book signature.

Directions: MN 23 and US 59 meet at the south side of Marshall. The brewery lies right here on the west side of the X they make. Go north on US 59/Main St, and turn left on Southview Dr. You can see the huge parking lot there on your left.

The Beer Buzz: Some people are just destined for things. Take Brewer Dustin's last name, the German word for beer? Dustin started homebrewing in college in the mid-90s and had the goal to open up a brewpub in a small town someday. He's been brewing commercially since 1999 when he operated a nanobrewery in a restaurant in nearby Lucan. But growth came fast—the system started with 15-gallons, then moved up to 2 barrels, then 15—and since a brewpub could not distribute, they decided to switch things up. In 2006 the brewery moved to a bigger location and got rid of the restaurant.

Thanks to the Surly Bill, the law was changed to allow production breweries to operate a taproom. So in October 2013, Brau Brothers moved into what used to be a large hardware store here in Marshall, and now he has a bottling line and the capacity to do up to 12,000 barrels in a year. He also was able to bring back a restaurant element. Along with Surly Brewing, this is one of (currently) two taprooms in Minnesota that also serve food.

Inside the taproom floors are polished concrete, and patrons sit at restaurant tables, booths and tall tables. The bar is a stainless steel top and behind it is a real 1956 fire truck functioning as the back bar. Dustin, a former volunteer firefighter, actually fought fires on that thing back in Lucan.

The brewery maintains a large hopyard—the largest in the upper Midwest—at the previous location, with 11 varieties, and grows barley as well. Dustin even built his own special hop picker. Rye grows within sight of the front door. The seasonal 100 Yard Dash was thus named because originally the hop fields were about 100 yards from the brew kettle. Lactose sugar for the highly popular Moos Joos comes from a local dairy, actually the first robotic dairy in Minnesota.

WiFi. Facebook.com/Brau-Brothers-Brewing-Co and Twitter @BrauBeer

Stumbling Distance: *Mariachi Fiesta* (329 W Main St, 507-532-2122) has great salsa and margaritas. If you prefer ribs and other barbecue, try *Hitching Post* (1104 E Main St, 507-929-2228). *Super 8* (1106 E Main St, 507-537-1461, super8.com) is a short walk from here if you need a place to stay. It's 42 minutes to *Bank Brewing* in Hendricks and another 35 minutes after that to *Wooden Legs Brewing Co.* (309 5th St, Brookings, SD, 605-692-2337, woodenlegsbrewing.com) if you want to make a hat-trick of your trip to SW Minnesota. It's 69 miles south to *Take 16 Brewing* (509 East Main St, Luverne, 866-663-9986, take16beer.com) which at the moment contract brews with South Shore Brewing in northern Wisconsin.

Montgomery Brewing

Opened: December 27, 2014
Head Brewer: Alan "AJ" Newton
Address: 306 2nd Street NW • Montgomery, MN 56069
Phone: TBD
Web Site: www.montgomerybrewing.com
Annual Production: 150 barrels
Number of Beers: 6 on tap

Staple Beers:
- » The Chief Beer (American Amber Ale with 4 hops)
- » Flag Street (American Pale Ale)
- » Northside (Blonde Ale)
- » Shelterbelt (Brown Ale)

Rotating Beers:
- » Double IPA
- » Imperial Stout
- » Kölsch
- » Lemon Beer (summer)
- » Pumpkin Harvest Beer

Courtesy Montgomery Brewing

Most Popular Brew: Shelterbelt and Northside

Samples: Yes, five 5-oz. pours for about $13

Brewmaster's Fave: Flag Street and The Chief

Best Time to Go: Open Wed–Sat 3–8pm, but watch website for expanding hours.

Where can you buy it? Here in pints and 13-oz pours, or to go in growlers and 750 ml "stubs." Some local draft accounts (check the website).

Got food? No, but food friendly.

Tours? No. But they might chat you up at your table and you can see everything from there anyway.

Special Offer: $1 off your first beer during your signature visit.

Directions: MN 13 and MN 21 pass north/south through Montgomery together as 4th St. At the corner of Boulevard Ave and 4th St, go east on Boulevard 2 blocks, and the brewery is at the corner on the right at 2nd St.

The Beer Buzz: Owner Charles Dorsey and Brewer AJ Newton went to high school together, and back in about 2005 they started homebrewing. They organized a homebrew club and after some time they were the only two left in it. Charles' family had already purchased the 25,000 sq. ft. building and Charles and AJ brought in a 40-gallon kettle and started brewing in here. They got to talking over beer and finally bit the bullet in October 2013 and started planning. They took over 1,500 sq. ft. of what was mostly storage space, and share the rest of the building with apartment units.

The original Montgomery Brewing Co. opened in 1882 and lasted until 1943, and at its height produced as many as 40,000 barrels. You can still see The Chief, the original flagship beer's logo painted on the side of the building. AJ and Charles have resurrected the name for their amber ale and are hoping to restore the paint job as well.

The beer names, such as The Chief, were part of the community. Shelterbelt is another name for a wind break which a farmer would create on the west side of the farm. They brew on a three-barrel system and their beers are unfiltered, malt forward, and approachable. With a town of only 3,000 they figured brewing would be a side project, something they could do a couple times a month just to keep a few taps on. But the locals picked up on it immediately and they may be brewing more than they anticipated. The taproom, located in the former brewery's former bottle shop, has a small bar and some tables and chairs, an intimate space.

Facebook/MontgomeryBrewing

Stumbling Distance: *Pizzeria 201* (201 1st St S, 507-364-5000, pizzeria201.com) has the best pies in town and delivers to the taproom. *Next Chapter Winery* (16945 320th St, New Prague, 612-756-3012, nextchapterwinery.com) is less than 5 miles north in New Prague.

COURTESY MONTGOMERY BREWING

August Schell Brewing Co.

Founded: 1860
Brewers: Dave Berg and Jeremy Kral
Address: 1860 Schell Road • New Ulm, MN 56073
Phone: 507-354-5528
Web Site: www.schellsbrewery.com
Annual Production: 135,000 barrels
Number of Beers: Taproom: 9 on tap plus 1919 Root Beer

Staple Beers:
- » FIREBRICK (Vienna-style amber)
- » SCHELL'S DARK
- » SCHELL'S DEER BRAND
- » SCHELL'S LIGHT
- » SCHELL'S PILS

Rotating Beers:
- » BOCK
- » CHIMNEY SWEEP
- » FRESH HOP EQUINOX
- » GOOSETOWN (gose)
- » HEFEWEIZEN
- » MAIFEST
- » SCHELL SHOCKED (grapefruit radler)
- » SCHMALTZ'S ALT
- » NOBLE STAR COLLECTION (various Berliner Weisse beers in 750ml bottles – brewed at *Star Keller Brewery* in New Ulm)
- » STAG SERIES (experimental, limited edition beers)

Most Popular Brew: Schell's Firebrick and Grain Belt Premium

Samples: Yes, with tours

Best Time to Go: Check the website for tour hours. Watch for Bockfest (the Sat before Fat Tuesday), Lager Lauf (a run in spring), Oktoberfest (early Oct), and the citywide Bavarian Blast in July. Also watch for Sundays in the Park, a family friendly event throughout the summer with live music, bread and cheese, and beer.

Where can you buy it? Distributed in bottles and cans (12- and 16-oz.) and 750 ml bottles in six states: IA, MN, NE, ND, SD, and WI. Also draft accounts.

Got food? Only a bit of spent-grain bread and local cheeses sometimes on summer weekends in the beer garden.

Tours: $3 per person, about one hour. From Memorial Day weekend through Labor Day weekend: Mon–Fri at 1, 2:30, and 4PM, Sat hourly 12–4PM, Sun hourly 1–4 PM. Off Season Tours: Fri 1 and 3PM, Sat hourly 12–4 PM, Sun 1 and 2:30PM.

Special Offer: A free beer during your signature visit.

Directions: US 14 runs right through New Ulm. From its juncture with Highway 37, take Hwy 37, which becomes 20th St, for 1 mile, crossing the Minnesota River. Turn right on Broadway St, go 0.2 mile. Turn left on 18th St, go 0.2 mile, and turn left on Washington St. Follow it to the brewery as it becomes Schell's Rd.

The Beer Buzz: At the edge of New Ulm, and at the end of a lovely little drive up a winding road into the woods, lies Minnesota's oldest brewery and the second oldest family-owned brewery in the US. (Yuengling of PA is the oldest.) Founder August Schell was born in Durbach, Germany, in 1828 but immigrated to the United States when he was 20, landing in New Orleans. He met his wife Theresa Hermann and they had two daughters before heading north to join other German immigrants in founding a new town in a territory that wasn't quite a state yet: New Ulm, Minnesota. The couple

had four more children. These were Germans, after all, so it isn't so surprising that August met a former brewmaster, Jacob Bernhardt. They partnered and built a brewery just outside town, overlooking the Cottonwood River. August bought out Jacob a few years later.

When August passed away at the age of 63, the brewery stayed with his wife and his son Otto, who had studied brewing back in Germany and took over. When Otto and his mother passed away, Emma, the eldest daughter inherited the brewery, and her husband George Marti took over in 1911.

Unlike so many other breweries that went beer belly up, Schell's survived Prohibition by making soft drinks, candy, and near beer. When George died in 1934, his son Alfred took over, and Alfred in turn passed the brewery to

his son Warren in 1969. By this time, New Ulm had had seven breweries, and the last of them was Hauenstein Beer which closed that same year. Schell's was the last game in town, and times were getting tough. For a long while Warren didn't take a paycheck just so he could keep the doors open. A massive black walnut tree on the grounds was cut down and made into planks to be sold off to make payroll. But the tightened belt paid off and the brewery survived. Warren's son Ted studied brewing at the Siebel Institute and took over as president in 1985. Jace Marti, one of Ted's three sons and representing the 6th generation, has also become a brewmaster for the brewery. In 1936, the brewery installed ten cypress lagering tanks, but took all but two out in 1993. Those two tanks were carefully restored so that Jace could make various versions of Berliner Weisse, a style he learned during his training in Germany. In 2015, all ten tanks moved to Schell's new *Star Keller Brewery* at the north side of town.

80,000 visitors come each year to see the stately brick buildings and the wooded 40 acres. Jace's brother Franz, who earned a Purple Heart serving in Afghanistan in the Army's 10th Mountain Division, keeps the gardens in order, and you can find deer and peacocks wandering the grounds. Beyond the gardens stands August's retirement home. What was originally stables for horses was converted to a garage, but now is the brewery's awesome little museum filled with antiques and breweriana from the brewery's storied past. Also inside is a beer hall where you may notice that Grain Belt is on tap along with the many other Schell beers. Schell's purchased this well known Minnesota beer and now produces it.

Trivia note: August's father was a forester, thus the crest with the Schell's deer on it.

Facebook.com/SchellsBeer and Twitter @SchellsBrewery

Stumbling Distance: Plan your trip to come when Schell's latest project *Star Keller Brewery* (next page) is open on the north side at Highland Ave and County Road 29. *Deutsche Strasse B&B* (404 S German St, 507-354-2005, deutschestrasse.com) is a perfect place to spend the night in New Ulm. *B&L Bar* (15 N Minnesota St, 507-354-2610, theblbar.com) is a friendly neighborhood tavern downtown with pool and darts, and enough Schell's on tap to serve as the brewery's unofficial taproom. *Lola – An American Bistro* (16 N Minnesota St, 507-359-2500, lolaamericanbistro.com) gets high praise for breakfast, lunch and dinner. If you are looking for German fare, there's *Veigel's Kaiserhoff* (221 N Minnesota St, 507-359-2071, kaiserhoff.org).

The Star Keller

Opened: 2015 (August Shell Brewing, 1860)
Brewmaster: Jace Marti
Address: At County Road 29 & North Highland Ave. • New Ulm, MN 56073
Phone: 507-354-5528 (Schell's Brewery)
Web Site: www.schellsbrewery.com
Number of Beers: 4-5 plus one-offs and variations

Staple Beers:
» STAR OF THE NORTH
» DAWN OF AURORA

Samples: Yes, flights are available.

Brewmaster's Fave: Star of the North (it was Jace's first)

Best Time to Go: When the taproom is open. Initially open one day a week, Saturday. Hours will likely expand, so check the website or phone first.

Where can you buy it? Here on tap and distributed in 750 ml bottles in 7 states, same as August Schell's Brewing.

Got food? Yes, but not a full kitchen or restaurant. Think small plate and cheese pairings.

Tours? Yes, check the website.

Special Offer: Not participating.

Directions: US 14 passes through New Ulm as 20th North Street. At its intersection with Garden St/County Road 29, go north out of town 0.5 mile and the brewery is at the Highland Avenue intersection. This is 4.3 miles from August Schell's Brewery on New Ulm's south side.

The Beer Buzz: Welcome to a new Schell's brewery. Owned and managed Schell's Brewing, this site is home to the historic brewery's sour program. Sour beers are risky if kept around your regular beers. An infection crossing over would be a disaster. So in 2015, the brewing of Schell's Noble Star Collection moved here to New Ulm's north side.

The ten 140-barrel lagering tanks here are the original 1936 cypress wood tanks from Schell's Brewery. Schell's was just coming off 13 years of Prohibition (ie. income limited to soft drinks, candy, and near beer) and though they were back in business with the beer, they needed to purchase economically and had to pass over the more expensive modern equipment of the time. Nevertheless, these tanks held beer as late as 1991! At that time, brewery president Ted Marti (Jace's father) retired them and had 8 of them removed from the brewery. But they were so special he couldn't dispose or recycle them, so he put them in storage with no intention of ever using them again.

Two of the cypress tanks still stood inside the brewery, and the idea came up to use them for beer again for the brewery's anniversary, but the wood had dried out. It took over a year of filling them with water to get the wood to expand and close the gaps—too late for the planned beer. Something else came up. Jace, who had gone to Germany to study brewing, really got into the Berliner Wiesse style while he was there. He spent time in Berlin, researching as much as he could about it. He realized these cypress tanks would be perfect for brewing one. Cypress is a neutral wood and durable, resistant to decay, but first they needed to remove 60 years of wax from the inside. They called in a company to dry-ice blast it off, and when it was ready, he brewed a basic beer as a test and let it sit for 4 months. The tanks proved beer-worthy, and so then Jace brewed his first batch of Berliner Weisse. Gradually he brewed other variations which have become Schell's Noble Star Collection.

The beers take six months to two years to finish aging. Dawn of Aurora is a recreation of a long-forgotten Berliner Weisse style of a traditional German strong beer called "Starkbier." The brewery is in a modern building and inside is a small room with the 1936 tanks along with tables and chairs in the middle and a bar at one end. The interior design is "steampunk speakeasy" and should be as cool and funky as the beer.

Stumbling Distance: Be sure to also visit the historical *August Schell Brewing Co.* on the south side of town.

COURTESY OF AUGUST SCHELL BREWING CO.

Reads Landing Brewing Co.

Founded: August 2011
Brewmaster: Bob Nihart
Address: 70555 202nd Avenue • Reads Landing, MN 55968
Phone: 651-560-4777
Web Site: www.rlbrewingco.com
Annual Production: 100 barrels
Number of Beers: 6 on tap (1–2 are guest brews)

Staple Beer:
  » Cremona Cream Ale

Rotating Beers:
  » American House Pale Ale
  » Black Leg Porter (with crème de leche)
  » Cap'n Amber (with Cap'n Crunch cereal)
  » Dead Head DIPA (aged on cedar)
  » ESB (on nitro)
  » Pullman Porter
  » Stout (on nitro)
  » Wagmu Ale (wagmu is Lakota for pumpkin)

Most Popular Brew: Cremona Cream Ale

Samples: Yes, sips for decisions, 7-oz. pours for about $2.50

Brewmaster's Fave: That changes, but he is a hophead.

Best Time to Go: Summer Hours (starting mid-March): Mon 11AM–9PM, Wed–Thu 11AM–9PM, Fri–Sat 11AM–10PM, Sun 12–9PM. Closed Tue; Winter Hours (after Thanksgiving): Mon–Wed Closed, Thu–Fri 12–9PM, Sat 11AM–9PM, Sun 12–8PM. Happy hour is Sun–Thu 3–6PM.

Where can you buy it? On here on tap or in growlers to go.

Got food? Yes, a full menu of appetizers, soups and salads, sandwiches and entrees, including daily specials. You might notice a southern cooking element to the food. Note the shrimp and grits.

Tours: By appointment or randomly if the brewer is free.

Special Offer: Not participating at this time.

Directions: US 61 along the Mississippi runs right through Reads Landing. Turn east toward the river on 9th Ave and the brewery is on the left just 250 feet down the hill.

The Beer Buzz: Back in its heyday, Reads Landing was a bustling river port with as many as 30 bars, 20 hotels, and a couple breweries. It was even considered as an option for the state capital. Bob's family and this building are a part of this town's history. This two-story 1869 building once housed a dry goods store, but Bob's grandfather bought it in 1937 and someone opened a bar there. Then his aunt managed it from the mid-50s, renting to The Anchor Inn, a pioneer in the all-you-can-eat model. But when they relocated to Wabasha in 1963, the building remained mostly empty, with the exception of some use as a family cabin.

Bob got his start homebrewing in college with extracts. Years later he decided he needed a hobby during winter and took up the brewing again but with grain. When he decided his beer was ready for a larger audience, he gutted the old building and put in the brewpub. Many homebrewers don't like to make the same beer over and over, and Bob doesn't want to give that up. Thus, the beers are always changing.

The brick building sits facing the Mississippi and an outside deck enjoys the same view. Only the railroad tracks lie between the brewery and the water, and trains still thunder past. Occasionally conductors or engineers call ahead for food orders (no beer, of course) and stop the train to pick them up. That perhaps makes this a locomotive drive-thru. Yes, the food's that good: He added a new kitchen built off the side of the original structure, and the chef trained at Le Cordon Bleu and the menu offers meat and seafood entrees with a southern twist to them.

The interior shows an old pressed tin ceiling, tables for dining, and a bar along the right corner wall with old beer labels under acrylic cover the bar top. Current brews are on an old church hymn board, and a chalkboard shows the day's food specials. Breweriana and historic photos decorate the walls inside and old beer signs hang on the outside of the building near the deck. That phone booth you see actually takes incoming calls.

The flagship beer's name has a story. A father and his two sons came here from Germany and wanted to start a newspaper. And so they did, but upon the printing of their first edition, they celebrated by going sailing. The boat capsized and the father and the youngest son drowned. Cremona was the name of the riverboat that carried them to Reads Landing from out east by way of the Ohio and Mississippi Rivers. One of the rotating beers, Black Leg, was slang for a riverboat gambler of dubious ethics who wandered up and down the rivers typically well dressed complete with gold pocket watch.

The giant sand dune you may (or may not) see across the water? That's sand and silt from the Chippewa River in Wisconsin which deposits it all when it meets the Mississippi just upstream of the dune. The Army Corps of Engineers dredges it and piles it on shore and then periodically spends 3–4 months pumping it, via a pipe laid across barges, downstream to a gravel pit in Wabasha. Barges are still hugely important for shipping, including grain, petroleum coke, and scrap metal heading south, and road salt and cement coming north. The Mississippi actually moves 60% of the export grain down through New Orleans.

WiFi. Facebook.com/rlbrewingco and Twitter @Rlbrewingco

Stumbling Distance: History buffs should swing by the *Wabasha County Historical Society Museum* (70537 206th Ave, wabashacountyhistory.org) in an old brick schoolhouse (weekends only May-Oct). The 19th century *American Eagle Bluff Bed & Breakfast* (70519 Highway 61, 651) 564-0372, americaneaglebluffbedandbreakfast.com) is a very nice place to stay just a short walk from the brewpub, and it has the longest website address ever. Birders flock here during migration periods. Wabasha is just a few minutes south and is home to the *National Eagle Center* (50 Pembroke Ave, Wabasha, 651-565-4989, nationaleaglecenter.org).

Red Wing Brewery

Opened: December 2012
Brewmaster: William "Norm" Norman
Address: 1411 Old W Main St. • Red Wing, MN 55066
Phone: 651-327-2200
Web Site: www.redwingbrewing.com
Annual Production: 300 barrels
Number of Beers: 8–9 on tap, plus guest beers, 13 beers per year

Staple Beers:
- » Barn Bluff Brown
- » Jordan Creek IPA
- » Pepie's Porter
- » Red Wing Premium (Kölsch style)
- » Remmler's Royal Brew
- » Stoneware Stout
- » Work Boot Red
- » Plus Good Ole Zimmie's Root Beer ·

Rotating Beers:
- » Anderson Wheat
- » Cokins Red Wing "Bavarian Style" Beer
- » ESB
- » Goodhue Farmhouse
- » Holiday Special
- » Ski Jump Special
- » Steamboat Scottish

Most Popular Brew: No front runner; a fan base for each.

Samples: Yes, build your own flights with 5-oz pours of any, including guest taps.

Best Time to Go: Open Tue–Thu 4–9pm, Fri–Sat 12–10pm, Sun 12–8pm. Growler Tuesdays.

Where can you buy it? Only here in pints and snits (half pints), and growlers to go.

Got food? Yes, primarily calzones and pizzas with handmade crusts made by a local bakery with the spent grain. Wings are local, and bottled beers include gluten-free and N.A. options.

Tours? Not formally, but there's info on the menu.

Special Offer: $2 off your tab during your signature visit.

Directions: US 61 passes right through Red Wing. Watch for Old West Main St and turn north (toward the river), and go 0.1 mile; the brewery is on the left.

The Beer Buzz: Red Wing hasn't had a brewery since the last one closed in 1951, but back in the beginning there were five brewers: four Germans and a Swede. Brewer Norm had his first homebrew experience when he was 21, when his younger brother bought their father a kit and they brewed over Christmas. He went out and got his own and has been brewing ever since. Co-founder Scott Kolby and Norm knew each other from working at a YMCA camp together and in 2000 they started brewing together on a stovetop. Both took a two-week course at Siebel in Chicago and after some long planning, they brought local beer back to Red Wing. Both are very passionate about their community, something you learn the minute you start talking with them.

All the beer names are relevant to Red Wing: Pepie's Porter is named after the Lake Pepin version of the Loch Ness Monster. (Lake Pepin is a 25-mile impoundment on the Mississippi River just down river from Red Wing.) Jordan Creek is a spring-fed stream that still flows, but since the days of development, *under* the city to the Mississippi. Cokins, Remmler's

and Red Wing Premium are a bit of beer history, local brews that the new brewery has resurrected. In fact, Remmler's is based on an 1896 recipe found at the Goodhue County Historical Society. A letter from the brewer to the American Brewing Academy in Chicago described his recipe in German.

The brewpub is a modern space with a long wood bar, some dining tables, and a window into the brewhouse facing the bar. There's no TV, but some games, cards and some books in the corner. A glass display cabinet is filled with breweriana, while there are some signs, bottles, cases and reprints of classic labels around the room.

WiFi. Also on Facebook.

Stumbling Distance: For the grape fans in your group, there's *Falconer Vineyards* (3572 Old Tyler Rd, 651-388-8849, falconervineyards.com). *Round Barn Farm B&B* (28650 Wildwood Ln, 866-763-2276, round-barnfarm.com) is 5 miles east of the brewery and a good place to stop for the night. You can tour, take a class, or just browse the merchandise at *Red Wing Stoneware & Pottery* (4909 Moundview Dr, 651-388-4610, redwingstoneware.com). *Red Wing Pottery's* showroom is a short walk from the brewery, and *Bob White Coffee & Candy Shop* (1920 Old West Main) is next door to that. Climb *Barn Bluff*—might be best before you have a couple. Cyclists/hikers can enjoy the 19.7 mile *Cannon Valley Trail* (cannonvalleytrail.com) connecting to Cannon Falls.

RED WING STONEWARE & POTTERY

PHOTO COURTESY OF RED WING STONEWARE & POTTERY

If you've made it to Red Wing, you should check out what the local potters are up to. Dating back to the 1800s, they were once the largest pottery producer in the nation. Notably, they produced special beer mugs for Hamm's and even some Hamm's bears. That little brown jug trophy passed back and forth between University of Minnesota and University of Michigan? That's them too. Back in 1877 Red Wing Stoneware Co. used the abundant clay of the area to fashion very utilitarian things needed by the settlers: crocks, jugs, and even sewer pipes. Changing time and needs forced them to merge with a couple other businesses to form Red Wing Union Stoneware, and with less need for crocks, they produced plant pots, tableware, and even more artistic creations. In 1936 they became Red Wing Potteries and found success with hand painting patterns on their works, but in the 60s cheap imports and a strike ended their good run and it became a retail store only. Red Wing Stoneware rose up from the ashes in the 80s and in 1996 Red Wing Pottery brought back the potters. In 2013 new owners bought both and merged them, but you can still visit both locations. Check out their 'Sotasteins and 'Sotashots. They also have a pilsner pint and 'Sotapitcher branded with one of eight Minnesota breweries.

Red Wing Stoneware & Pottery
800-352-4877
redwingstoneware.com

The Pottery store (1920 Old West Main) Mon–Sat 9–6, Sun10–5
Here potters do daily demonstrations near the showroom

The Stoneware store (4909 Moundview Dr.) Mon–Sat 9–5
Weekdays at 1PM there are 25-minute factory tours for a nominal fee (which gets you a coupon worth more than the fee).

Kinney Creek Brewery

Opened: December 2012
Brewmaster: Donovan Seitz
Address: 1016 7th Street NW • Rochester, MN 55901
Phone: 507-282-2739
Web Site: www.kinneycreekbrewery.com
Annual Production: 180 barrels
Number of Beers: 9–12 on tap; 24 beers per year

Staple Beers:

- » Abyss American Stout
- » Black Ice IPA
- » Centennial Blonde
- » Darca-Doo Imperial Stout
- » Grappler
- » Lady Liberty
- » Log Cabin
- » Opener IPA
- » Smoked Porter
- » Strong Ale
- » Sunny Days Light
- » Timber English Brown Ale

Rotating Beers:

- » American Ale
- » Canoe the Zumbro (IPA)
- » Controlled Burn
- » El Dorado
- » Eye Opener (IIPA)
- » Honey Blonde
- » Lost Elf
- » Old Town Ale
- » Sippn' Sour (bottle release)
- » Squirrel's Delight
- » Rochtoberfest
- » Rockin' Wheat
- » Tessalation (IPA)
- » ... plus barrel aging and sours

Most Popular Brew: Eye Opener (IIPA)

Samples: Yes, flights of 4 ($6), 5 ($8), or 6 ($10).

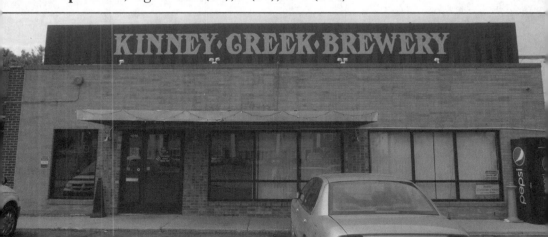

Brewmaster's Fave: "I love all my children. I drink them all." (Eye Opener if forced to choose.)

Best Time to Go: Taproom is open Thu–Sat 12–10PM, Sun 12–6PM. Growler sales/exchanges Mon–Wed 12–6PM, Thu 12–8, Fri 12–9PM, Sat 12–10PM—all subject to change. Live music on Saturday nights.

Where can you buy it? Here in pints and growlers and 750s to go. Select liquor stores from the Twin Cities to the River Valley may carry 22-oz. bombers.

Got food? Just snacks such as salted peanuts, jerky, and pretzels, but food friendly, so order in. They serve their own root beer and ginger beer. Caterers may come in some evenings from Thu–Sat.

Tours: No.

Special Offer: A free pint glass with your book signature.

Directions: From US 63/US 52, take Exit 56A (where it meets US 14 coming from the west) and merge onto Civic Center Dr. Go 0.5 mile, turn left on 11th Ave, go 0.2 mile, and turn right on 7th St. The brewery is 250 feet from the corner on your right.

The Beer Buzz: Donovan called homebrewing his mistress, but it wasn't always so: he had first spent many years making wine. When he took

a trip to Boston Brewing Co., however, he became inspired to go beer and go pro and started planning in August 2009. His day job (at the time of printing) was still in construction, but this is "the most fun I've ever had." This was a pawn shop and restaurant supply shop before the brews moved in to create Rochester's first brewery since Prohibition. The half-barrel system on display is where this all started. And while it doubled to a one-barrel, expectations are they will go even bigger by 2016. His styles are many and varied, as he hopes to provide a little something for everyone.

The taproom is spacious with light gray interiors with many tables, cocktail tables with stools, and a center island bar, and the serving bar has corrugated zinc and lights up blue from behind. For entertainment there are games such as foosball, washer & hook, board games, Giant Jenga, and Hammer Schlagen (pounding a nail into wood with one swing). Parking is in the lot outside where you can see some hop vines growing on the building.

WiFi. Facebook.com/kinneycreekbrewery and Twitter @KinneyCreekBrew

Stumbling Distance: *The Tap House* (10 3rd St SW, 507-258-4017 taphousemn.com) has 50 on tap, wine, appetizers and a lovely rooftop patio. *The Thirsty Belgian* (2650 S Broadway Suite 600, 507-258-4402, thirstybelgian.com) has good beer, good food. *The Doggery* (18 3rd St SW, 507-289-2742, thedoggerybar.com) for killer cocktails in a speakeasy environment.

LTS Brewing Company

Opened: Spring 2015 (Taproom by summer 2015)
Brewmaster: Brandon Schulz
Address: 2001 32nd Avenue NW • Rochester, MN 55901
Phone: Check the website
Web Site: www.ltsbrewing.com
Annual Production: 450 barrels
Number of Beers: 12 on tap

Staple Beers:

- » Belgian Blonde
- » 80 Shilling Scottish Ale
- » IPA
- » Kölsch
- » Pale Ale
- » Oatmeal Stout

Rotating Beers:

- » Bock
- » Brown Ale
- » Dark Ale (with maple syrup)
- » Porter
- » Saisons
- » Wild Rice Brown Ale
- » …Belgian and traditional German styles, plus casks and infusions

Most Popular Brew: IPA for now

Samples: Yes, sample flights.

Brewmaster's Fave: Farmhouse, Saisons and Belgian styles

Best Time to Go: Taproom hours Mon–Fri 3–11PM, Sat–Sun 11AM–12AM. Be sure to check the website or call.

Where can you buy it? Draft accounts and growlers to go. Small batches in taproom only.

Got food? Yes, some small plates. Food friendly as well.

Tours? Yes, by chance or appointment.

Special Offer: $1 off your first pint or sample flight during your signature visit.

Directions: US 52 and US 63 meet up and run north-south through Rochester together. Heading north from where they cross US 14, go 0.5 mile and take Exit 56C for 19th St. Turn left (west) and go 1.2 miles, turn right on 32nd Ave and the brewery is 400 feet along on the left.

The Beer Buzz: Brandon had been homebrewing about a decade before LTS opened its doors. Good friends at work were homebrewers; he had some, like it, figured he could do the same. Suddenly, things get out of hand. "Your garage is now full of stuff. It kinda took off," he says. He had planned for five years and looked for a business partner. Jeff Werning, a friend from work, stepped up. For now, they are keeping their day jobs. Why the name? Brandon was on a brewery road trip with best friends hitting the highlights of Michigan—Ann Arbor, Kalamazoo (Bell's), and more. Beer tends to unleash ideas, and they were talking about opening a brewery. Said one friend, "Well, life's too short, so if you're going to do it, do it." That stuck in Brandon's head, so when it came time to name his creation, LTS it was. Life's Too Short. This is about following your dreams.

They converted an old industrial building, an excavator's garage with a large workshop and office space which became the brewery and taproom.

WiFi. Facebook/ltsbrewing and Twitter @ltsbrewing

Stumbling Distance: *John Hardy's Bar-B-Q* (929 W Frontage Rd, 507-288-3936, johnhardysbbq.com) serves some excellent wood-smoked Southern-style barbecue. *Mr Pizza North* (4040 28th St NW, 507-252-9400, northmrpizza.com) does good casual pizza and other Italian, plus cheesecake, oddly enough.

OLVALDE FARM & BREWING CO.

Founded: 2011
Brewmaster: Joe Pond
Address: 16557 County Road 25 • Rollingstone, MN 55969
Phone: 507-205-4969
Web Site: www.olvalde.com
Annual Production: 100–150 barrels
Number of Beers: 4 but more in the works

Beers:
- » THE AUROCH's HORN (aged on fresh rhubarb – summer)
- » BRYNHILDR's GIFT (Minnesota Farmhouse Juniper Ale – spring-summer)
- » ODE TO A RUSSION SHIPWRIGHT (Imperial Stout Porter – winter)
- » RISE OF THE BURGHERS AND THE FALL OF THE FEUDAL LORDS (herbed ale – fall)

Most Popular Brew: The Auroch's Horn

Best Time to Go: Not open to the public at this time, but check the website as that may change!

Where can you buy it? In 750 ml bottles in the Twin Cities and Rochester areas. See website for specific outlets.

Tours: Not without special arrangements.

The Beer Buzz: This unusual little farm brewery is in a utility barn on Joe's in-laws' farm. This used to be a dairy farm, but they wanted to try something different. Now Joe is surrounded by ingredients and aims to add a hop garden and malting house. Joe graduated from University of Minnesota with a chemical engineering degree, and got his first professional brewing experience in Chicago. While the brewery is not open to visitors, you can find where his beer is for sale on his website. These are farmhouse ales and bottle conditioned.

Twitter @Olvalde

ZONE 4
Central and Northwest Minnesota

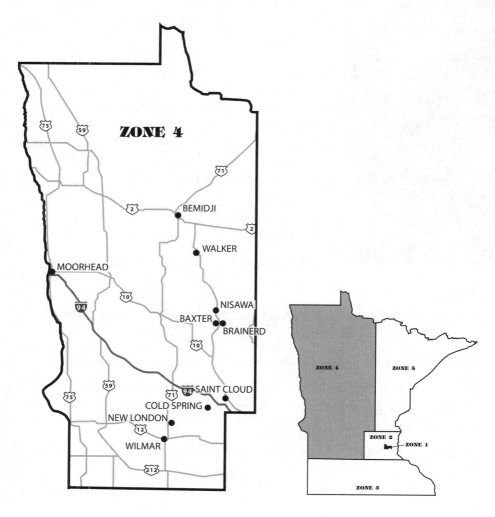

JACK PINE BREWERY

Founded: 2013
Brewmaster: Patrick Sundberg
Address: 7942 College Road, Suite 115 • Baxter, MN 56425
Phone: 218-270-8072
Web Site: www.jackpinebrewery.com
Annual Production: 350 barrels
Number of Beers: 7 on tap, 10 per year

Staple Beers:
- » DEAD BRANCH CREAM ALE
- » DUCK POND NUT BROWN ALE
- » FENCELINE PALE ALE
- » VENGEANCE! (Dead Branch infused with fresh jalapeños)

Rotating Beers:
- » BARBWIRE IMPERIAL IPA
- » BIG BUCK BARLEYWINE (late winter)
- » HARVEST RED ALE (early October)
- » HORNETS NEST HONEY LEMON WHEAT (summer)
- » ICE OUT WHITE IPA (spring)
- » JACKTOBER (fall)
- » OATMEAL STOUT (winter)
- » TRESPASS PORTER (winter)

Most Popular Brew: Fenceline Pale Ale

Samples: Yes, five 4-oz. pours for about $9

Brewmaster's Fave: Fenceline or Dead Branch when it's hot, Big Buck in winter

Best Time to Go: Taproom open Wed–Thu 4–9PM, Fri–Sat 2–9PM.

Where can you buy it? In the taproom in pints and half pints, or growlers and the occasional 750 ml bottle to go. Also on tap in several area establishments.

Got food? No, but there's root beer and the taproom is food friendly and good for delivery. Food trucks on occasion.

Tours? No, but you can see it all from the taproom and chat with him if he's free.

Special Offer: A free bottle opener with your book signature.

Directions: MN 371 runs north-south through Baxter and crosses MN 210. From that intersection, head south 1.1 miles and go east on College Rd 0.5 mile and the brewery is on the left. (If you are coming from the south, turn right on College Rd.)

The Beer Buzz: Patrick worked a series of jobs "vaguely related" to his double major of math and physics. But a desire to start his own business and his "overgrown hobby" of homebrewing eventually won out and thus Jack Pine came to be. He wasn't always convinced his beer was good enough. Sure, when he gave some to friends they said it was good, but when he started winning homebrew competitions, he started to see he was on to something. So he immersed himself in the brewing. He went through the Beer Judge Certification Program, and after four years of planning, he set up a three-barrel system inside what had been a vacant storage space in an industrial building.

A garage door opens into the brewery and the taproom is more a tap area set aside from the brewhouse by a low wall. There's a nice wooden bar and some tall cocktail tables and from there one can see everything that's going on in the work area. In winter, it's mostly locals, but summer brings tourism to the area and the taproom is busier. While the patrons eagerly drink Patrick's beer, the spent grain goes to a local pig farmer and a worm farm.

Facebook.com/JackPineBrewery and Twitter @JackPineBrewery

Stumbling Distance: Get fantastic wood-fired pies at *Boomer Pizza* (14039 Edgewood Dr N, 218-454-4900, boomerpizza.com). A bit less casual over in Brainerd is *Prairie Bay Grill* (15115 Edgewood Dr N, Brainerd, 218-824-6444, prairiebay.com). Though at the moment it's being contract brewed, *Brainerd Lakes Beer* (brainerdbeer.com) is locally developed and for sale in local liquor stores and has some draft accounts.

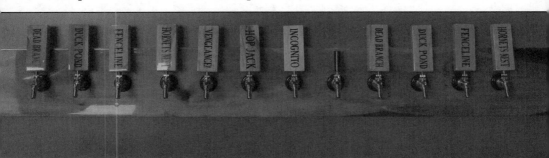

Bemidji Brewing Company

Founded: 2012
Head Brewer: Tom Hill
Address: 401 Beltrami Avenue, North West Suite A• Bemidji, MN 56601
Phone: 218-444-7011
Web Site: www.bemidjibeer.com
Annual Production: 450 barrels
Number of Beers: 6–9 on tap, at least one on nitro, and one cask per month. Many styles each year.

Staple Beers:
»   IPA
»   Robust Porter

Rotating Beers:
»   Dog Day IPA
»   English Mild
»   Pub Ale
»   Smoked Brown Ale
»   Belgian Farmhouse Ale
»   Single hop series of IPAs
»   Stout
»   … plus various sours, saisons, and hoppy brews in summer

Most Popular Brew: IPA and anything hoppy

Samples: Yes, free sips for decision making, and flights of six 5-oz pours for about $12

Brewmaster's Fave: Any of the single-hop series beers

Best Time to Go: Hours vary seasonally so confirm on the website. Summer: Wed–Thu 2–10PM, Fri–Sat noon–11PM. Winter (Jan–Apr): Wed–Thu 4–9PM, Fri–Sat 3–11PM.

Where can you buy it? In the taproom in Short Pours (10-oz.) and pints, and growlers to go, plus a few draft accounts downtown.

Got food? No, but food friendly, and there are menus from local places for delivery. Craft soda served as well.

Tours? Yes, nothing formal, but randomly when someone is available.

Special Offer: A high five from one of the staff (optional fist bump available while supplies last).

Directions: US 2 passes just the west of Bemidji. Take the County Road 7 exit and go east toward downtown Bemidji about 1.7 miles as it becomes 5th St. Turn right (south) on Beltrami Ave, go to the end of the block, and the brewery is on your right.

The Beer Buzz: The birth of this brewery is a bit unusual. Sure, Tom had been a homebrewer since college and brewed nearly a decade before he decided to open a brewery. But they were one of the first craft breweries to run a successful Kickstarter campaign to get the funds for equipment and ingredients. And then they started brewing double batches on a 25-gallon system—in a commercial kitchen at the local Harmony Cooperative. Clever. In fact, they brewed this way for about the first seven months, then took a break in April 2013 while they secured a lease and built out the brewery. They opened in July 2013 in this renovated corner drugstore. Back in the early 1900s it was a creamery. When they pulled up the carpeting during the remodeling, they found the beautiful terrazzo floors you see now. Perfect for a brewery and a taproom. The landlord installed big windows in front to let in lots of light as well.

After opening, they expanded to a 1.5-barrel system, and in summer of 2014, moved up to a 3-barrel system. While winter might be a little slower in this destination town, the local beer fans are numerous and loyal enough to keep those doors open and the lights on. During those colder months, Tom likes to rotate through more brews, trying out things he might bring on in summer. His love of hops inspires the single-hop

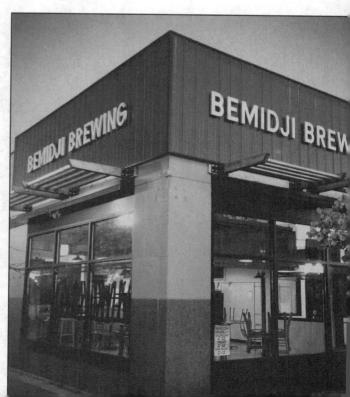

series of IPAs, and there is always something hoppy on besides their staple IPA. Tom is also quite adept at making sours, and you can expect to see one or more of these special brews on tap just about anytime.

WiFi. Facebook.com/BemidjiBeer,
Twitter @BemidjiBrewing, and Instagram BemidjiBrewing

Stumbling Distance: Don't miss your photo op with the giant *Paul Bunyan and Babe the Blue Ox* (300 Bemidji Ave N) just a couple blocks away at the lakeside *Paul Bunyan Park.* Visit *Lake Bemidji State Park* (3401 State Park Rd NE, 218-308-2300) five minutes north over the lake for camping, hiking, paddling and more, or *Diamond Point Park* in town just off Birchmont Dr. Tutto Bene (300 Beltrami Ave NW, 218-751-1100, tuttobene.us) a block away, is a foodie's dream and gets raves. They occasionally do beer dinners with the brewery. *Brigid's Pub* (317 Beltrami Ave, 218-444-0567, brigidsirishpub.com) is a pleasant Irish pub with food (including fish & chips, of course), great music. Both places serve Bemidji beers.

PHOTOS COURTESY BEMIDJI BREWING

PAUL BUNYAN AND BABE THE BLUE OX

A bunch of tall tales have become a number of tall statues. Paul Bunyan, the enormous lumberjack of lore, strode the lands with his companion Babe the Blue Ox in search of lumber, presumably. Stories of superhuman feats, fighting off beasts as big as he, and consuming large amounts of food were common and shared among loggers. After perhaps 30 or 40 years of oral tradition, the stories made it to newspapers and books, and eventually, advertising: Red River Lumber Co. began using him in ads.

But now the image of the bearded axe-wielding giant in the checkered flannel shirt is as much a symbol of the north woods, especially Minnesota. He also makes for a good photo op on the roadside. There's one right here in Bemidji (300 Bemidji Ave N), in fact, and another just south of Paul Bunyan State Forest (trees he apparently missed) in Akeley. Pass through town and right on Highway 34 you can find Paul Bunyan's Cradle behind a 30-foot-tall Paul Bunyan down on one knee with his axe in one hand and his palm out for you to sit in. The cradle might seem a bit much, but in fact Red River Lumber was based here.

And his connection to a beer book? There was a Paul Bunyan beer. While this was first brewed in Waukesha, Wisconsin, then later in Marshfield, Wisconsin, Minneapolis' Gluek Brewing used Bunyan in the 1950s to market Stite Malt Liquor, a "Paul Bunyan Kind o' Drink." Or as some lovingly referred to it, Green Death.

PHOTO COURTESY EXPLORE MINNESOTA

THIRD STREET BREWHOUSE / COLD SPRING BREWING CO.

Founded: 2011
Brewmaster: Horace Cunningham
Address: 219 Red River Avenue N • Cold Spring, MN 56320
Phone: 320-685-3690
Web Site: www.thirdstreetbrewhouse.com
Annual Production: 15,000 barrels of their own (up to 185,000 with contract brewing)
Number of Beers: 5 on tap, 8 beers plus specialty brews

Staple Beers:

»   BITTER NEIGHBOR BLACK IPA
»   LOST TROUT BROWN ALE
»   RISE TO THE TOP CREAM ALE
»   THREE WAY PALE ALE

Rotating Beers:

»   HUNNY DO WHEAT BEER (May-Jul)
»   JACK'D UP AUTUMN ALE (Aug-Oct)
»   RYE IPA
»   SPOTLIGHT IPA (Mar-Aug)
»   SUGAR SHACK MAPLE STOUT (Nov-Feb)
»   ...some barrel aging and one-offs as well

Samples: Yes, flights of five 3-oz. pours for about $5.

Best Time to Go: Taproom hours are only Fri 4–8PM, Sat 12–5PM, but growler sales (only filling Third Street-labeled growlers) are available Mon–Thu 8AM–5PM, Fri 8AM–8PM, and Sat 12–5PM. Watch for Firefest (firefestmn.com) at the end of July, a ticketed event hosted at the brewery and drawing over 10,000 people to benefit the Cold Spring Fire & Rescue Dept.

Where can you buy it? On tap on site and in growlers to go, but distributed in bottles and kegs throughout Minnesota and eastern North Dakota, and growing. Limited beers come in 750 ml bottles. Variety 12-packs include the 4 staples plus a seasonal.

Got food? Just pretzels, but food friendly and occasional food trucks or vendors come in on taproom nights and serve in the courtyard and patio.

Tours? Yes, Sat 12PM, 1PM, 2PM, 3PM. Reservation can be made online or call 320-685-3690. Tours are free and include five samples. Hours change seasonally so check website.

Special Offer: A free pint of beer for the book owner during your signature visit.

Directions: From where MN 23 intersects with Red River Ave, turn north and go 0.4 mile and the brewery is on the left.

The Beer Buzz: There is a long history of beer here: Cold Spring Brewery opened in 1874 and lasted as such into the late twentieth century, getting some extra notoriety at the end of the 1970s when they brewed Billy Beer, named for President Jimmy Carter's infamous brother. In 2011 the owners approved a new brewhouse for $14 million which was completed in June 2012 to bring their beers into the craft beer world. The new brand was Third Street Brewhouse and it seeks to differentiate itself from the old-school beers. The world-class bottling, canning, and packaging operation made them well positioned for distribution. Cold Springs Brewing still does its own beer and a variety of contract brewing plus some nonalcoholic beverages as well.

The name comes from Third Street, a street the city actually abandoned, a sort of alley between the brewhouse and Cold Spring Brewery. (You won't find an official street sign there any longer, though the brewery is working on setting up a decorative one.)

Mike Kneip, a former president of the Master Brewers Association of the Americas, was the longtime Director of Brewing at Cold Spring Brewing, serving over 40 years. He retired and the brewery brought in Horace Cunningham to transition to the new technical state-of-the-art brewhouse and to help hire a brewing team—a changing of the guard.

Sap from the local arboretum is used to make the syrup in Sugar Shack Maple

Stout. Specialty beers may come and go and may never return, brews such as Cool Beans Imperial Coffee Porter which was made with beans from Muggsy's Beans (muggsysbeans.com) in St. Cloud.

The taproom has some tall communal tables and heavy wooden stools, and looks out toward the trees through big windows behind the marble-top bar. The windows opposite offer a view into the adjacent brewhouse. There's a fireplace by the door, and during business hours, a receptionist desk at the end of the room. Off-street parking is in the adjacent lot.

Facebook.com/thirdstreetbrewhouse,
Twitter @3rdStBrewhouse and Instagram.com/thirdstreetbrewhouse

Stumbling Distance: *Cold Spring Bakery* (308 Main St, 320-685-8681, coldspringbakery.com) does some mighty fine cookies, donuts, breads and cakes. If you need a place to stay, *The Pillar Inn* (419 Main St, 320-685-3828, thepillarinn.com) is a good bed & breakfast option. *The Great Blue Heron Restaurant* (305 5th Ave S, 320-685-3831, blueheronsupperclub.com) is a supper club option, or pizza over at *Marnanteli's Pizza & Grille* (314 3rd St S, 320-685-3083, telispizza.com).

Junkyard Brewing

Founded: 2012
Brewmaster: Aaron Juhnke
Address: 1320 1st Avenue North • Moorhead, MN 56560
Phone: 701-261-8403, Aaron 701-261-5861, Dan 701-261-5861
Web Site: www.junkyardbeer.com
Annual Production: 1,000 barrels
Number of Beers: 10 on tap, 20 beers per year

Staple Beers:
- CoachGun IPA
- Top Gorilla Belgian Tripel
- Whistle Wetter Double IPA

Rotating Beers:
- Flying Tiger Black IPA
- Hatchet Jack Baltic Porter
- Hop Habit
- Ugly Ted's Buffalo Brown Ale
- The Coalminer's Daughter (Russian imperial stout)
- Prairie Shaman English IPA
- Free Candy Belgian-style Quadrupel
- Scrounger (cream ale)

Most Popular Brew: Coach Gun IPA

Samples: Yes, free sips for decision-making, flights for sale

Brewmaster's Fave: Whistle Wetter Double IPA

Best Time to Go: Taproom open Mon–Thu 4–9PM, Fri 4–12AM, Sat 12PM–12AM, subject to change.

Where can you buy it? Pints in the taproom with growlers to go when beer supply is ample, plus some Fargo-Moorhead, Detroit Lakes, and Grand Forks draft accounts.

Got food? No, but food friendly, and Rhombus Guys pizza (606 Main Ave Fargo, ND, 701-540-4534, rhombuspizza.com) delivers free to the taproom.

Tours? Kinda. It's pretty small, but the brewer may be free to chat, otherwise make an appointment.

Special Offer: A free pint glass with your book signature.

Directions: From US 10, stay on the posted highway until you reach 21st St. Turn right, go 0.5 mile continuing onto 1st Ave and the brewery is on the right. From I-94 from the east, take Exit 2 and follow 34th St 2.0 miles to US 10, turn left, and pick up the US 10 directions from there.

The Beer Buzz: You might think, gees, it's practically in North Dakota, but believe me it is worth the drive. What started out as a nanobrewery has become something a bit bigger thanks to some great beer and the locals who support it.

Aaron was a freshman in college and his brother Dan was still in high school in 2007 when they decided to take up homebrewing because they couldn't afford the good stuff and wouldn't drink the lousy stuff. By 2012

they were both out of college and figured why not start a brewery? They didn't have a lot of funds but they had the passion and the creativity to scrounge it all together. They built their own 50-gallon system and approached Country Cannery, the homebrew supply store in town, about the idea. Both parties agreed that the old wood shop in the back of the store would work, and the brothers started the paper chase to legally brew.

In August 2013, their first commercial beer was served. In less than a year, they were ready to expand, and they found a place just down the road which could be remodeled to create a larger brewery and taproom. They opened in their new location, a former warehouse for a beekeeper, in November 2014. A better-than-expected Kickstarter campaign kicked up their new facility to a 7-barrel system.

The brewery is a bright red cinderblock building with white double garage doors that open in front to a picnic table patio area right off the street. Inside the taproom is a central bar facing the street and some long communal tables, plus booths with old church pews, beer logos painted on the walls, open beam ceiling, reclaimed wood, and bar stools like the seat of an old-school tractor.

The name of the brewery is a nod to the brothers' methods of cobbling together what they needed as they got started and grew. "Junkyards are places to find cool stuff," says Aaron. A junkyard is also a decidedly local sort of place and typically quite interesting—like the brewery. Aaron has gotten the occasional call to his cell phone from someone searching for an actual junkyard. Hatchet Jack was their first beer on tap. Ugly Ted is named after Teddy Roosevelt.

Facebook.com/JunkyardBrewery and Twitter @JunkyardBrewing

Stumbling Distance: *Burger Time* (1620 1st Ave N, Moorhead, 218-233-9641, itsburgertime.com) is an old-school burger drive-thru one block away. Check out the awesome replica of a Viking ship and a Norwegian stave church at *Heritage Hjemkomst Interpretive Center* (202 1st Ave N, Moorhead, 218-299-5511, hcscconline.org). A good bottle shop is *99 Bottles* (924 Main Ave, Moorhead, 218-284-0099, 99bottles.biz). For homebrew supplies, of course, there's *Country Cannery* (1320 1st Ave N, Moorhead, 218-291-0678, countrycannery.com).

Goat Ridge Brewing Co.

Founded: April 16, 2015
Brewmaster: Josh Reed
Address: 17 Central Avenue W • New London, MN 56273
Phone: 320-354-2383
Web Site: www.goatridgebrewing.com
Annual Production: under 300 barrels
Number of Beers: 6 on tap; every 2–3 weeks a new style
(plus craft root beer, ginger soda, and cold press coffee on nitro)

Possible Beers:
   » Belgian Strong Golden Ale
   » Double Honey IPA
   » Kölsch
   » Rye IPA

Samples: Yes, four 5-oz. pours for about $6.

Brewmaster's Fave: Double Honey IPA or Rye IPA

Best Time to Go: Thu 3–9PM, Fri–Sat 12–10PM.

Where can you buy it? Here in imperial pints and half pints, (higher alcohol beers may be served in 10-oz tulip glasses), and growlers and half growlers to go. Some local draft accounts possibly.

Got food? No, but food friendly.

Tours? Yes, by appointment.

Special Offer: $1 off your first beer during your signature visit.

Directions: MN 23 passes just south of New London. Take MN 9 north through town and pass the water and turn left on Central Ave. The brewery is on the left.

The Beer Buzz: Brewer Josh has a background in water resources, and water is a very important ingredient for beer. So I guess we shouldn't say we're surprised he ended up opening a brewery. He grew up on a ranch in nearby Brooten but moved around a lot as an adult. When he and his wife lived in Washington and Oregon in the 90s, he got into brewing. He did so sporadically as they traveled but got serious in 2004, and took some Siebel coursework.

Josh and his wife moved back to her family's farm right off Glacial Ridge, where an offshoot ridge backs up to their land. The old Norwegians used to call that *geita ruggen* which directly translates as 'goat back' or in this case, Goat Ridge. They planted a hop yard in 2010 and sold their crop to Indeed Brewing in Minneapolis. Now Josh will be using them for his own beers.

This is a small town (population: 1200) just getting into craft, so Josh is testing the crowd. He aims to always have some German-style, sessionable, easy drinking beers on tap, but also will have an IPA, a Belgian, something dark, and will try his hand at barrel-aging as well. He may settle on a few regular brews, but for now you can expect new things frequently. He uses local ingredients whenever he can.

His business partner Kelly Asche helps out in the taproom and oversees the books. He is originally from Hancock, Minnesota, but his girlfriend's family is from Brooten, and Josh is old friends with her dad and uncle. I mentioned this was a small town, right? It's all about community. Josh used to run into Kelly at local events and talk beer and politics with him from time to time. At a festival in 2013 he brought up his brewery

COURTESY GOAT RIDGE BREWING

plans and Kelly wanted to help. Kelly also still works at the University of Minnesota-Morris, Center for Small Towns.

Josh and his wife bought this building a few years before. He saw the property and said "We're going to put a taproom in here." Originally a garage for the DOT, the room was most recently a pottery workshop. Josh took it over in August 2014 and started remodeling. He vaulted the low ceilings for a 14 foot clearance.

The brewery is right on the Middle Fork Crow River, and they have a beer garden overlooking the water. The Dam Taproom (named for the dam 300 feet from here) has a rather eclectic design, or as Josh calls it, "old-school rock-and-roll meets bachelor farmer." There are maps and old concert posters on the wall, a growler collection, even a small library. A carpenter friend brought in reclaimed barn wood for the bar, and the back bar has a frame made out of old gas pipe. The bar seats eight, plus there are tables and chairs, a foosball table, pool table, and dart board giving it an old tavern feel. There are no TVs, as they are trying to build community, but they have cribbage and other board games, some books, and occasional live music. "Beer from Here" is their motto.

WiFi. Facebook/goatridgebrewing

Stumbling Distance: *Jack's Coffee Shop* (32 Main St N, 320-354-7017, jackscoffeeshop.com) for your caffeine fix plus sandwiches. *Middlefork Café* (34 Main St S, 320-354-2124) is great for breakfast/lunch. Vino fans, head out to *Glacial Ridge Winery* (15455 Co Rd 131, Spicer, 320-796-9463, glacialridgewinery.com). Family-owned *Redhead Creamery* (31535 463rd Ave, Brooten, 920-691-2154, redheadcreamery.com) has fresh curds in nearby Brooten and gives tours but is open limited hours; check site or call.

Goat Ridge is 20 minutes from *Foxhole Brewhouse* in New London, 35 minutes from *Third Street Brewhouse* in Cold Spring, and 1.5 hours from *Brau Brothers Brewing* in Marshall to the southwest. This is 100 miles west of Minneapolis.

GULL DAM BREWING, INC.

Founded: 2014
Brewmaster: Luke Steadman
Address: 23836 Smiley Road • Nisswa, MN 56468
Phone: 218-963-2739
Web Site: www.gulldambrewing.com
Number of Beers: about 9 on tap

Staple Beers:
  » AMBER ALE
  » IPA
  » RYE PA
  » SCOTCH ALE (with maple syrup)
  » STOUT (with vanilla bean)
  » WHEAT

Rotating Beers:
  » WINTER LAGER

Samples: Yes

Best Time to Go: Winter: Thu–Fri 4–9PM, Sat 12–10PM. Call or check website for current hours.

Where can you buy it? Here on tap and to go in growlers.

Got food? No.

Tours? By appointment.

Special Offer: Not participating at this time.

Directions: MN 371 runs north through Nisswa and the brewery is on the east side of the highway on a frontage road, just south of the juncture with County Roads 77 and 13. Watch for the big waterwheel out front. Coming from the south, there is a short lane to Smiley Rd, but from the north it is best to go east (left) onto County Road 13 and take the first right on Smiley Rd.

The Beer Buzz: Mark and Barb Anderson have been craft beer lovers since before they were even married. Their mutual interest led them to homebrew together, and their enthusiasm grew until they decided maybe this was a good business opportunity. Mark is a business jet pilot, but he had had a bar and restaurant here years ago. They settled on this location amid lakes in the north woods and chose a catchy clever and yet entirely local name for it. It's not just the cutesy way we cuss without cussing, but it's also an actual dam on the Gull River a half mile from the outlet of East Gull Lake (8 miles south of the brewery).

They brought in Brewer Luke who got his experience brewing at Sprague Farm and Brew Works near Erie, Pennsylvania, and completed the Siebel Institute World Brewing Academy Concise Course in Brewing Technology.

Quite an auspicious building, the brewery was actually a woodstaining company before this. You can't miss the big water wheel and pond out front. The taproom bar is made with 100-year-old wood from Luke's family's barn out in Pennsylvania and shows a stainless steel counter. The brewery has a mascot named Gully, naturally.

WiFi. Facebook/gulldambrewing, Twitter @GullDam_Brewing and Instagram @gulldam_brewing

Stumbling Distance: *Grand View Lodge Golf Resort & Spa* (23521 Nokomis Ave, 866-801-2951, grandviewlodge.com) is just a few minutes from here. *Zorbaz on Gull Lake* (8105 Lost Lake Rd, 218-963-4790, zorbaz.com) has 45 on tap at least half from Minnesota and mixes a menu between Mexican and pizza. From May to October, the *Nisswa Farmers Market* (nisswafarmersmarket.com) is worth a visit Thursdays 8AM–12:30PM at the American Legion Parking Lot at 25807 Main St.

BEAVER ISLAND BREWING CO.

Opened: February 21, 2015
Brewmaster: Chris Laumb
Address: 216 6th Avenue South • St. Cloud, MN 56301
Phone: 320-253-5907
Web Site: www.beaverislandbrew.com
Annual Production: 1,000 barrels
Number of Beers: 4 on tap with room for 4 more

Staple Beers:
  » RIPPLE (Kölsch-style)
  » '39 RED IPA

Rotating Beers:
  » ALT
  » LANE 5 IIPA (spring)
  » MÄRZEN
  » OKTOBERFEST
  » UNION SUIT OLD ALE (imperial porter – winter)

Most Popular Brew: Ripple and '39 Red IPA are neck and neck.

Samples: Yes, free sips for decision-making.

Brewmaster's Fave: '39 Red IPA

Best Time to Go: Open Thu–Sat 4–10PM. Happy hour Thu–Fri. But check the website as they may add other days.

Where can you buy it? Here on tap and limited pre-filled growlers to go. Some local draft accounts as well.

Got food? No, but food friendly, plus there are local menus on site.

Tours? Yes, by chance or by appointment.

Special Offer: $1 off your first pint during your signature visit.

Directions: From US 10, exit on MN 23 toward St. Cloud. Go 1.3 miles, turn left on 7th Ave, left again at 3rd St, and left again on 6th Ave. (You've come around the block due to a median on MN 23/3rd St.) Brewery will be on the right.

The Beer Buzz: St. Cloud Brewery closed its doors in 1939 and that was the last time this town had its own beer—until now. Co-founder Nick Barth wanted to get into homebrewing and set friend and co-founder Matt Studer up with a kit. So they brewed every Tuesday. A few drinks in and it's natural that a fellow starts talking of bigger and better things. What's bigger and better than a brewery?

Chris Laumb got his start back in the 90s brewing at O'Hara Brothers which transitioned to McCann's brewpub in St. Cloud, and then he brewed at the much larger Third Street Brewhouse in Cold Spring. Matt knew Brewer Chris through the local music scene and some mutual friends. Chris is a singer-songwriter and plays mandolin and guitar in some area bands. He used to manage other bars and Matt knew those bars as well. When the time was right, they brought Chris back to his roots on a smaller 15-barrel system.

PHOTO COURTESY BEAVER ISLAND BREWING

This 5000 sq. ft. building operated as a storage facility for Chrysler distribution until 1940. Then it became Pickard Motor Co., a dealership that survived into the 80s. The Pickard family still owns it. There used to be a head shop next door and a sandwich shop in here, but during the build out, the partners opened it all up. But there's still another 11,000 sq ft in the complex. You'll find lots of repurposed stuff in here: The tap tower is an old lubrication table. The wood from Lane 5 from a bowling alley, reclaimed barn wood and tin, a red cedar strip canoe on the wall, St. Cloud bricks, and even the lights from an old cattle barn at the Minnesota State Fair. There's no TV here, but background music is always playing and live music is common. Plus there are board games and the requisite cribbage board. The taproom offers a mix of low-top and tall tables. There's a parking lot out front and some spots in back.

The Beaver Islands are a cluster of islands just below the dam on the Mississippi River in St. Cloud. When looking for the source of the Mississippi, Zebulon Pike named them. Beavers were choking out the river and he could barely get through.

WiFi. Facebook/beaverislandbrew, Twitter @BeaverIslandSTC and Instagram @beaverislandbrew

Stumbling Distance: *Pioneer Place on Fifth* (22 5th Ave S, 320-203-0331, ppfive.com) is a 1913 Elks Club turned theater, great for live music, and its *Veranda Lounge* is an excellent wine bar. *The Pickled Loon* (715 W Saint Germain St, 320-281-3581, thepickledloon.com) is not your regular humdrum sort of eatery but offers eclectic seasonal menus and features DJs and live music on weekends. *The White Horse Restaurant & Bar* (809 W St Germain St, 320-257-7775, whitehorsemn.com) offers some fine dining. *Clear Waters Outfitting Co.* (100 Pine St, 320-558-8123, Clearwater, cwoutfitting.com) sets up outings on the Mississippi River. They drop you off below the dam and let you paddle south to their place in Clearwater.

GRANITE CITY FOOD AND BREWERY

Founded: June 1999
Brewmaster: Cory O'Neel
Address: 3945 2nd St. South • St. Cloud, MN 56301
Phone: 320-203-9000
Web Site: www.gcfb.net
Annual Production: 700 barrels
Number of Beers: 5

Staple Beers:
- » BATCH 1000 DOUBLE IPA
- » BROAD AXE STOUT
- » BROTHER BENEDICT'S BOCK
- » DUKE OF WELLINGTON IPA
- » NORTHERN LIGHT LAGER

Samples: A tray for about $4.95 for eight 3-oz. samples.

Best Time to Go: Open daily; Mon–Thu 11AM–1AM, Fri–Sat 11AM–2AM, Sun 9AM–10PM. Happy hour runs weekdays 3–6PM, Sat–Sun noon–5PM, and every night 9PM–close.

Where can you buy it? Growlers on site (or any of the other 34 Granite City locations in 14 states)!

Got food? Yes, flatbread pizzas, soups and salads, seafood, pasta, burgers, steaks and monthly specials. There are also a gluten-free and kids' menus.

Special Offer: Not participating.

Directions: From MN 15 heading north into St. Cloud, watch for MN 23 West / 2nd St. Turn left and the entrance to the brewery is on the right.

The Beer Buzz: This brewpub franchise was first founded right here in St. Cloud in 1999 but has since expanded throughout the Midwest. Part of their ease of expansion was streamlining the brewing process and eliminating some of the need for equipment at each location. One of the co-founders was a bit of a legend in the craft brewing scene in the Twin Cities: Bill Burdick was the guy behind Sherlock's Home Restaurant Pub and Brewery, which made a lasting impression on brewers and beer drinkers during its run from 1989 to 2002. At Granite City, Burdick developed a process they called Fermentus Interruptus™. The wort is actually prepared in their central brewing facility—a brewhouse in Ellsworth, Iowa—and then shipped to each location where it is fermented. The result is consistent staple beers and less investment in multiple brewhouses. The Granite City name comes from the 19th century industry that built St. Cloud: quarrying granite.

Granite City offers a Mug Club loyalty program wherein you receive points for what you spend at the brewpub and discounts on food purchases.

The restaurant is a stand-alone building just off the intersection of Highway 15 and 2nd St. Plenty of parking.

Stumbling Distance: See *Beaver Island Brewery* here in town.

FOXHOLE BREWHOUSE

Opening: July 2015
Brewmaster: Ryan Fuchs
Address: 313 4th Street SW • Willmar, MN 56201
Phone: 320-295-6294
Web Site: www.foxholebrewhouse.com
Annual Production: 750 barrels
Number of Beers: up to 6 on tap No flagships, rotating

Rotating Beer Styles:
» BARLEYWINE
» BRANDY BARREL AGED AMBER
» COFFEE STOUT (with local THE GOODNESS)
» DOUBLE IPA
» GALAXY PALE ALE
» HEFEWEIZEN
» IPA
» PECAN PORTER
» PUMPKIN ALE
» RHUBARB WHEAT

Samples: No.

Brewmaster's Fave: Rye IPA with Rhubarb Wheat in a close second

Best Time to Go: Open Wed–Fri 4–9PM, Sat 12–10PM to start. Check website to confirm.

Where can you buy it? Only here on tap in pints and half-pints, and growlers to go.

Got food? No, but food friendly.

Tours? Yes, by appointment.

Special Offer: $1 off your first pint during your signature visit.

Directions: US 12 passes east-west through Willmar as Litchfield Ave but briefly become Pacific Ave. From here go south on 2nd St SW and turn right on Litchfield Ave SW. Go two blocks west and turn left on 4th St SW and the brewery is on the left.

The Beer Buzz: This whole thing started with Ryan realizing he loved beer enough to brew it at home with a kit. But extracts did nothing for him, so then it was all grain. Friends liked it and gave him the encouragement. Ryan used to build bridges for a living, and he started to wonder: can I do this all my life? He was away from home a lot, so maybe beer was the way to go. He could be doing what he loves and staying close to the people he loves. Liv, his wife, is partner in this and her brother Stevin signed on as assistant brewer.

They found space in an historic 1926 building—it was once a soda shop but now the 20,000 sq. ft. space is divided up for the brewery and a planned neighboring restaurant. The brewery took over 2,000 sq. ft. of what was storage space in recent years. It's an open floor plan so you can see the 5-barrel brewhouse.

Ryan and Liv have traveled to England and Europe, and Liv loved the look of the pubs, the cozy, dim lighting, so they decided not to go for the usual industrial look. There are seats at the bar and a long bench on one wall facing tables and chairs that can be combined for larger groups, plus some standard tables. Music plays in the background and the taproom hosts occasional local musicians. Board games, such as cribbage, are also on hand. Parking is on the street or a city lot a half block away at 4th and Trott Ave.

WiFi. Facebook/foxholebrewhouse

Stumbling Distance: *Jake's Pizza* (316 Litchfield Ave SW, 320-235-1714, jakespizzaofwillmar.com) delivers. Two great choices for Mexican: *Rosita's* (304 4th St SW, 320-235-1072, rositasinwillmar.com) or *Azteca Mexican Restaurant* (215 4th St SW, 320-262-3920). Since 1964 *The Barn Theatre* (321 4th St SW, 320-235-9500, thebarntheatre.com) has been doing community shows. Roadside attraction fans should see the 17-foot statue of *Chief Kandiyohi* (the name of the county, not an actual chief) near the public library (505 Becker Ave SW).

Foxhole is 20 minutes from *Goat Ridge Brewing* in New London, less than an hour from *Third Street Brewhouse* in Cold Spring, and just over an hour from *Brau Brothers Brewing* in Marshall to the southwest.

ZONE 5
Northeast Minnesota and the North Shore

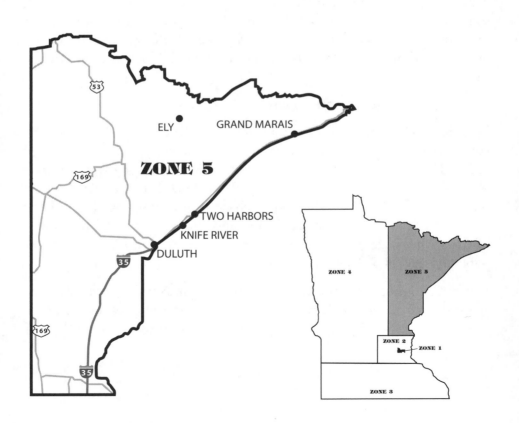

BREWERY TOURS: THE DULUTH EXPERIENCE

The Duluth Experience is a full-service tour agency with trained guides, a comfortable bus, and plenty of good knowledge of what Duluth is all about. And they do **brewery tours**. Not only is this a great way to see the Duluth area breweries without having to drive yourself around—and thus either not drink or find a designated driver—but in some cases it is the only way you can visit that brewery. *Blacklist Brewing* and *Borealis Fermentery* up in Knife River are **not** typically open to the public. You gotta know someone—and that someone is anyone working at The Duluth Experience.

Their Craft Beer Brewery tours take you behind the scenes at the area breweries and brewpubs and include samples and a lunch or dinner at a great local restaurant. There are several tours to choose from and some go beyond the city limits, including over the bridge to Superior's *Thirsty Pagan* and up the North Shore to *Castle Danger Brewing* and *Borealis Fermentery*. You might also visit *Vikre Distillery* and in the summer, stop at a local hops farm such as *Harbor Hops* up in Two Harbors.

In addition to the brewery tours, The Duluth Experience also guides historical tours, as well as biking, mountain biking, and kayaking tours.

Call or book online:
The Duluth Experience
218-464-6337 | info@TheDuluthExperience.com
TheDuluthExperience.com

PHOTOS COURTESTY OF THE DULUTH EXPERIENCE

GROWLER BAGS

Minnesota—and in particular, Duluth—is a pretty outdoorsy place. So how to pack that growler of your local brew along on your hike/paddle/ride? Frost River in Duluth has you covered. The Single Wide is like a daypack for your growler. The Double Wide is similar but holds two growlers and adds a foam divider to keep them from banging together. The SlingPack has only one strap, a bit more casual, and a ZipUp is also on offer.

Shoulder straps and handles make them easy to carry and they are all made with brass hardware, leather and waxed canvas. In the R&D phase, a Frost River user had a growler leak half a glass into the pack and even overnight it didn't leak out and make a mess of his car. No clinking bottles or brown paper bag, so onlookers don't know you're hauling suds. Discreet, eh? Plus, these are American made: New Jersey canvas; Red Wing, Minnesota leather; and Duluth assembly. Buy at Frost River directly or find some branded bags at some of the local breweries.

Frost River
1910 W. Superior St | Duluth, MN 55806
1-800-FROST-84 | www.frostriver.com

PHOTO COURTESY OF DEWEY KOSHENINA

Bent Paddle Brewing Co.

Founded: 2013
Brewmaster: Bryon Tonnis and Colin Mullen
Address: 1912 West Michigan Street • Duluth, MN 55806
Phone: 218-279-2722
Web Site: www.bentpaddlebrewing.com
Annual Production: 6,500 barrels
Number of Beers: 4 flagships, 8 beers per year, 10 on tap in taproom

Staple Beers:
» Bent Hop (Golden IPA)
» Black (Black Ale)
» 14° ESB
» Venture Pils

Rotating Beers: (seasonals and limited-release specialty beers)
» Barrel-Aged Double Black
» Cold Press Black (Black with cold press coffee)
» Day Pack Pale Ale
» Harness the Winter IPA (Feb–Apr)
» Winter Ale
» …plus nitro taps, barrel-aging, alternate versions of staple beers, casks in the tap room

Most Popular Brew: Bent Hop

Samples: Yes, flight of six 5-oz. pours for about $8.

Best Time to Go: Open Wed–Thu 3–10PM, Fri 3–11PM, Sat 1–11PM. Closed Sun–Tue. Watch for live music and cask tappings. (There may be yoga classes here on weekends as well.)

Where can you buy it? In Minnesota and Wisconsin in cans and on tap, plus the occasional limited specialty beers in 750 ml bottles. In the taproom they sell 10-, 16-, and 20-oz pours and take-away growlers.

Got food? No, but it is food friendly, with a few delivery menus on hand, and there are food trucks in summer.

Tours? Every Saturday at noon by pre-registration on the website. The one-hour tour includes samples, and while it is free, the brewery would appreciate a nonperishable food item donation for a local food pantry.

Special Offer: A free Bent Paddle sticker with your book signature.

Directions: From its juncture with I-35 in Duluth, take Exit 255 for US 53 north and immediately watch for the 21st Ave West ramp. Take this and continue onto N 20th Ave West for 0.1 mile, then turn left onto Michigan St and the brewery is on the right.

The Beer Buzz: Founded by two couples—Karen and Bryon Tonnis and Laura and Colin Mullen—this large production brewery, with light-colored metal siding and a brick façade to the taproom, is on the West End of town in a sort of industrial warehouse zone not far from the port and rail yards. Bryon spent several years as the head brewer at the Minneapolis Rock Bottom Brewery, and Colin did the same at Barley John's Brew Pub in New Brighton. Laura was an event coordinator for the Minnesota Craft Brewer's Guild. When the two couples got together, they discovered they had the same goals: start their own brewery.

Bryon calls beer and canoeing his two passions, and for years he's used a bent paddle for mashing during the brewing process—thus the name. Additionally, the name goes well with Duluth's reputation as an outdoors sports mecca and its proximity to the famous Boundary Waters. A paddle blade is worked into the logo, and for a time a tiny hiker graced the labels as well. A brewery in Vermont asked them to remove the little guy, however, for being too similar to their own logo. The brewers decided to go with cans rather than bottles for the flagship beers, not only because of technical advantages, but also because they work better for hikers and paddlers. Glass is often prohibited in paddling areas, in fact. They also sell non-glass growlers.

The taproom has concrete floors, high industrial ceilings, exposed brick, and metal siding as wainscoting that extends out along the front of the bar. Tables are up front and the bar stands along the back wall in front of a walk-in cooler. A glass garage door on the left opens into the brewery proper. Available beers are displayed on boards on the back wall. Parking is on the street.

WiFi. Facebook.com/bentpaddlebrewing and Twitter @bentpaddlebeer

Stumbling Distance: A popular stop for baked goods is *Johnson's Bakery & Coffee Shop* (2230 W 3rd St, 218-727-1889, johnsonsbakery.com). Looking for high-quality, locally made packs? Visit *Frost River* (1910 W Superior St, 218-727-1472, frostriver.com). *Randy's* (2125 W Superior St, 218-727-1144) is a great sort of hole-in-the-wall place, good for cheap and satisfying eats, popular with locals.

DOGGIE BREW BITES

It's not uncommon for spent grain to make it out to a local farmer's livestock for a bit of recycling, but here's an idea your dog may like better: Doggie Brew Bites. This company out of Duluth has developed a doggie snack fashioned out of spent grain and peanut butter. Grains come from Lake Superior Brewing, Bent Paddle Brewing, and Canal Park Brewing, and the manufacturing is done in town as well. The peanut butter is made only with peanuts and sea salt—no crazy chemistry lessons on the label—and it is American made at a worker-owned cooperative in Missouri called East Wind Nut Butters.

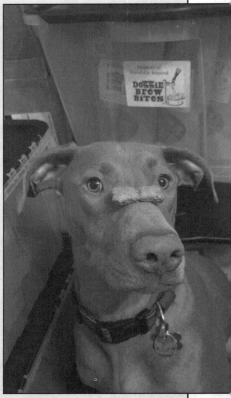

Owner and creator Matthew Barthelemy developed this recipe on his own and has kept it simple: peanut butter, malted barley, whole wheat flour, and eggs. He found a basic recipe for spent grain dog treats online but spent two months reworking it until it was just right. I asked him if he had ever tried his

PHOTO COURTESY OF
DOGGIE BREW BITES

own treat. Actually, he's eaten many. "It's really a part of our production process. Every batch we make, a treat or two is consumed by the baker for quality control—and a quick snack. The ingredients we use are all-natural and human grade. My dogs eat a higher quality peanut butter than I do."

His first delivery was to *Canal Park Brewery* but now they are for sale at 5 local breweries and several other craft stores. He also has a foldable waxed canvas dog bowl which works for either food or water and is perfect for anyone who takes their dog everywhere.

Brewfully Inspired
1218 ½ E. 4th Street, Duluth | 218-673-0606
doggiebrewbites.com

BLACKLIST BREWING

Founded: 2013
Brewmaster: Brian Schanzenbach
Address: 211 East 2nd Street • Duluth, MN 55805
Phone: 218-831-2767
Web Site: www.blacklistbrewing.com
Annual Production: 250 barrels
Number of Beers: 10+

Staple Beers:
» OR DE BELGIQUE (Strong Belgian Golden)

Rotating Beers:
» BELGIAN-STYLE SOUR WIT (lacto-soured – summer, fall, winter)
» COCO NOIR (weizenbock with cocoa nibs and coconut – fall, winter)
» HEFE (imperial hefeweizen with grapefruit zest – summer)
» MAIDENS D'OR SERIES:
» CRAN (Or with cranberries – summer, fall, winter)
» VERTE (dry hopped Or – summer, fall, winter)
» RHUBARB WIT (Thanksgiving season)
» SPRUCE TIPPED (imperial IPA with fennel – fall, winter, spring)
» TRIPEL (with green tea, lemongrass and honey – summer, fall)
» WIT NOIR (Belgian-style dark wheat ale – summer, fall, winter)

Most Popular Brew: Or de Belgique

Samples: On a Duluth Experience tour.

Brewmaster's Fave: Flemish style Sour Red aged in wine barrels

Best Time to Go: When you've booked a tour through The Duluth Experience.

Where can you buy it? For sale in 750 ml bottles in major liquor stores and on tap in a few select places in Duluth and the Twin Cities. Use the Locator on their website.

Got food? No.

Tours? Typically only available through The Duluth Experience, but groups of 6 or more can contact them for an appointment.

Special Offer: Not participating at this time.

Directions: *Remember:* you need to be on a Duluth Experience tour to visit. From I-35 heading north through downtown Duluth, take Exit 256B for 5th Ave West toward Lake Ave. Turn north on Lake Ave, drive 5 blocks and turn right on 2nd St and the brewery is on the left.

The Beer Buzz: Owners Jon Loss and Brian Schanzenbach have been friends since junior high back in Brainerd, MN. Brian came to Duluth to study, while Jon attended art school in the Twin Cities before moving here to join Brian in this endeavor. Jon now handles the business, marketing, and design elements of the brewery, and he is a Certified Cicerone®. Brian interned at Duluth's Lake Superior Brewing and studied at Siebel before finishing the program in Germany. His travels there inspired his beers: he likes wheat beers and sours and likes to play with fruits and spices.

In 2012 they initiated a Kickstarter campaign and by April 2013 they were brewing for the market. Blacklist has produced 20 different beers since then. They started as a members club sort of brewery, and those members today function as a sort of test kitchen for "crazy things we never made before," says Jon. The hits with the members are the beer we mass produced," says Jon. "And by mass produced I mean very small amounts."

Blacklist brews "experience beers," and they are meant for special occasions, perhaps as a substitute for champagne.

A fire in February 2014 caused them to close until July that year, and they had to dump everything but the stainless steel equipment. They overcame the loss and have been right back at it. The brew kettle sits right over an open burner. Much of the space is taken up by the barrels the brews are aging in. Beers are aged at least four months, and customers are advised to wait a minimum of 8 weeks after purchasing a bottle. These are not your everyday beers, and you can cellar them for 1–3 years.

Plans are to expand and move at some point, to have a beer garden, to be a destination, but for now public visits are limited to the Duluth Experience and group tours by appointment.

Facebook.com/BlacklistBrewing and Twitter @BlacklistBeer

Stumbling Distance: *Zeitgeist Arts Café* (222 E Superior St, 218-336-1360, zeitgeistarts.com) offers lunch and dinner with local emphasis and also acts as Blacklist's home base for beer releases. *Sarah's Table* (1902 E 8th St, 218-724-6811, astccc.net) is a wine bar and farm-to-table eatery serving breakfast, lunch and dinner. MN beers on tap.

CANAL PARK BREWING CO.

Founded: 2013
Head Brewer: Ryan Woodhill
Address: 300 Canal Park Drive • Duluth, MN 55802
Phone: 218-464-4790
Web Site: www.canalparkbrewery.com
Annual Production: 1,700 barrels
Number of Beers: 10 on tap, plus 2 casks

Staple Beers:

- » ANKLE DEEP PILSNER
- » DAWN TREADER TRIPEL
- » HANK AND DAB'S PALE ALE
- » NUT HATCHET BROWN
- » STONED SURF IPA

Rotating Beers:

- » ESB
- » FOGGY JACK PORTER
- » 40 ACRE SAISON
- » GENERAL STERLING PRICE AMERICAN AMBER
- » GREEDY BASTARD BLACK IPA
- » MAIBOCK
- » OKTOBERFEST
- » OLD AVALANCHE BARLEYWINE
- » SCOTTISH ALE
- » WETSUIT MALFUNCTION WIT

Most Popular Brew: Nut Hatchet Brown

Samples: Yes, four 4-oz pours for about $6.50

Best Time to Go: Open Sun–Thu 11AM–11PM, Fri–Sat 11–12AM. A great happy hour runs Mon–Fri 4–6PM and 9PM–close. See the website for other weekly specials and trivia night.

Where can you buy it? Here in imperial pints and growlers to go.

Got food? Yes, full family menu, with soups, salads, sandwiches, build-your-own burgers, fish & chips, porter-braised pork poutine, pretzel with IPA mustard, pickled herring, beer-can chicken, a wild rice and black bean burger, plus a kid's menu

Tours? Yes, 45-minute tours scheduled Fri–Sat. Check website or call. $10 for the tour, pint glass and a pint of beer. Junior package for $8.

Special Offer: A free pint when you get your book signed.

Directions: From I-35 heading north through downtown Duluth, take Exit 256B for 5th Ave West toward Lake Ave. Follow signs for Lake Ave and merge onto Lake Ave. (From the north, take the same exit and you'll turn left on Lake Ave.) Go 0.1 mile southeast on Lake Ave and turn left on Canal Park Dr and the parking lot and brewery are on your right.

The Beer Buzz: It's a family affair: Rockie Kavajecz, Tracy Uttley, Diane Kavajecz, Kim Kaz, Sara Kavajecz, Paul Kaz, and Ted Kavajecz took part in founding this Lake Superior-side brewpub that celebrates what it is to be a Northcoaster. On this site once stood Duluth Spring Co.; they used to make parts for the famous ice resurfacer Zamboni. Unfortunately, they left behind an environmental mess, and to build the new brewery, the construction had to start from 15 feet below ground level as they cleaned it up.

The brewhouse is a real beauty, a customized 20-barrel system from DME (Diversified Metal Engineering) they refer to as "Gus," atop an Argelith tile floor from Germany. The hot liquor tank pulls heat from the city steam system. Be sure to get the tour. Canal Park Won Silver at the World Beer Cup for the Nut Hatchet Brown in 2014. The brewing

team uses some local hops for wet-hopped beers. Their most recent brewer Ryan is a native of Minnesota, but they found him brewing in New Orleans. He moved back for the job.

The bar area has views of the serving tanks through windows behind the wood and blue-tile bar, and growler lamps hang above. Along with the tall tables there, you can find proper restaurant seating in the next space. The dining area has plenty of glass windows so you can see the view. Rockie's son Luke, a journalism major, took all the photos you see. Matt Tetzner did the metal work for the tap handles and the keg chandeliers. Menus at the tables and bar feature detailed beer descriptions. In season (or even when it's chilly a bit), you can enjoy the outdoor terrace with a view out to Lake Superior. The deck features a fire pit and a fountain made out of a keg. The location is just off the boardwalk along the lakeshore, an easy walk from the old Fitger's Brewery (now a hotel with a retail complex, museum and brewpub). You can see Uncle Harvey's Mausoleum (or "The Cribs") from the patio. The brewpub has its own parking lot.

ATM on site. WiFi. Facebook.com/Canalparkbrewingcompany and Twitter @canalparkbrew

Stumbling Distance: A good place to crash is *Canal Park Lodge* (250 Canal Park Dr, 218-279-6000, canalparklodge.com) right next door. Try *Northern Waters Smokehaus* (394 South Lake Avenue #106, 218-724-7307, northernwaterssmokehaus.com) for local smoked meats, fish and sandwiches. Check out the tipple at *Vikre Distillery* (525 S Lake Ave #102, 218-481-7401, vikredistillery.com). A locavore fine-dining option is *Lake Avenue Restaurant & Bar* (394 S Lake Ave, 218-722-2355, lakeavenuerestaurantandbar.com).

UNCLE HARVEY'S MAUSOLEUM

Less than 100 feet out into the cold waves of Lake Superior, just off the Duluth Lakewalk along Canal Park, there stands a bleak concrete box. This is Uncle Harvey's Mausoleum.

But no one's remains lie here. Nor was it a speakeasy or gambling house back during Prohibition, and it wasn't an icehouse, as it is sometimes called. Lake charts mark it as "the cribs," but in fact, these are the ruins of a sand and gravel hopper. Today, scuba divers like to poke around it, and swimmers climb up and dive off.

The structure, most of which is now gone, was built in 1919 by "Uncle" Harvey Whitney of Superior, Wisconsin. The building business was booming in Duluth, so it seemed to Harvey a good idea to set this up to receive sand and gravel shipments from the South Shore over in Wisconsin, namely the Apostle Islands area, and Grand Marais up the North Shore. A boat would moor up here, a crane would unload it into the hopper, and trucks at the end of a tunnel would haul it off to the next building project. If the city of Duluth went ahead and built a breakwater for the harbor, Harvey would be sitting pretty with an abundance of the materials they needed. The trouble is that plan never came to fruition and by 1922 it was abandoned. Concrete doesn't wash away so easily, so here it still stands about a century later—although it is showing signs of deterioration and buckling. A pillar—still visible in this 2014 photo—sank into the ice on February 7, 2015.

BEER ON THE TRACKS

Back in 1886, a new rail line called the Lake Division finally connected the Duluth & Iron Range Railway, which stopped in Two Harbors, into Duluth and on to the rest of the country's rail system. The Lakefront Line, as it was eventually known, offered an important service to the iron ore industry, then the timber industry, and until 1961, for passengers. In the 1980s it was to be abandoned, but members of the Lake Superior Railroad Museum saved it and it was renamed the North Shore Scenic Railroad.

Today the museum operates the train and offers several different excursions. But if you are on a beer hunt, there's one excursion that might be of most interest to you. *Castle Danger Brewery* is located north of Duluth in Two Harbors, and the train makes that 28-mile run departing Duluth at 10:30AM and returning between 4 and 5PM. This leaves you a two-hour stay in Two Harbors, enough time to stop in and **visit the brewery**.

Other trips are shorter—one or 1.5 hours—and run through downtown, staying close to Duluth. Fully narrated tours tell the history of Duluth, the harbor, and the stories of the railroads that built northern Minnesota and Wisconsin. Trains operate starting in May and run until October. The Music & Pizza Train includes Domino's Pizza, soda, and live music for the return ride.

In September, watch for the **Fall Beer Tasting Train**. Brews are provided by area breweries. The 2.5 hour run includes all-you-can-try tastings in two bar-cars with a coach ticket or free food, a seat in the Dining Car, and table service beer tasting with a first-class ticket. Needless to say, this special train ride sells out every year, so book early.

There are several other special event train excursions, including private reservations for the Birthday Caboose. Check the website for more information. You can also check out the Lake Superior Railroad Museum (lsrm.org) (not included in the tour price).

North Shore Scenic Railroad
506 West Michigan St, Duluth
218-722-1273 | 800-423-1273 | northshorescenicrailroad.org

CARMODY IRISH PUB & BREWING

Founded: St. Patrick's Day, 2006
Brewmaster: Rick Sauer
Address: 308 East Superior Street • Duluth, MN 55802
Phone: 218-740-4747
Web Site: www.carmodyirishpub.com
Annual Production: 350 barrels
Number of Beers: 4–7 on tap plus guest beers totaling 32; 20–30 brews per year plus weekly small batches

Staple Beers:
- » AGNES IRISH RED (Ed's grandmother's niece b. 1892)
- » DEWEY SCANLON IPA
- » FAMINE BLACK 47 (stout)
- » PEOPLE'S PUB ALE
- » OLD SWILL (six-grain high-gravity)

Rotating Beers:
- » WINTER ALE

Most Popular Brew: Dewey Scanlon IPA

Samples: Yes, four 4-oz. pours for about $5

Brewmaster's Fave: Derailed Ale

Best Time to Go: Open daily 3PM–2AM. Watch for small batch releases. Occasional live music.

Where can you buy it? Only here, and to go in growlers, but also on tap at the sister pub in Two Harbors.

Got food? Yes, a full menu with bangers and mash, sandwiches, wraps and appetizers, plus signatures such as Chicago beef and Cuban and Reuben sandwiches.

Tours? If someone is free and available, sure. See also The Duluth Experience tours.

Special Offer: A free flight (paddle) of four samples when you get your book signed.

Directions: From I-35 heading north through downtown Duluth, take Exit 256B for 5th Ave West toward Lake Ave. Follow signs for Lake

Ave and turn left onto Lake Ave. (From the north, take the same exit and you'll merge to the right onto Lake Ave.) Turn right on Superior and go 0.3 mile and the brewery is on your right.

The Beer Buzz: Now this is a bit of a serious Irish pub, history-wise. Ed Gleeson, who owns this with his wife Liz, has strong ties to Ireland. Ed's an interesting character. His grandparents came from Ireland and settled here. His grandmother hailed from County Kerry, and his father was four when he came across the pond. Born in Duluth, Ed lived here until he was 12 when his mom, by then a widow, saw the National Guard shooting at Kent State and packed up and moved to Belfast, Ireland. Ed grew up there drinking European beers. He's served in the Canadian army and worked as a cop in Chicago.

He ended up marrying a gal from Oak Park, Illinois, and entered the corporate world. Years later, as a traveling salesman, he found himself in Superior, Wisconsin, with a flat tire, two weeks before Christmas. Nearby he saw a simple cement block building and went over to ask if he could use the phone to call AAA. This was Twin Ports Brewing, and the fellow he spoke to for the next six hours was the brewer Rick Sauer. A few weeks later he wrote a check and became a 20% owner of a brewpub. He had had a passion for beer much of his life. "Why did I wait until I was 48 to do it?" But the ball—or the barrel?—was rolling now.

In 2005 he and Liz moved up to his childhood hometown and opened this Irish pub. He brought in Rick Sauer to start the brewery. Rick, who has done well as a consultant starting up a number of breweries around Wisconsin, didn't end up staying long. Jason Baumgarth took the job, brewing a slew of interesting beers (his Carmody Lavender Ale was licensed to Rock Bottom Brewery) before heading up the North Shore for Voyageur Brewing in Grand Marais. Now Rick is back.

Ed loves his history. The beer names reflect that a bit. Dewey Scanlon IPA is named after the Duluth Eskimo's player/coach/manager who was also Ed's dad's second cousin. His grandparents, Irish immigrants, started People's Brewery here in Duluth back in 1907 (thus People's Pub Ale), and it survived until Prohibition. (Longer than his grandfather who perished during the influenza epidemic in 1918.)

A fly-fishing outfitter and an electronics repair outfit previously occupied the space. Dollars and foreign currency decorate the ductwork above and

A *People's Brewery* company picnic in Duluth's West End. Carmody owner Ed's father, Ed Gleeson is second from the right standing with a dark tweed scally cap next to his cousin. Ed's grandmother, Margaret Carmody is the next one to the right of the cousin. Her husband, Michael "Big Mike" Gleeson is on the opposite side standing, fourth man from the left with a mustache and a picnic basket in front of him.

flags hang from the ceiling. The previous brewer affectionately called it a "living room with a bar," and that captures the pub's essence. This is a comfortable local hangout, great for a pint and a chat (no TVs), and functions as a good "last call bar" when food trucks pull up in front at the end of the night. The back corner has a gas stove as does the Irish-style stone hearth up front.

ATM on site. Free WiFi. Facebook.com/CarmodyIrishPubAndBrewery and Twitter @CarmodyIrishPub

Stumbling Distance: You may hear of *The Rathskeller* as being a very cool sort of speakeasy place in an historic building. Do check it out, in the basement of *Tycoons Ale House* (132 E Superior St, 218-623-1889, tycoonsalehouse.com). Sister pub *Carmody 61* (1102 7th Ave, 218-834-1102, carmody61pub.com) also serves food and Carmody's beer. This is a short walk from *Fitger's Brewhouse*.

FITGER'S BREWHOUSE
Founded: 1996
Brewmaster: Dave Hoops
Address: 600 East Superior Street • Duluth, MN 55802
Phone: 218-279-2739
Web Site: www.fitgersbrewhouse.com
Annual Production: 3,000 barrels
Number of Beers: 14 on tap, 80 styles per year

Staple Beers:
- » APRICOT WHEAT
- » BIG BOAT OATMEAL STOUT
- » EL NIÑO DOUBLE HOPPED IPA
- » LIGHTHOUSE GOLDEN
- » STARFIRE PALE ALE (NORTH SHORE-STYLE HOPPY PALE ALE)
- » WILDFIRE LAGER
- » WITCHTREE ESB

Rotating Beers:
- » BEAVER BAY BROWN ALE
- » EL DIABLO (Belgian Strong Ale)
- » HOPPELUJAH IPA
- » SUPERIOR TRAIL IPA
- » …constantly changing seasonals and Brewer's Choice, with cask-conditioned ales, occasional sours and barrel-aged brews

Most Popular Brew: Starfire Pale Ale

Samples: Yes, a flight of seven 3-oz. pours for about $8.

Brewmaster's Fave: "I can only say one??"

Best Time to Go: Sun–Mon 11–12AM, Tue–Thu 11–1AM, Fri–Sat 11–2AM. Live music most days of the week.

Where can you buy it? Only by the glass and to go in growlers, or at several sister establishments in Duluth (see Stumbling Distance). *Note: The Brewhouse beer is not to be confused with Fitger's brand beer in bottles, which is a contract brew associated with the hotel, a separate entity.*

Got food? Yes, "Duluth pub food" and much of it is locally sourced. Wild rice burger, smoked fish, fish and chips, burgers, sandwiches, salads (Maple

Salad is a highlight), appetizers, and vegetarian options. Also house root beer and Woodchuck Granny Smith Hard Cider.

Tours: Sat 2 & 3:30PM, $8 for age 21+ (3 samples, a glass, and coupon), $5 for all others. Sign up at the beer store or call 218-625-8646.

Special Offer: A free sticker with your book signature.

Directions: From I-35 heading north through downtown Duluth, take Exit 256B for 5th Ave West toward Lake Ave. Follow signs for Lake Ave and turn left onto Lake Ave. (From the north, take the same exit and you'll merge to the right onto Lake Ave.) Turn right on Superior and go 0.5 mile and the brewery is on your right.

The Beer Buzz: Often referred to simply as The Brewhouse, the city's first brewpub (and the state's largest) is appropriately renting space in the Fitger's complex—the old Fitger's Brewery turned into a hotel, shopping space, and offices. The building itself has a small museum and is on the National Register of Historical Places, while the Brewhouse occupies a sizable space spread out on two floors including their Beer Store on the lower level.

Mike Hoops, now at Town Hall Brewing in Minneapolis, was the original brewer and opened the place with owner Tim Nelson. He passed the paddle and gumboots to his brother Dave in late 1999 when annual production hit about 200 barrels. Now they are approaching their 3,500 barrel limit. Dave was work-

ing in the California wine industry when he picked up homebrewing in the late 80s. He made more than he could drink and would give it away as Christmas gifts. Then he decided to go pro, and in the heart of the Cali craft beer country, he went to brew school. He helped open Pyramid Brewing's plant in 1995, but then he and his wife, a Duluth native, moved here to raise their children.

The beer has been winning awards since the 90s, including some medals at the Great American Beer Festival, and Dave's creativity is pushed by the locals. "We have the best beer consumers in the state," says Hoops. "The weirder the beer, the more they want to go out of their way to get it." He calls Duluth a "beer educated community" and notes that drinkers are hop driven. He's brewed 33 different IPAs in one year.

Spent grain feeds their Scottish Highland cattle where the beef for the menu comes from.

ATM on site. Free WiFi. Facebook.com/FitgersBrewhouse and Twitter @DuluthBrewhouse

Stumbling Distance: As a brewpub, *The Brewhouse* can only distribute to its sister restaurants or "tied houses," and fortunately, these are all nearby. Check out the rock club *Redstar Lounge* (same as The Brewhouse, 218-723-7827, duluthredstar.com), *Burrito Union* (1332 E 4th St, 218-728-4414, burritounion.com), and American chophouse *Tycoons Alehouse & Eatery* (132 E Superior St, 218-623-1889, tycoonsalehouse.com). Each of these have their own special brews. And if you need a place to crash, you don't even have to go outside to get to *Fitger's Inn* (218-722-8826, www.fitgers.com). This is a short walk from *Carmody Irish Pub & Brewing*.

LAKE SUPERIOR BREWING CO.

Founded: 1994
Head Brewer: Dale Kleinschmidt
Address: 2711 West Superior Street • Duluth, MN 55806
Phone: 218-723-4000
Web Site: www.lakesuperiorbrewing.com
Annual Production: 2,500 barrels
Number of Beers: 9 beers+

Staple Beers:
- » DEEP WATER BLACK IPA
- » KAYAK KÖLSCH
- » SIR DULUTH OATMEAL STOUT
- » SPECIAL ALE

Rotating Beers:
- » MESABI RED
- » NORTH SHORE WHEAT (May-Aug)
- » OKTOBERFEST
- » OLD MAN WINTER WARMER (barleywine)
- » SPLIT ROCK BOCK

Most Popular Brew: Kayak Kölsch

Samples: Yes, $1 each or just a free sip to help you choose.

Brewmaster's Fave: Special Ale unless the North Shore Wheat is on

Best Time to Go: Open Fri 4–9PM, Sat 3–9PM.

Where can you buy it? Any liquor store from Hinckley to Grand Marais, most places statewide, parts of northern Wisconsin (Superior, Hayward).

Got food? Just a few bagged snacks. Food friendly—carry in or have it delivered. They brew their own High Bridge Root Beer.

Tours? By appointment, and during tap room hours if not busy. Free and includes sample and insults.

Special Offer: A free pint during your signature visit.

Directions: From its juncture with I-35 in Duluth, take Exit 255 for US 53 north and immediately watch for the 21st Ave West ramp. Take this and continue onto N 20th Ave West two blocks and turn right on Superior St. Drive 0.7 mile and the brewery is on the right behind a parking lot there.

The Beer Buzz: Named for the lake they call gitche gumee, Lake Superior Brewing was founded by Bob Dromeshauser, a scientist who found himself out of research work. With a bit of help from University of Minnesota-Duluth's small business incubator, he and a partner opened a homebrew supply and microbrewery in the Fitger's Complex downtown, becoming the first brewery in Duluth since Fitger's closed its doors in 1972. Dale Kleinschmidt, current co-owner and operations manager, was one of the homebrewer types who kept hanging around until they invited him to help out as an apprentice. It was a tiny space, about 200 square feet, but not so tiny that The Beer Hunter Michael Jackson didn't take notice and pay a visit. (Actually, Bob had taken his homebrew to a sampling at Sherlock's Home Pub & Brewery near the Twin Cities in 1991, and Jackson had been the guest host.) With popularity growing, it became harder to keep up with demand—they had started with just one fermenter and a soup burner. In 1999, they converted this warehouse space into a brewhouse, doubled their size, and started bottling as well. Bob moved on in 2001, and the current owners Don and Jo Hoag, John Judd III and Karen Olsen were founding members of the local homebrew club, Minnesota's first: the Northern Ale Stars. In 2014, the brewery opened its taproom.

Dale is quite a character if you get a chance to chat with him, and he's one of four Master Slivovitz Judges in the world. "Smells like lighter fluid and ether, and tastes just like it smells."

The brewery sits in an industrial space with an office. Inside malt bags hang above the taproom area like a canopy where there's a small wood bar made of oak and maple left over from a photo shoot of floor samples at the commercial photographer's next door. Posters on the walls—complete with spelling errors—are some design samples from an ad agency that wanted $55,000 for them, and when the brewery decided that was a bit too steep for their budget, they were allowed to just keep them for the taproom.

The taporoom has some cocktail tables and bar stools and is separated from the brewing operations by a low wall. Beers on tap are listed on a chalkboard across the room. Come for growler fills and doggie bites (see text box). You may notice a canoe and some kayaks hanging from the ceiling. These belong to Dale and the head brewer and are being stored when not in use. This is the Best Town Ever according to *Outside* after all.

Facebook.com/LakeSuperiorBrewing and Twitter @LkSuperiorBrew

MERCH

GROWLER FILL - $10 / $6 (Beer / Root Beer)
GROWLER GLASS - $5
T-SHIRT or HAT - $15
LONG SLEEVE - $20
PINT GLASS - $5
KOLSCH GLASS - $7
LSB PATCH - $4
STICKER - $1

BEERS

KAYAK KOLSCH
SPECIAL ALE
OATMEAL STOUT
BLACK IPA & NITRO
Seasonal → North Shore Wheat
ONLY $1 → HIGH BRIDGE ROOT BEER
St. Louis IPA

Stumbling Distance: The 1898 *Clyde Iron Works* (2920 W Michigan St, 218-727-1150, clydeironworks.com) is now a restaurant and a very cool place for a concert or wedding. Good for a beer-battered fish fry on Fridays. The brewery makes a Negro Modelo clone for them called Clyde Dark, and other area brews are also on tap. Happy hour is Sun–Thu 4–6PM. *Duluth Grill* (118 S 27th Ave W, 218-726-1150, duluthgrill.com) is a great food option as well.

SLIVOVITZ! SLEEVE – OH WHAT?

As you drink around Northern Minnesota, you are likely going to come across a local favorite called Slivovitz. The people of Eastern and Central Europe know this one too. It's brandy made from Damson plums, and it packs a wallop—often boasting 100-140 proof. And if you ask Brewer Dale Kleinschmidt from *Lake Superior Brewing*, he'll tell you:

"Smells like lighter fluid and ether, and tastes just like it smells," says Dale. "Absolute bottom of the barrel."

What does Dale know? He is one of four Master Slivovitz Judges in the world. (Ask, and again he'll tell you.) His buddy Bill Radosevich, a lead contamination specialist from Minneapolis, was a big fan of the stuff. Bill decided they needed to found The International Slivovitz Tasters Association, and of course they had to have a festival. His pal Jerry Kortesmaki brought out a big tent, and Dale brought the beer. In 2004, Two Harbors, Minnesota became home to the first Slivovitz Festival. The three of them acted as judges. The event repeated a few years, growing in popularity until one day Bill received a call from the Polish consulate. Poland had gotten wind of the festival and wanted in. Did no one know that Polish slivovitz was the finest in the world? The trouble was the Polish slivovitz industry didn't have the permissions to import into the US. So the consul general himself drove to Minnesota with a diplomatic pouch of four cases of his nation's tipple. Diplomatic immunity. True story. So while we know you are here for the beer, be sure to knock back a shot of slivovitz and celebrate your initiation into Northern Minnesota life.

www.slivovitz.us

Boathouse Brewpub & Restaurant

Founded: 2007
Brewmaster: Ben Storbeck
Address: 47 East Sheridan Street • Ely, MN 55731
Phone: 218-365-4301
Web Site: www.boathousebrewpub.com
Annual Production: 300 barrels
Number of Beers: 7 beers plus one guest beer on tap; no flagship beers, always varying

Beers: (always varying)
» 1160 Porter
» Blueberry Blonde
» Entry Point Golden Ale
» ESB
» Ginger Binger Belgian Copper Ale
» Katzenjammer IPA
» Pyro India Red Ale
» Scottish Wee Heavy
» Smokey Off Kilter
» …plus so many more

Most Popular Brew: Blueberry Blonde

Samples: Yes, a flight of four samplers for about $6.

Brewmaster's Fave: Katzenjammer IPA at the moment. (The newest one.)

Best Time to Go: Open daily year round, but may close earlier in winter. Restaurant: 11AM–9PM Tavern: 11AM–11PM. Summer midnight. Growlers: 8AM–10PM (not Sundays). Happy hour is 4–6PM weekdays. Occasional live music. Watch for Blueberry Art Fest the last week of July.

BEER FOR THE BOUNDARY WATERS CANOE AREA

Be aware that metal and glass containers are never allowed in the BWCA. Be sure to pick up a BWCA-legal plastic growler for your trip. Boathouse Brewpub sells (and fills) them.

Where can you buy it? Only here and in growlers to go, including full-size and 750 ml/25 oz. plastic growlers.

Got food? Yes, a full menu including burgers and sandwiches, but also many vegetarian, gluten-free, and vegan choices.

Tours? By appointment or random luck to catch the brewer free.

Special Offer: Not participating at this time.

Directions: MN 1 connects Ely from the North Shore's MN 61 and from US 53 (merging with MN 169) to the west. From either direction it becomes Sheridan St and the brewery is at the corner of Sheridan and 1st Ave East.

The Beer Buzz: Welcome to the gateway to the Boundary Waters. But before becoming a mecca for paddling, mining put Ely on the map. Almost a dozen mines were dug here in what is part of the Vermilion Iron Range. Miners, paddlers, and… physicists?—they all need beer.

When longtime bar and restaurant Cranberry's went up for sale, Andrew Sakrison, the original brewer, was brewing at Fitger's Brewhouse and approached his uncle to get some seed money to start it. Mark and Lani Bruzek decided to purchase it. Minnesota natives, they had lived in Wausau, Wisconsin, for 23 years where Mark had a dental practice but kept a cabin on Lake Vermilion. They figured they'd become a silent partner in a new brewpub but ended up taking over the reins. Andrew left and a couple other brewers passed through, updating the equipment a bit before Brewer Ben was hired. Ben, a homebrewer, went through the

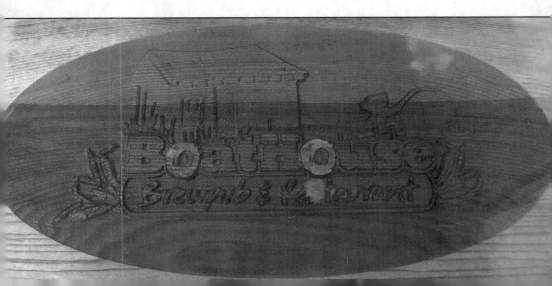

Beer Judge Certification Program (BJCP) and when an opportunity to clean kegs at Lake Superior Brewing came up, he took it and began his professional brewing life.

This is the oldest running commercial building in town, dating back to the nineteenth century, and it's been everything from a mortuary to a head shop and a hardware store in between.

Despite being deep in the northland, Ely is an active tourist destination year round: paddlers flock here in summer, snowmobilers in winter. One night at the bar might see a bunch of oil drillers, the next night might be the physicists from the lab at the Soudan mine, fifteen minutes down the road.

Ben likes to "roll fast and loose with the styles." He's always switching around the beers because his local happy hour crowd appreciates variety. As he puts it, there is always, "something boring, something fruity, something hoppy, and something malty." (Those are air quotes around "boring.") He prefers hoppier stuff, but his Blueberry Blonde is a big hit when it's on—plus they plop a blueberry into it and you can watch it rise and fall in the glass.

The restaurant dining room is to the left as you walk in, separate from the bar, but also connected from the back of the bar side. There's a stage back there for the occasional live music performance. Mounted trophy fish adorn the wood-plank walls where you can also see a map of Superior National Forest (www.fs.usda.gov/superior). The tables are fashioned out of reclaimed dock wood, and you've got darts, a pool table, five TVs and

DRINK LIKE A RANGER

Have a shot of Pelinkovac, a bitter liqueur unique to northern Minnesota. Like slivovitz (see the Duluth section), the origins of this drink lie in Europe, particularly in Serbia, Bosnia-Herzegovina, Croatia, Slovenia, and Montenegro. At 70 proof, it's not quite as potent as slivovitz. Its flavor has been compared to Jägermeister, and like that German concoction it contains herbs, in this case, wormwood, the ingredient said to make absinthe hallucinogenic. (It doesn't.) While absinthe was banned for its mind-altering reputation, this wormwood drink somehow got a pass and has been intoxicating the Iron Range for years. And like all things wicked bitter, it was believed to be medicinal. Go ahead, try it if you have a cold. The herbal blend, which includes cinnamon, anise and more, does seem to work as a digestive at least. *Boathouse Brewpub* in Ely has it behind the bar if you're curious.

a jukebox to keep you entertained. Before you leave, be sure to try the traditional northern Minnesota fire water: Pelinkovac.

ATM on site. WiFi. Facebook.com/boathouse.brewpub.ely

Stumbling Distance: *Ely Safe Ride* can help if you had too much: 248-235-7109. For a good and early breakfast, *Britton's Café* (5 E Chapman St, 218-365-3195) opens in the wee hours through lunch. Those in awe of nature need to visit the *International Wolf Center* (1396 Highway 169, 218-365-4695, wolf.org) and the *North American Bear Center* (1926 Highway 169, 218-365-7879, bear.org). If you're heading into the Boundary Waters, *Ely Outfitting Co.* (529 E Sheridan St, 218-343-7951, elyoutfittingcompany.com) is a recommended outfitter. *Soudan Underground Mine State Park* (1302 McKinley Park Rd, Soudan, 218-753-2245, www.dnr.state.mn.us) has historical tours of the mine and also science tours of the high energy physics lab here conducting the Cryogenic Dark Matter Search and Main Injector Neutrino Oscillation Search.

Gun Flint Tavern & Brewpub

Founded: 1998 (opened the brewery November 2014)
Brewmaster: Paul Gecas
Address: 111 West Wisconsin Street • Grand Marais, MN 55604
Phone: 218-387-1563
Web Site: www.gunflinttavern.com
Annual Production: 200 barrels
Number of Beers: 5–6 on tap; plus guest taps (total 24 taps)

Staple Beers: 3
  » Cascade River Ale Cream Ale
  » Jasper Ale English brown
  » Sawtooth Mountain Pale Ale
  » (always something dark, something hoppy, and something sessionable)

Rotating Beers:
  » IPA
  » Porter (always something dark in winter)
  » …plus cask ales

Most Popular Brew: Sawtooth Mountain Pale Ale

Samples: Yes, four 5-oz. for about $6.50.

Brewmaster's Fave: "At the moment, Whiskey Jack Porter"

Best Time to Go: Open 11AM–1AM. Happy hour in winter only.

Where can you buy it? Only here on tap and to go in growlers.

Got food? Yes, a full menu and bar. Main entrees range from sirloin and Dungeness crab to walleye, ribs and pasta. Bangers and mash, chicken molé, and other Mexican dishes as well, plus sandwiches, pizzas, soups and salads, desserts, and appetizers.

Tours? Unofficially, yes. It's pretty small but if the brewer's free, he'll chat or show you around.

Special Offer: Not participating at this time.

Directions: MN 61 runs along the North Shore and passes right through Grand Marais. Turn southwest toward the lake on Wisconsin St and the brewery is on the left after 500 feet.

Cyclists: *Gitchi-Gami State Trail is right across the street.*

The Beer Buzz: The original Gunflint Trail was an old logging road, and resorts for fishing, hunting, and paddling popped up around it in the 1930s. Now the trail is Cook County Road 12, and it lends its name to this long-standing tavern that rather recently added a brewing component. Owners Jeff and Susan Gecas wanted something different for Grand Marais. Susan loves to cook and designed the menu, which aims for something more adventurous and that emphasizes organic, locally sourced food. Jeff insisted there be no macro beers on tap, only quality craft brews. They took it one step further by brewing their own.

Jeff and Susan's nephew Paul Gecas was looking for work in the Twin Cities when Jeff called and asked him back to take on the brewing. Paul's dad homebrewed all his life, and Paul would help grind the grain. Growing up always around it, he started brewing on his own in college. In 2012, his uncle and aunt talked to him about the idea. He had been job shadowing at breweries and had taken an internship at *The Thirsty Pagan* in Superior, Wisconsin, and found he had the vision to experiment and do small batch stuff, an artistic and innovative approach. He traveled to Scotland where cask ales made a great impression on him as well, so expect to find some here. Barrel aging will depend on space.

This building used to be a sort of little mall. There was a bank, and the tavern had just one small dining area when it opened and started expanding. The brewery area used to be a clothing store and flower shop. Now Gun Flint has the entire building. The Raven Pub is a sort of pirate-themed bar a couple steps down from the dining room in the lower level and features a few tall tables, a TV, plus one long booth with a bench. The bar has money hanging from the ceiling above it. The Raven's Nest on the roof doesn't serve food and has a limited bar, but carry up your wares and enjoy the view of Lake Superior and live music every day in summer. A cribbage board is on hand, plus a few other games.

No WiFi. ATM on site. Facebook.com/GunFlintTavern

Stumbling Distance: Production brewery *Voyageur Brewing* is one block away. Paul's parents run *Heston's Lodge* (579 S Gunflint Lake Rd, Grand Marais, 218-388-2243, hestons.com) a collection of log cabins along the Gun Flint Trail. *Superior North Outdoor Center* (3 Broadway, 218-387-2186, velomarais.com) is a great resource and offers road- and mountain-bike rentals, tours, and climbing gear.

GRAND MARAIS, GRAND OUTDOORS

Tourists crowd up this quirky little town on Lake Superior, which is best known as a hub for great outdoors experiences. *National Geographic Adventure Magazine* has listed it in its Top 100 Adventure Towns. The *Gitchi-Gami State Trail* (ggta.org) is partly complete and will run 88 miles from Two Harbors to Grand Marais. (Bike between the breweries!) Mountain bikers can find many miles of single-track out in the woods. Hiking and rock climbing are huge here, but this is also a gateway to the Boundary Waters. In winter, it gets quieter, but good cross country and downhill skiing and great trails for snowshoeing and snowmobiling still draw visitors.

ARTS AND CRAFTS

In town one still can enjoy great dining, local beer, and a collection of art galleries, but there are ways to get even more involved in the creativity. *North House Folk School* (500 W Hwy 61, 888-387-9762, northhouse.org) is a fantastic educational opportunity, with courses in a whole variety of crafts from music, storytelling, and knitting to blacksmithing, boatbuilding, and shoemaking. Since 1947 the *Grand Marais Art Colony* (120 W 3rd Ave, 218-387-2737, grandmaraisartcolony.org) hosts events and exhibits and offers classes for all levels of artists in a variety of mediums.

Stop in at the *Grand Marais Visitor Information Center* (13 Broadway, 888-922-5000) to get more information about the wealth of options this little town has to offer.

VOYAGEUR BREWING CO.

Opened: February 12, 2015
Brewmaster: Jason Baumgarth
Address: 233 West Highway 61 • Grand Marais, MN 55604
Phone: 218-387-3163
Web Site: www.voyageurbrewing.com
Annual Production: 1,500 barrels
Number of Beers: 6 on tap

Staple Beers:
> » BOUNDARY WATERS BRUNETTE WILD RICE BROWN ALE
> » DEVIL'S KETTLE IPA
> » PALISADE PORTER
> » TRAILBREAKER BELGIAN WHEAT

Rotating Beers:
> » SMOKED MAPLE RYE
> » Brews with blueberries in summer
> » Brews with local fresh hopped beers in fall

Most Popular Brew: Devil's Kettle IPA or Boundary Waters Brunette

Samples: Yes, free sips for decision-making, and flights of six 5-oz. for about $11.

Brewmaster's Fave: He's pretty proud of his Beglian Wit

Best Time to Go: Open daily in summer: Mon–Thu 4–11PM, Fri–Sat 12–11PM, Sun noon–until? Winter: Thu–Fri 4–11PM, Sat 12–11PM. Watch for live music on weekends. As always, check website for most current opening/closing times.

Where can you buy it? Here on tap and in growlers (pre-filled, exchanged, or bring your own) to go. Growlers come in glass as well as three other options—Nalgene, stainless steel, and Hydro Flask. They distribute from Grand Marais down to Duluth, with eyes on the Twin Cities in the near future. Draft accounts and 6-pack 12-oz. bottles

Got food? Yes, appetizers in house: wings, pub pretzels, charcuterie, curds, etc. Food friendly as well.

Tours? Yes, scheduled on the website, typically Saturdays at 11AM, more often in summer. Make a reservation online. Suggested donations (a couple bucks) collected for local non-profits.

Special Offer: A free pint of beer with your book signature.

Directions: MN 61 runs along the North Shore and passes right through Grand Marais. The brewery is right on the highway opposite the lake between 4th and 5th Ave.

Cyclists: *Gitchi-Gami State Trail is right across the street.*

The Beer Buzz: Three couples—Mike and Sue Prom, Paul and Cara Sporn, and Bruce and Ritalee Walters—have traveled together for a long time. As beer connoisseurs they used to always find the best taproom and brewpubs on their peregrinations. All of them were from the Twin Cities metro area but frequently came up to Grand Marais for outdoor adventure and simply fell in love with it. In 1993 Sue and Mike were just out of college and bought an outfitter shop from the original owner, servicing paddlers heading into the Boundary Waters. But if there was one thing lacking up here, it was some local brew.

For three years they worked on the plan, and for another year and a half they put it together in a former appliance storefront. They added on, doubling the size of the original building by expanding out the front for the taproom.

Grand Marais has a strong locavore movement—local art, local food, a local dairy and a co-op—which guided their efforts. The taproom focuses on sustainability, and they spent the extra money on everything from all American-made equipment, kegs and ingredients to energy efficient LED lighting. Reclaimed barn wood supplied the wainscoting, local pine gleams on the bar top, and old wood barrels adorn the walls.

Brewer Jason ran the show at *Carmody Irish Pub & Brewing* in Duluth for six years before moving up the North Coast. They brought in Turnkey Brewing Consulting from Portland to help set up the 20-barrel system.

The taproom features a TV for the occasional sporting event, background music, and a real fireplace. Board games and cribbage are on hand as are bigger challenges such as cornhole (beanbag toss) and human-size Jenga. Sit out on the rooftop in the summer and enjoy the beautiful view of Lake Superior.

WiFi. Facebook/voyageurbrewing and Twitter @VoyageurBrewMN

Stumbling Distance: *Gun Flint Tavern & Brewpub* are a block away. *My Sister's Place* (401 E Hwy 61, 218-387-1915, mysistersplacerestaurant. com) does burgers (Wild Rice and Juicy Lucy versions), a variety of hot dogs, pizzas, and salads. *Sven & Ole's Pizza* (9 W Wisconsin St, 218-387-1713, svenandoles.com) delivers to the taproom. *Mike and Sue's Voyageur Canoe Outfitters* (189 Sag Lake Trail, 218-388-2224, canoeit.com) does full service outfitting for the Boundary Waters including permits. Looking for local maple syrup? *Maple Hill Sugarbush* (321 Co Rd 60, 218-387-2186) has it plus a lot of other great produce, plus they do weekend workshops and tours of their farm.

THE PADDLER'S HOLY PILGRIMAGE

Situated in northeastern Minnesota along the border of Canada and within the Superior National Forest, the Boundary Waters Canoe Area Wilderness (BWCAW) is one of those must paddles. 250,000 annual visitors think so anyway. And for those who love it, a trip there can become an annual thing. Protected since 1926, over a million acres of primitive lake and forest offers a lot of space to disappear into. Canoe routes offer a network greater than 1,200 miles and over 2,000 campsites accommodate those on longer trips. Quota permits, associated with specific entry points, are required from May through September and planning ahead is necessary as the permit numbers are limited. (Off season permits are free and self-issued.) Permits are awarded on a lottery system and you must apply during the monthlong application period starting in mid-December prior to your trip! Paddling is hardy and portages are part of the experience. Careful planning is necessary—for example, you need to hang your provisions in a tree so as to keep resident bears out of them—and if you're packing beer, you need to know there is no glass or trash allowed. *Boathouse Brewpub* in Ely is at one entry point. *Gun Flint Tavern & Brewpub* and *Voyageur Brewing* are closer to an eastern entry point. The latter brewery also operates an outfitter. How convenient!

Superior National Forest—Supervisor's Office
8901 Grand Ave Place
Duluth, MN 55808
218-626-4300 | www.fs.usda.gov/superior

Borealis Fermentery

Founded: April 2012
Brewmaster: Ken Thiemann
Address: P.O. Box 130 • Knife River, MN 55609
Phone: 218-834-4856
Web Site: www.borealisfermentery.com
Annual Production: 90 barrels
Number of Beers: 5

Staple Beers:
  » La Lune Special Ale
  » Mon Cherries Cherry Dubbel
  » Raisin Liaison Saison
  » Speckled Ghost Abbey Ale
  » White Throated Wit (with kaffir lime leaves and lemongrass)

Most Popular Brew: Mon Cherries

Samples: On a tour.

Brewmaster's Fave: Raison Liason Saison

Best Time to Go: On a scheduled tour with The Duluth Experience

Where can you buy it? In 750 ml bottles in liquor stores in Duluth and the Twin Cities, and on tap in just a few Duluth establishments.

Got food? No.

Tours? The only way to tour here is to join a scheduled tour with **The Duluth Experience** (218-464-6337, theduluthexperience.com).

Special Offer: A highly prized trinket of the brewer's choosing.

Directions: This is off the map as he doesn't have regular visiting hours. If you want to see it, contact The Duluth Experience!

The Beer Buzz: When making beer, many will tell you it's all about the water. Ken Thiemann's brewery is sitting right on top of an artesian well. An actual "water witch" found it for him using a divining rod. You've heard of brewers who practically live at the brewery? Well, Ken here literally does. He built this post and beam, timber frame home himself, and the brewhouse and living quarters are sharing the space. It's surprisingly well suited for the tough winters, with 435 straw bales inside the stucco-covered walls providing great insulation. And he didn't use a single nail in the construction, just wooden pegs. He credits Belgian monks for the building style.

Ken is a Detroit native, and he found a homebrew club when he attended Michigan Tech for engineering in the early 90s. Later, while working an engineering job in the Netherlands, Ken traveled into Belgium on a regular basis and clearly was inspired. It's no coincidence he only brews Belgian styles and bottle conditions them.

He's won awards for his beer, but he keeps a low profile. He does not open the brewery to the public except for organized tours, currently only from The Duluth Experience. Not only is he secretive about his location, but he also seals his lips when asked about some of the secrets he picked up in Belgium and worked into his beers. One thing he is outspoken about, however: "Bottle conditioning is the way to go." You may agree once you try his beer.

Facebook.com/borealisbrew and Twitter @borealisbrew

Stumbling Distance: *New Scenic Café* (5461 N Shore Dr, Duluth, 218-525-6274, sceniccafe.com) is the closest place to Knife Harbor serving Borealis brews, and the food there is divine. *Beaner's Central Coffee House* (324 N Central Ave, Duluth, 218-624-5957) typically has Borealis' beer, as does fine-dining option *Lake Avenue Restaurant & Bar* (394 S Lake Ave, Duluth, 218-722-2355, lakeavenuerestaurantandbar. com). *7 West Taphouse* (7 W Superior St, Duluth, 218-727-2494, 7westtaphouse. com) also typically serves it.

CASTLE DANGER BREWERY

Founded: 2011
Brewers: Clint MacFarlane, Mason Williams, and Jeremy King
Address: 17-7th Street • Two Harbors, MN 55616
Phone: 218-834-5800
Web Site: www.castledangerbrewery.com
Annual Production: 6,000 barrels
Number of Beers: 6–10 on tap; 3 in cans plus seasonals

Staple Beers:
- » DANGER ALE
- » 17-7 PALE ALE

Rotating Beers:
- » CAMP DEPRESSION LAGER (mid-winter)
- » CASTLE CREAM ALE (summer)
- » DOUBLE CROSSING IPA (spring)
- » GALE FORCE WHEAT (spring)
- » GEORGE HUNTER STOUT (winter – also in cans)
- » NESTOR GRADE AMBER ALE (fall)
- » NORDIC LAGER (spring/summer – Finnish Sahti made with rye and juniper)
- » RED HOP RISING IPA (summer)
- » WIMPY LAGER (spring)
- » *London Crossing IPA Series* (many variations)
- » *Freestyle Series* are one-offs, experimental brews that allow them to learn new techniques and test new beers. These may include barrel-aged versions, examples being Gentleman George, stout aged in Jack Daniels barrels, and Sommelier George, stout aging in red wine barrels

Most Popular Brew: Danger Ale

Samples: Yes, flights of four 5.5-oz. pours for about $9.

Best Time to Go: Open daily June–September from noon–9PM (until 11PM Fri–Sat). Winter hours may lose a couple days and some hours: Wed–Thu 3–9PM, Fri–Sat 12–10PM, Sun 12–5PM. Check website to confirm.

Where can you buy it? On tap in 11-oz. and 18-oz. pours and to go in growlers (64-oz. and 750 ml) in the taproom. Find it in six-pack 12-oz cans and some draft accounts along the North Shore of Lake Superior and as far away as St. Cloud and Brainerd, but generally northern Minnesota for now.

Got food? Only chips along with 10 different salsas made by Clint's cousin (some are "weapons grade" hot). But the taproom is food friendly, plus the occasional food truck shows up and local menus are on hand for delivery.

Tours? Yes, usually Friday nights and Saturdays for a fee. Check website for scheduled times.

Special Offer: $1 off your first beer during your signature visit.

Directions: MN 61 passes right through Two Harbors (as 7th Ave). At 7th Street, turn south (toward the lake) and go 6 blocks and the brewery is on the right at the corner of 1st Ave. See biking option in the Stumbling Distance.

The Beer Buzz: The brewery takes its name from its original location, Castle Danger, MN. This tiny town along the shore of Lake Superior was settled in 1890 by Norwegian fishermen, though loggers were already around taking timber and rafting it down the coast to Duluth and its fifteen lumber mills. The name origin is uncertain but many believe the shoreline cliffs resembled a castle and sailors knew these marked a dangerous offshore shoal. At least one ship, the Criss Grover was lost near here.

Danger be damned, Brewer Clint and Jamie MacFarlane built a modest 700 square-foot building here for a 3-barrel system and brewed the first batch on March 1, 2011. Clint had started with homebrewing in 2006, making 5 gallons at a time with a kit on the kitchen stove, and within the year had started developing original recipes. Danger Ale and George Hunter were among them. Longtime friend Mason Williams became their first employee, learning brewing from Clint and later taking coursework with the Siebel Institute. Success was quick, but the system limited production, so they took a big leap forward when they moved into a brand new building in Two Harbors in August 2014—with a 30-barrel system. Bigger batches meant more work, so they also added Jeremy King, previously with Canal Park Brewing and Northern Brewer (where he famously isolated a Wisconsin yeast strain for Milwaukee's Lakefront Brewing.) The new brewery occupies what was a parking lot, but long before that a railroad clubhouse sat on this site. The railroad still comes here in summer but now for the brewery (see tours below). The taproom is a huge space—about 1,500 square feet—with tables and seating for 100 people. Polished concrete floors and a lot of wood and metal give the place character, and a 300-lb slab of maple with the brewery logo hangs behind the bar. There are no TVs but a view of Lake Superior. Board games and, of course, cribbage are on hand.

The beer names correspond to local places, but George Hunter is Clint's great-great-grandfather, an Irish immigrant who settled in Tower, Minnesota, and was himself part owner of a brewery, Iron Range Brewing Co.

WiFi. Facebook.com/castledangerbrewery and Twitter @cdangerbrewer

Stumbling Distance: Check out the train tour from Duluth to here for a brewery visit. *North Shore Scenic Railroad* (506 W Michigan St, Duluth, 218-722-1273, northshorescenicrailroad.org) does a variety of tours but the Beer Tasting Train may be one you ought to check out. *Carmody's 61* (1102 7th Ave, 218-834-1102, carmody61pub.com) has that Duluth brewer's beer on tap and serves food, notably a spent-grain burger. They deliver to the brewery here, as do *Do North Pizzeria* (15 Waterfront Dr, 218-834-3555, donorthpizza.com) and *The Vanilla Bean Bakery & Café* (812 7th Ave, 218-834-3714, thevanillabean.com). *Note to cyclists:* the *Gitchi-Gami State Trail* (ggta.org) is partly complete and will run 88 miles from Two Harbors to Grand Marais so you can bike between the breweries in each!

HARBOR HOPS

This husband and wife team Ryan and Lori Melton had been growing hops for years, and they grew so well up here along the North Shore that they thought to scale it up a bit and start providing hops to the quickly growing craft brewing scene in the area. Originally from Rochester, they were living in Duluth when they decided to purchase this 10-acre farm just outside of Two Harbors along the Stewart River. Lori works in communications for the University of Minnesota-Duluth, but Ryan quit his position with the US Forest Service to devote extra time with their move "back to the land."

Hops are not like your garden vegetables. You don't just drop a seed and expect a harvest come fall. In fact hops take three years before they offer up a significant amount. The Meltons have 20 varieties of hops on a half acre of land but will phase out the varieties that don't produce well or lack demand. They plan to keep things organic, and in the past they have used smelt guts from Lake Superior Fish Co. as fertilizer. They originally hoped to offer a pick-your-own arrangement for local homebrewers, but that plan is currently on hold. For now the only way to visit here is on a tour with The Duluth Experience (218-464-6337, theduluthexperience.com).

Harbor Hops
Twitter: @HarborHops | harborhops.com

Beer Festivals

Festivals and tasting events are many in the great state of Minnesota, and with new ones popping up all the time, it's impossible to list them all. Plus, some of them change dates from year to year. Here are some of the biggest and best known. Check your local brewery for others or pick up a copy of *The Growler*.

MINNESOTA CRAFT BREWERS GUILD

Founded in 2000, the Minnesota Craft Brewers Guild has a mission to promote Minnesota beer and the brewers who make it. They bring the brewing industry together and invite beer-related businesses and entities to join as well. And for you, dear reader, they host some spectacular beer festivals every year. mncraftbrew.org/events
Facebook.com/MinnesotaCraftBrewersGuild
Twitter @MNcraftbrew
Instagram: mncraftbrewersguild

Winterfest (February)
Over 60 guild member breweries and brewpubs break out the Winter Warmers for this two-night St. Paul event which honors a Best Beer. Expect a lot of food, education events, and exhibits from industry partners, plus live music and other entertainment.

10,000 Minutes of Minnesota Craft Beer (May)
This craft beer week is celebrated statewide with tap takeovers, beer tours, firkin tappings and special brew events. #10000Minutes, #MNCraftBeer, #MNBeerWeek

All Pints North (July)
Held up north (naturally) in beer mecca Duluth. Plenty of food and live music, plus education and over 60 great breweries. Tickets go on sale in April.

Land of 10,000 Beers / Minnesota State Fair (August)
The Land of 10,000 Beers Craft Beer Hall exhibit at the Minnesota State Fair features flights and special tastings from over 30 Minnesota brewers, loads of history, education, and brewcation information, and some root beer for the kids. The State Fair runs the 12 days leading up to Labor Day.

Autumn Brew Review (September)

This massive Minneapolis fest brings together over 110 craft breweries, with live music, food, competitions for food and table display, and beer education sessions.

THE BEER DABBLER FESTIVALS

Matt Kenevan founded The Beer Dabbler (beerdabbler.com) in 2008 with the idea that he could create some craft beer festivals and take them and a "caravan of craft brewers" out into the smaller communities of Minnesota to spread the gospel of good beer. He brought on Joe Alton who also liked the idea, but they found the rural world wasn't ready for it. With Minnesota being such a passionate IPA culture all of a sudden, that may be hard to swallow. So they stuck to the Twin Cities and introduced two festivals that have become staples in the beer event calendar: Summer Beer Dabbler (with Highland Business Association as a partner) and Beer Dabbler Winter Carnival (paired up with the Saint Paul Winter Carnival). With the success that followed, they added a third in 2012: The Beer Dabbler at Twin Cities Pride. These festivals are highly anticipated each year, and it's a good idea to get those tickets well in advance. Sign up on their website at beerdabbler.com to receive email notices.

Beer Dabbler Winter Carnival (January)
Over 120 local, regional, and national craft breweries, live music, gourmet food from local food trucks, and even some cheese and artisan meat vendors hosted by Lunds & Byerly's. Minnesota's largest outdoor (you read that correctly—outdoor) beer festival.

Beer Dabbler at Twin Cities Pride (June)
The ultimate pairing: 25 local breweries and 25 local food trucks and carts, plus live music, Silent Disco, and many games and activities.

Summer Beer Dabbler (Aug or Sept)
With over 65 local, regional, and national craft breweries, live music, gourmet food from local food trucks, and more.

A SAMPLING OF OTHER FESTIVALS

Mankato Craft Beer Expo (January)
mankatocraftbeerexpo.com
Over 45 breweries, plus music and food.

Northern Lights Rare Beer Fest (March)
rarebeerfest.com
Benefitting Pints for Prostates, this limited ticket St. Paul fest features vintage and specialty beers.

Rochester Craft Beer Expo (May)
rochestercraftbeerexpo.com
Dozens of breweries on hand for tastings plus seminars

St. Paul Summer Beer Fest (June)
stpaulsummerbeerfest.com
Featuring over 100 breweries, music, good, seminars and a charitable silent auction.

Hopped Up Caribou Beer Festival (July)
Facebook.com/hoppedupcaribou
Just over a dozen breweries but a fun one up on the North Shore in Lutsen, MN.

Glossary of Beers

Ale — Short answer: beer from top-fermenting yeast, fermented at warmer temperatures. Long answer: see Ales vs. Lagers in the History of Beer Section.

Altbier means "old" beer—as in a traditional recipe, not a brew that's gone bad. It's a bitter, copper-colored ale.

Amber is that funny rock-like stuff that prehistoric bugs got trapped in and now makes great hippie jewelry; or that pretty girl you were sweet on in middle school. But here I think they're just talking about the color of a type of American ale that uses American hops for a bitter, malty and hoppy flavor.

American IPA is generally a term used for an IPA recipe made with American ingredients, especially the hops.

APA (American Pale Ale) is a pale ale using American hops. The hops flavor, aroma, and bitterness are pronounced.

Barley wine is like precious gold wherever it's brewed. This ale jumps off the shelves or out of the tap. It is strong, sweet, a bit aged, and those who know are waiting to pounce on it.

Berliner weisse is a wheat ale made a bit tart or sour with lactic acid bacteria.

Bitter is part of the family of pale ales, cousin perhaps to the IPA. Like folks in a small Minnesota town, all beer is related in some way, I guess. This brew has a wider range of strength, flavor, and color than the IPA. See "ESB." You'll be back.

Blonde or Golden Ale is a lighter form of pale ale usually made with pilsner malt. It's a popular Belgian style, and gentlemen prefer them.

Bock is a strong lager darkened a bit and brewed in the winter to be drunk in spring. Monks drank it during the Lenten fasting period because it had substance to it, you know, like liquid bread? The name comes from the medieval German village of Einbeck. So, no, it does not mean Bottom of the Keg or Beer of Copious Kraeusening. Bock means goat in German. Thus the goats on so many of the labels and the popularity of headbutting at fraternity bock parties.

Brackett (also called braggot) is the first form of ale and a sort of beer and mead hybrid. It was first brewed with honey and hops and later with honey and malt—with or without hops added.

Cask ale or **cask-conditioned ale**: see **Real Ale**

Cream Ale is a smooth and clean, light-colored American ale similar to a pale lager. Cleaner flavor than your usual ale.

Doppelbock see "Bock" and read it twice. Seriously, just a bock with a stronger punch to it though not necessarily double.

Dunkelweiss is a dark wheat beer, a German style. "Dunkel" means dark.

Eisbock if you say it outloud is probably easier to guess. No, it's not beer on the rocks. Take a bock, freeze it, take the ice out, and you have a higher alcohol content bock. Weizen eisbock then is a wheat version of this beer and it's delicious.

ESB (Extra Special Bitter) see "Bitter" and add some more alcohol. Isn't that what makes beer special?

Gose is an unfiltered 50% malted wheat beer style still found in Leipzig, Germany. Some lactic acid and the addition of ground coriander seeds and salt make an unusual sour beer.

Gueze is a blended beer made by combining a young 1-year-old lambic with an older one of 2 or 3 years.

Gruit or **Grut** is a mixture of herbs that beer makers used to use before hops came into favor. It added bitterness and in some cases preservative qualities, and the unique blends offered a variety of flavors for beers. Some brewers might do unhopped beers and use things like juniper berries, chamomile, heather, or other things that sound like lawn clippings.

Hefeweizen (German Wheat Beer) is *supposed* to be cloudy—it's unfiltered. Don't make that face, drink it. That's where all the vitamins are and stuff. See also "Weisse" et al. It's recommended not to drink beers directly from the bottle, but to use a proper glass, but especially in this case. Germans even write that on the bottle sometimes in case you forget.

Imperial Stout see "Stout." The Brits originally made this for the Russian imperial court. It had to cross water as cold as International Falls so the high alcohol content kept it from freezing. Expect roasted, chocolate, and burnt malt flavors and a strong left hook. Also called **Russian Imperial Stout.**

IPA (India Pale Ale) is what the Brits used to send to India. The long journey spoiled porters and stouts, and so this recipe calls for lots of hops. Did you read that part yet? About hops as a preservative? You can't just skip parts of the book. I'll catch you. And there will be a quiz. Don't say I didn't warn you.

Irish-style Stout is a dry version of stout, typically served under nitro for the creamy special effect. However, it's very dark and thus too difficult to dye green on St. Patty's Day.

Kölsch is just an excuse to use those little dot things—"What is an umlaut?" for those of you looking to score on *Jeopardy*—and a difficult-to-pronounce-correctly-and-still-retain-your-dignity name for a light, subtley fruity ale that originated in Cologne... the city in Germany; please don't drink your aftershave no matter how nice it smells.

Lager — Short answer: beer with bottom-fermenting yeast, fermented colder than ale. Long answer: see Ales vs. Lagers in the History of Beer Section.

Lambic — Let's just call this the Wild One. It's a Belgian ale with a bit of unmalted wheat and it uses naturally occurring yeast, the kind that's just floating around out there. The brew is tart and may have a fruit element added such as raspberries or cherries.

Low alcohol — See "Near Bear."

Maibock is not your bock and if you touch my bock, there's gonna be trouble. This is the lightest of the bocks and is traditionally brewed to be drunk in May, but we're not always hung up on tradition and it is often around whenever you want it.

Märzen takes its name from March, the month in which this lager is typically brewed so it can age in time for Oktoberfest when it magically becomes Oktoberfest beer.

Mead is honey fermented in water. It ain't beer, but it's good. And there's plenty of honey in Minnesota to make it. The word "honeymoon" comes from a tradition of gifting a newlywed couple a month's worth of mead to get things off to a smooth start. From this you can guess why we say "the honeymoon's over" with such lament.

Near Beer — Let's just pretend we didn't hear this and move on, shall we?

(Nut) Brown Ale uses brown roasted malt, and a bit of hops brings some bitterness. Brown ales can be a bit malty sweet or a bit hoppy; the style varies even from London to Newcastle (malty, almost nutty) where the term originated. Originally it was simply a description of the color (of porters, stout), but it has evolved to be a style. In America they tend to be a bit hoppier and stronger. *Does not contain nuts or is processed in a facility that uses nuts.*

Oktoberfest is Märzen after the 6–7 month wait as it ages a bit.

Pilsner is a style that comes from Plzen, a Czech version of Milwaukee. Dry and hoppy, this golden lager is hugely popular, and most of the mass-produced versions fail to imitate the Czech originals. Best to try a handcrafted version at your local—or someone else's local—brewpub. Also a term I use to describe residents of Moquah, Wisconsin, which is also the Township of Pilsen where my grandparents lived. Interestingly, the first pilsner was brewed in Plzen in 1842 by Josef Groll, a brewer hired from Bavaria. The pale malt, the Saaz hops, bottom-fermenting yeast (lager), and the super soft water of Plzen created a very different brew from the (until then) top fermenting ales of Bohemia, and it quickly became a sensation.

Porter is a fine, dark ale made with roasted malt and bitter with hops. Baltic Porter (a bit stronger to be shipped across the Baltic Sea) and Robust Porter (may be stronger, more aggressive with the hops).

Rauchbier is beer made with smoked barley malt. It may be an acquired taste, but if you like bacon… Back in the day, when open fires were sometimes used to dry malt, most beers likely had some smokiness to them. Beginning in the 1600s, the use of kilns eliminated this effect. This intentional style is associated with Bamberg, Germany, where it is still done.

Real ale is another way of referring to **cask ale**. It is unfiltered and unpasteurized and completes its secondary fermentation in the cask it is served from, without the use of carbon dioxide or nitrogen pressure "pushing" it through a serving line. They are either hand-pulled (on a hand pump or "beer engine") or gravity fed.

Rye beer substitutes some malted rye for some of the malted barley. Remember in that "American Pie" song, the old men "drinking whiskey and rye?" Yeah, that's something else. This gives a distinct slight spiciness to the beer.

Sahti is an old Finnish style of beer, herbal in its ingredients, typically employing juniper berries but not always hops.

Saison is French for "season" (those people have a different word for everything it seems) and this beer was intended for farm workers at the end of summer. It's Belgian in origin and the yeast used ferments at a higher ale temperature. It's generally cloudy and often has something like orange zest or coriander in it. While it was originally a low-alcohol brew so the workers could keep working, many American revivals of the style are packing a bit of a punch.

Saké — This is more of a trivia note than anything. It's not wine or rice wine; it's actually a Japanese rice beer, technically, as it is a fermented grain. And you can actually have Minnesota saké—*moto-i* in Minneapolis, the sister restaurant to the brewpub *The Herkimer*, brews it just a couple doors down from the brewpub.

Schwarzbier is the way they say "black beer" in Germany. This lager is black as midnight thanks to the dark roasted malt and has a full, chocolatey or coffee flavor much like a stout or porter.

Scotch Ale or Scottish-style Ale is generally maltier than other ales and sometimes more potent. The FDA insists it be labeled "Scottish-style" as it is not actually from Scotland if brewed here in Minnesota. Fair enough.

Smash is a slang term for "single malt, single hop" referring to the brew recipe.

Sour Ale is a variety of beer that uses wild yeasts and bacteria to get a brew that makes you pucker a bit. Beer can become unintentionally and unpleasantly sour when bacteria infect it. This is different; it's intentional and when done traditionally, it's kinda risky to other nearby brewing, so steps must be taken to keep unintended infections from happening. A lambic fits this category.

Stout is made with dark roasted barley and lots of hops, and it is a black ale most smooth. It can be bitter, dry, or even sweet when it's brewed with milk sugar (lactose). On occasion brewers add oatmeal for a smoother and sweeter ale, and you have to start wondering if there is something to that saying, "Beer, it's not just for breakfast anymore." Imperial Stout is a strong variation on the recipe first done up by the English exporting to the Russians in the 1800s. The real fun of it is when it is on a nitrogen tap. Look that up!

MEASURE FOR MEASURE

A **growler** is a half-gallon (64 oz.) jug, refillable at your local brewpub. Many brewers sell them to you full for a few dollars more than the refill. Typically made of glass, some are stainless steel or even insulated. Frost River of Duluth even makes a great carrying bag for them.

A **howler** or **grumbler** or **squealer** is a term coined variously for a container that is a 32-oz. or **half growler**. This may vary, however, as state law in Minnesota allows for **750 ml** sales at taprooms, which is not exactly half of a growler. So you may see 750-ml refillable containers here.

A **bomber** is a 22-ounce bottle.

One **US barrel** (1 bbl) is two kegs or 31 gallons or 248 pints, so you better start early.

A **keg,** sometimes casually and inaccurately referred to as a barrel, holds 15.5 gallons—this is the legendary half-barrel of the college party fame

A **Cornelius keg** is a pub keg, similar to one of those soda syrup canisters and holds 5 gallons.

A **US pint** = 16 oz. = a proper US beer. (Also defined as 1/8 of a gallon)

Tripel is an unfiltered Belgian ale that has a very high alcohol content. The combination of hops and large amounts of malt and candy sugar give a bittersweet taste to this powerhouse. Many brewpubs will only allow you to drink one or two glasses to make sure you can still find the door when you leave.

Wheat Beer is beer made with wheat. You didn't really just look this up, did you? Dude.

Witbier, Weisse, Weizen, Wisenheimer — three of these words are simply different ways of saying white wheat beer that originated in Belgium. They are sometimes flavored with orange peel and coriander and are mildly to majorly sweet. The fourth word describes the kind of guy that would write that Wheat Beer definition.

A **can** = 12 oz. or 16 oz. This used to be a sign of cheap beer, but many craft brews are moving to this.

A **UK or Imperial pint** = 20 oz.* (lucky chumps) and there are laws protecting the drinker from improperly filled pints! Look for that little white line on the pint glass.

Ah, but wait. Imperial pints are 20 Imperial ounces, which are different from the American ounces. The imperial fluid ounce is 28.4130625 ml while the US fluid ounce (as opposed to the dry ounce) is 29.5735295625 ml exactly, about 4% larger than the imperial unit. And if that isn't clear, be aware that the US also defines a fluid ounce as exactly 30 milliliters for the purposes of labeling nutrition information.

A **firkin** is a small cask or barrel, usually the equivalent of a ¼ barrel or about 9 gallons (34 liters)

A **buttload** is a real thing. In wine-speak, a butt was a large cask with the volume of four standard wine barrels, just about 480 liters. In US gallons, that would be about 126. So just over 4 barrels of beer would truly be a buttload of beer.

Getting confused yet? I gave up at "pint" and drank one. And don't even get me started on the whole metric vs. Imperial gallon vs. US gallon vs. 10-gallon hat conundrum.

Index

Index

Signatures

56 Brewing

612Brew

Able Seedhouse & Brewery

Angry Inch Brewing Co.

August Schell Brewing Co.

Bad Weather Brewing Co.

Badger Hill Brewing Co.

Bang Brewing

Bank Brewing Co.

Barley John's Brew Pub

Bauhaus Brew Labs

Beaver Island Brewing

Bemidji Brewing Co.

Bent Brewstillery

Bent Paddle Brewing Co.

Big Wood Brewery

Blacklist Brewing

Boathouse Brewpub & Restaurant

Boom Island Brewing Co.

Borealis Fermentery

Brau Brothers Brewing Co.

Bryn Mawr Brewing Co.

Burning Brothers Brewing

Canal Park Brewing Co.

Carmody Irish Pub & Brewing

Castle Danger Brewery

Dangerous Man Brewing Co.

Day Block Brewery

Eastlake Brewery

ENKI Brewing

Excelsior Brewing Co.

Fair State Brewing Cooperative

Fitger's Brewhouse

Foxhole Brewhouse

The Freehouse

F-Town Brewing Co.

Fulton Brewing Co.

Goat Ridge Brewing Co.

Granite City Food & Brewery (Eagen)

Granite City Food & Brewery (Maple Grove)

Granite City Food & Brewery (Roseville)

Granite City Food & Brewery (St. Cloud)

Granite City Food & Brewery (St. Louis Park)

Great Waters Brewing Co.

Gull Dam Brewing, Inc.

Gun Flint Tavern & Brewpub

HammerHeart Brewing Co.

Harriet Brewing Co.

Hayes' Public House

The Herkimer

Indeed Brewing Co.

Insight Brewing

Jack Pine Brewery

Junkyard Brewing

Kinney Creek Brewery

Lake Monster Brewing Co.

Lake Superior Brewing Co.

Lakes & Legends Brewing Co.

Lift Bridge Brewing Co.

LTD Brewing Co.

LTS Brewing Co.

Lucid Brewing Co.

Lupine Brewing Co.

Lupulin Brewing Co.

LynLake Brewery